PEASANTS IN ASIA

PEASANTS IN ASIA

PEASANTS IN ASIA:
SOCIAL CONSCIOUSNESS AND
SOCIAL STRUGGLE

By

Zhanna D. Smirenskaia

Translated by

Michael J. Buckley

Ohio University Center for International Studies
Center for Southeast Asian Studies

Monographs in International Studies
Southeast Asia Series Number 73

Athens Ohio 1986

Library of Congress Cataloging-in-Publication Data

Smirenskaia, Zhanna Dmitrievna.
    Peasants in asia--social consciousness and social
struggle.

    (Monographs in international studies. Southeast Asia
series ; no. 73)
    Translation of: Krest´ ianstvo v stranakh Azii--
obshchestvennoe soznanie i obshchestvennaia bor´ba.
    Bibliography: p.
    1. Peasantry--Asia. I. Title. II. Series.
HD1536.8.S6513 1986   305.5'63   86-14733
ISBN 0-89680-134-9

ISBN: 0-89680-134-9

To Leslie and her "miracle"
operation

CONTENTS

This Soviet study of the reasons behind modern peasant rebellion differs considerably in its theoretical and methodological assumptions from Western analyses on the subject. The author, Zhanna D. Smirenskaia, searches for the preconditions of the birth of peasant class consciousness, which, from the Marxian perspective, constitutes the correct explanation of rebellious behavior. In her analyses of Java, West Bengal, Kerala, Punjab, Iran and the Philippines, the author shows what different paths Asian peasants took while overcoming traditional horizontal relations and "progressing" to societal structures dominated by economic or vertical relations.

Smirenskaia assumes the researcher can bridge the gap between the individual and the societal levels of analysis through an analysis of social relations. Methodologically she focuses on changes in patterns of landownership and land usage and in leadership and administrative positions, analyzing how changes in these variables interact with the influence of community, clan, caste and religion to produce different types of class consciousness. Thus, the most clear-cut example of class-oriented behavior, the Hukbalahap rebellion in the Philippines, is not analyzed according to whether it succeeded or failed, but rather, according to what changes occurred in horizontal and vertical relations among the peasantry. I considered these methodological and theoretical principles of high enough interest to warrant translation.

Scholars should not be discouraged by the difference in Soviet scholastic techniques evident in the work. Although not nearly as rigorous as what is expected in the West, the study is still highly interesting for the reasons mentioned above. Additionally, hardly any Soviet material on this subject is translated into English, and so this study represents one of only a few works Western scholars can use to assess Soviet explanations of why peasants revolt--or why they do not.

Born in 1938, Zhanna Dmitrievna Smirenskaia graduated from the the philogical department at Ural State University in Sverdlosk in 1960, specializing in Russian Languages and Literature. In 1965-1968 she was a graduate student at the Institute of Latin America, USSR Academy of Sciences. In 1969 she defended her dissertation as a Candidate in Historical Sciences on "Problems in Modern Northeastern Brazil: Features of the Socio-Economic Development and Revolutionary Process in the Region during the 1950's-1069's."

Since the early 1970's she has been a research worker at the Institute of Eastern Studies, USSR Academy of Sciences, specializing in the study of traditional village relations and peasant consciousness.

Her publications in Soviet journals include the following articles:

"The Awakening of the Northeast: Several Features of Peasant Development in Brazil at the End of the 1950's and Beginning of the 1960's" in Modern and Recent History, No. 5, 1968.

"On the Evolution of Socio-Economic Structures in Northeast Brazil in the XVI-XVIII Centuries" in The Middle Ages: A Collection, Issue 35, 1973.

"The Green Revolution and the Problem of the Decay of Traditional Relations (Based on Three Regions of Hindustan)," in Developing Countries and the "Green Revolution," 1974.

"The Heritage of the Traditional Community and the Communal Peasantry: Features of Communal Consciousness (Based on Several Regions of Java in the Mid-Twentieth Century)," in Agrarian Structures of Eastern Countries: Genesis, Evolution and Social Transformation (An article included as a chapter in a monograph on peasants), 1977.

"Traditional Relations in the Village and Peasant Consciousness (Based on a Number of Asian Countries)," in <u>Asia and Africa Today</u>, No. 4, 1978.

THE PEASANTRY ISOLATED BECAUSE OF THEIR
SOCIAL CONSCIOUSNESS AND SOCIAL BEHAVIOR

The relatively violent character of socio-political life in Asian countries in modern times is related in some degree to the social position of the great majority of the population in these countries, the peasantry. This can be seen in either activity and protest or in passivity and conformism, in the movements for traditionalism or for idealism and leadership. Accordingly, the peasant can play either an active or a passive role in the vicissitudes of socio-political life in these countries.

A correct understanding of the events taking shape in the village and beyond its borders then is impossible without comprehensive research on the peasantry as a social force. It is impossible to restrict this research to an analysis of the objective role of the peasantry in times of great political progress. It would also be incorrect to limit it to a study of the most visible peasant movements and actions. The many millions of the masses remain "behind the scenes" in such a case, their role in the struggle unmentioned. Analysis of these movements would lead inevitably to an exaggerated estimate of the willingness of peasants to protest. Such an approach in general sharply restricts the scope of research in which the social personality of the peasant is manifested.

The study of the peasantry "from within," as it appears firsthand in the social life of the village, in its daily forms of economic, cultural, domestic and religious life, is very important. The main objective of the analysis here will be to see the peasant as an individual, as a social person acting in multi-faceted bonds and relations, the holder of

a definite group of ideas, suppositions and concepts. Knowledge of the full scope of relations in
which the peasant acts has been supplemented by
knowledge of his ideas on the world and society and
about his place in it. It allows us to describe his
social attitude.

The realm of the social consciousness of the
individual, to a significant degree concealed from
observation, presents the most difficulty for research. Contemporary research has shown that the
motivational reasons for individual behavior lie in
this area, social psychology. Categories of social
psychology, such as environment, value orientation
and value system act as a bridge between consciousness and behavior, and regulate individual behavior
(24, p. 50; 53, p. 470).

In what way are we able to research peasant
consciousness today? The social interrelations of
the peasant will, apparently, be the first objective
of study. In the research of these relations among
the peasantry, it is most important that they are
directly interrelated with the social ideas of the
undeveloped societies in which they have appeared.
This was emphasized by Marx: "A spontaneous primary
consciousness is woven into material action and into
the material relations of the people, in the language of real life." The language of the real life
of the peasant and concrete forms of his social intercourse in this way is inseparable from the study
of consciousness.

Social consciousness, as is well known, pos-
sesses a significant stability and has its own regu-
larities of development. Because of this, it does
not at all automatically reflect any change in the
real relations which gave birth to it. Marx and
Engels spoke repeatedly about the "overdue nature"
of social consciousness and the "firmness of this
system" of ideas created by society (5, p. 21; 7, p.
36). Without exaggeration we can say that the past,
in view of historically formed practices of everyday
economic, administrative, cultural, religious and
domestic relations, as well as experience in social
struggle, continues to be an important factor in the
formation of peasant consciousness today.

The ideological heritage of the past is another
powerful factor which has been exerting a great influence on peasant consciousness in modern times.
For centuries traditional ideological, philosophical
and religious conceptions, which had created the
peasant's fundamental value system, prepared and
sanctified mores and norms (on the role of ideology
in the formation of social psychology see 70, pp.
108-109, 113), formed his consciousness, his relation to the world and his place in it. The importance of research into the ideological heritage of
the past has not diminished in modern times while
new forms of ideology influence the peasantry, because inherited conceptions of activity act on perceptions of new ideas by the peasant consciousness.

Whether we study a "theoretically valid" social
struggle in Asian villages depends greatly upon some
perceptible degree of approximation of the peasant's
social attitude to a class type of attitude. The
class type, in the ideal sense, assumes domination
of class features in the consciousness and in the
behavior of the peasantry. These features are hostility toward direct exploitation and primarily
class motivated social behavior. It should be kept
in mind that the class attitude of the peasant in
the strict scientific sense is the independent action of every individual, for whom action in the social struggle is an act of personal choice. The
consolidation of the peasantry is, in such a way, a
uniting of individuals who are realizing their class
interests. From the analysis of different forms of
social struggle of the peasant we can see that the
"irresoluteness" of which V.I. Lenin wrote: "that
irresoluteness is the very thing that makes it possible to call a revolutionary movement a revolutionary onslaught" (8, p. 28).[1]

---

[1] We fully share in the enthusiasm of the article of
Rakhmatullin, which showed how high a priority
V.I. Lenin gave to an understanding of the "revolutionary movement," "political consciousness,"
"political peasant movements" and "struggle" (See
62).

The first step on the path of formation of the
peasant's class consciousness is the semiconscious
hostility to direct exploitation. In this case socio-psychological factors of social behavior rather
than socio-political are relevant. For this reason,
the peasant's struggle assumes the character ". . .
of riots, devoid of any kind of political consciousness. . . ." Historical practice shows that eventually this spontaneous feeling of hostility toward
exploitation, free of any kind of archaic motivations, is itself a product of long historical development and relatively mature social attitudes.

The problem of peasant consciousness is closely
related to the problem of isolating the "real peasantry" in the strict scientific sense. The beginning of the peasantry as a "special social grouping"
is related to the ". . . division and development of
segments (isolated groupings) which stifles the initiative and creative energy of the working individual. A segment can find its adequate class form only
where the worker is the free private owner of the
means of production" (27, p. 78).

In the research of peasant consciousness in
Asian countries we apparently are not able to find
the "real peasant" for several reasons. Above all,
segments have for centuries existed in society
(which, using an expression of Engels, we can call
"fragments" of the kin strata in society) (7, p.
155), and, accordingly, we cannot find their adequate class form. Consequently, the revolutionary
potential, unused initiative and creative energy of
the individual cannot unfold.

Furthermore, the independence of segmented
peasants can be and often is a historically recur-
ring phenomenon, particularly in the East, because
of the influence of despotic governments.

Finally, in a given situation it is more important that the economic isolation of the individual
is mostly a gradual and not an immediate phenomenon.
It is in no way accompanied by the disappearance of
diverse multi-faceted relations, including important
areas of activity in the peasantry's lifestyle which
nourish peasant consciousness. Consciousness itself
is closely related to the past.

We will use, then, an understanding of "peasant" and "peasant-like" in the widest sense of these words, having in mind the entire multi-layered mass of rural workers. In this mass the consciousness of the "real peasant" is in no way always divided from or opposed to other categories of rural peoples.

The starting point for the development of peasant consciousness in the East is that of tribal-kin society. We term this kind of consciousness archaic. At any given time, the tribal-kin layer of society acts as a unified body reproducing the patriarchal family. Society has the total use of its natural productive powers organized on this basis. Property, according to Gavrilenko, "is coextensive with its labor" (25). The end result of labor is alienation. The collective forms of labor are a necessary attribute of society. The product of labor leads more or less to the centralization of distribution. Consumption also leads to a significant degree of collective character.

Any separation of economic, administrative, organizational and ritualistic relations is often absent. Economic relations are complicated by religion. Labor itself is often still carried out in a ritualistic mode, and is to a significant degree an imperative of tradition, oriented "toward the welfare of all society."

The leadership of society was centralized in the hands of the keepers of traditional knowledge and experience, the council of elders.

Bonds of solidarity, which at first firmly united the kin group, the tribe and later the clan, were especially traditional. They were based on the idea of a "natural" unity, a blood or symbolic (mythological) family of all members of society, closely related to the archaic religious beliefs of society. These were combined into magical rituals, and were sacred, having an all-embracing and necessary character. In the peasant consciousness these ideas of village society as a unified family, with its "father," its inner-family laws and familial methods for the resolution of conflicts, were deeply imbedded.

In such a model of societal relations, based on the lineal family, every member of society became firmly "soldered into" the naturally forming collective, and acted, as Marx noted, "as a member of a defined, organized personal conglomerate" (4, p. 17). Engels provided a profound characterization of the social attitude of the members of such a society: "The tribe retained the same kind of restrictions on people in their relations to foreigners as in their relations with themselves--tribe, family and its institutions . . . are naturally given the highest priority, under which the individual personality remains uncomfortably subordinate to in its feelings, thoughts and actions. . . . The people of this era still do not cut loose, according to Marx's expression, from the umbilical cord of primitive society" (7, p. 99).

The absorption of the individual into society, with the most important guide to behavior being the good of the family; the lack of diversity in relations; their personal character--at any one time all these excluded any conception by any member of the community that society might be unequal, of the exploited and the exploiters, and about class antagonisms.

For many, many centuries the peasantry has, in order to realize its class interests, been overcoming these archaic notions from earlier times. An alteration of the social attitude among members of tribal-kin society included above all else a radical restructuring of what had been dominant in their earlier relations. It is known what great significance Marx gave to the problem of the individual's social relations. "The disintegration of old social relations Marx considered a necessary characteristic of active capitalistic production" (3, p. 559; see also 2, p. 146). A true understanding of mature civil society was considered by Marx as necessarily inseparable from an understanding of the individual person who had been liberated "from natural relations," that in earlier historical periods had made him an inseparable part of an already described, greatly organized personal conglomerate.

The peasantry stood on the verge, therefore, of overcoming kin, tribal, clan and other "natural" relations. These relations maintained their natural and necessary character. They succeeded the archaic model described above, or, alternatively, reproduced the separate components of the archaic model on a grander scale in a later period of development. We term such relations traditional.

The many centuries of the evolution of rural society's social relations included a gradual, step-by-step destruction of the monolithic, inner structure of archaic types of society.

The decay of traditional collective forms of ownership (and later property), labor and distribution was a precondition for the unraveling of exploitive relations, for any decisive improvement in the realm of consciousness. The economic liberation of the individual was an important step in this process. However, institutions inherited from the archaic ages, the regulatory mechanisms of social life and stereotypes of behavior acted as conservative factors restraining the creative initiative of the individual. Ethnic, social and religious internecine dissension; despotic government with its powerful administrative, political and ideological influence; and much later, in many countries of Asia, subjection to colonial exploitation--all these factors stood as barriers to the economic liberation of individuals. These factors hindered as well the consolidation of traditional types and slowed down the radical reconstruction of the peasant's social consciousness for many centuries. Nevertheless, this reconstruction went on, but was extremly uneven in the diversity of Asia.

Even the most superficial glance at the huge peasant mass in Asian countries--we include in it the landowning as well as the landless working strata of any country--allows us to delineate groups or segments of the peasantry. Their existence defined the dominating features of their social attitude. These features are the forms of social intercourse in the village, the level of development of social consciousness and the predominant forms of social behavior. In every island, territory and geographical region we can find this "mosaic."

A large number of rural workers are included in
societal structures which in many ways are preserving features of the above described archaic model.
These tribal and tribal-kin societies have little
ethnography.[2]

But even if we put this large segment of the
rural working mass aside, we find in modern Asia
models of peasant social relations where the archaic
features are not fully but only partially overcome.
Here, archaic and traditional elements act not in a
chaotic manner, not in the manner of isolated "remnants," but in the form of a more or less coherent
system. The communal peasantry forms a special segment from this point of view. The communal form of
organization is quite typical for Asian peasants.
For centuries Asian countries were an area of communities of very diverse kinds of lifestyle. Their
special stability and conservativeness led these
communal institutions--for example, the clan, as
well as earlier familial communities--to an existence where they were ruled by despotic governments,
where they fulfilled the function of the lowest "administrative" link. In this analysis the subject of
research is the communal peasantry of several

---

[2] Even though formally it was impossible for this
population to move at will into the peasantry, a
number of important factors lets us see them as a
kind of peasantry: agrarian reforms in tribal
zones acted toward a transformation of the working
peoples into "typical" peasants; a large portion
of the tribal population was already integrated
into the economic structure of the non-tribal
zones as agricultural workers and tenants, and
this tendency grew; the specific number of Asian
peasants who were still members of tribes in their
social attitude was very old; finally, "the tribal
character" of the social attitude of these workers
had great significance in the political struggle
of many countries. Even in conditions of a significant degeneration of the tribal stratum, the
presence of tribal relations, tribal (ethnic)
self-consciousness and tribal (ethnic) consolidation lets us see these rural workers as a special
segment of peasants.

regions of Java in the 1950's and early 1960's.

We will analyze the caste peasantry of India during the time when caste relations were the most important factor in social behavior[3] (here we also include the mass of rural workers, a significant portion of which never, within the limits of caste society, owned land). Overcoming the peasantry's caste ideas and relations and progressing to a class position is a problem of unusual difficulty. Nevertheless, the experience of present-day India shows that such progress may take any number of different forms. It seems we can raise the possibility of the presence of a tendency toward formation of different types of peasant consciousness, within the limits of caste strata, from paternalistic to petite bourgeoisie. We will examine different aspects of caste relations with the goal of delineating preconditions for peasant class self-definition in three examples from Indian villages.

In isolated segments of Asian peasants we can find those for whom class direction and an orientation of hostility to direct exploitation, uncomplicated by clan, caste or religious motivations, is an important feature of their social attitude. Such peasants (particulary tenants) are primarily found in those regions of Asia where private landownership and private forms of exploitation had rather deep historical roots. We will examine such a situation in the analyses of Iran and the Philippines.

The enumeration and examination of such a small sample of peasant societal types does not to the slightest degree exhaust the variations of peasant social attitudes in modern Asia. The characteristics of the social attitude of the described segments is far from complete. This study is only a trial run, a first step toward research, which allows us to understand better the inner springs of modern peasant behavior. One of the main problems

---

[3] Accordingly, from this segment are excluded those masses of the Indian peasantry in whose social attitude caste relations and caste membership were not defining variables.

was to unveil how heterogeneous the peasantry was in
its historical legacy, in its social habits, social
ideas and stereotypes of behavior. In other words,
the problem was to show how much specificity there
is in every situation of the historical socio-cultural "complex" which for centuries created this
consciousness, especially in the formation and evolution of social relations in particular regions of
Asia.

Materials largely related to the decades of the
1950's and 1960's will be used to describe the characteristics of the social philosophy of the peasantry in contemporary times. This period is a model
lesson to a great degree since it mostly corresponds
to the first decade of independence for many Asian
countries. In this era a most important transformation of socio-economic and administrative-political
character occurred. It exposed the many weaknesses
of the peasantry as a social force and the hetero-
genic response of several of its segments to the
transformations in the village. The timeliness of
research into these segments has not diminished today. Additionally, the material of the period is
reflected relatively well by sources foremost in the
field of inquiry.

We have attempted to maximize the use of Soviet
sources, in which social relations, consciousness
and the peasant's struggle are to one degree or
another highlighted. This will be especially evident in the chapter devoted to the Iranian peasantry
(18; 30; 31; 64), as well as the Philippine (49; 50;
51; 58) and Indian chapters (13; 14; 45; 46; 52;
65).

Zhanna D. Smirenskaia

USSR Academy of Sciences

TRADITIONAL PEASANT SOCIETY (JAVA)

Historical Features of the Evolution of Javanese Society: the Spiritual Heritage of Society

Many existing features of public life in Javanese society and in the traditional Javanese village had formed primarily in the central and partially in the eastern portions of the island. This was in isolated, set apart areas where the Javanese people preserved, right up to the middle of the twentieth century, features that were similar to very remote eras, or the time early government was formed on the island in the first century. Research has delineated mainly two varieties: so-called agricultural ("irrigated") governments and commercial, littoral urban governments (43, pp. 520-521, 523; 66, p. 9, 12). The first was closely related to an earlier level of social development and was an archaic theocracy.[4] It played an important role in the formation of Indonesian civilization and traditional Javanese culture.

In the inner regions of the irrigated ricelands of central Java and parts of eastern Java, a new (compared with tribal-kin communities) type of society arose, based primarily on territorial and

---

[4] We use the terms "archaic" and "theocratic" to refer to certain early-governmental formations, having in mind the presence of a government with centralized magical-religious functions, allied with the sacred character of power itself in the eyes of the masses--features that were inseparably linked with the dominance of magical-religious ideas in the masses.

familial relations--the <u>desa</u>. Here the relatively
large product (thanks to natural factors and labor
cooperation), combined with a high density of population, created the preconditions for an active social life in rural villages. In the final analysis
this accounted for the origin of early government
organized on a special ruling class, isolated from
the basic mass of the population. The need for
cooperative labor and the institutionalization of
the desa into the governmental system hindered any
further disintegration of society in the isolated
peasant economy.

The stability of land as the natural, economic,
social and religious organism prolonged the life of
<u>adat</u>. Adat was the norm of common law which had
combined in different ways with the archaic stages
of rural society's evolution, during which animistic
beliefs were dominant in the people's consciousness.
As a code of unwritten rights and norms, regulating
the activity and behavior of all society, its separate members and groups, adat reflected archaic
ideas about the isolated inner order, of self-governing society, acting as a collective with natural
functions and organizing material resources (land,
forests, water) and spiritual resources (sacred objects and so forth). Adat was in a special relation
with the supernatural world and its powers. The
bond of the tribe to its land was sacred. The right
of the tribe to its territory had been passed down
by its ancestors, the spirit of which supposedly remained with the members of society. It was just
these spirits, as well as territorial spirits, that
were the natural guardians of the earth. For that
reason the land was to the people of this remote
time a receptacle of spirits and protective powers.
The welfare of society was directly related to its
relations with supernatural powers. These relations
were realized in collective magical rituals. Ritualistic functions were the main function of society
in the minds of its members. The unity of society
was interpreted above all else as a spiritual and
magical unity.

The bases of the rural population's economic
practices remained unchanged, especially cooperative
labor and ritualistic collective practices, which

had been ingrained into the functions of early
government since they were so closely tied in with
the economy. The rural population invariably preserved such important features of consciousness as
the special "symbolic" mode of world vision, resulting from its magical-religious interpretation of
life, social processes and so forth. The "symbolic"
mode of world vision meant the conjecture of the existence of a secret supernatural power for all outer
material objects. Such objects acted in this way
only as a covering or a symbol of more important,
"magical" objects, powers and relations. The Indonesian researcher Soemasaid described the "symbolic, projective, imaginatory" character of traditional forms of Javanese thought. For the Javanese
everything had a secret meaning which they were always ready to search for in actions, words and situations. "Apparent and comprehensible subjects were
considered as possible projections (or reflections)
of more abstract and secret meanings, denoted by the
word _surasa_, meaning sense or inner destination"
(111, p. 15, pp. 21-31). The division of the world
into the microcosmos, or the world of people and the
macrocosmos, the "extra-person," supernatural world,
was the central ideal of the Javanese world vision.
Faith in the spirits was the most important manifestation of the idea of the supernatural world. For
the Javanese, the world was "filled with a myriad
number of invisible local spirits and ancestral
spirits, pervading through all natural objects, personal lives, and subjects." The spirits were always
potentially ready to lead one into misfortune (89,
p. 44; 91, pp. 20-27).

With such an understanding of the world, the
formation of ancient ideas about laws governing usage of particular plots of land and natural resources in general were related to belief in spirits: "every part of earth having a physical
border--a plot of irrigated land, the place under-
neath a home, an intersection--all had a locality
spirit, a _danyang_" (94, p. 326).

A village, as a territory, also had its own
spirit. Local spirits were the objects of worship,
and gradually the spirits of the founders of the
community, the common ancestors of the community, or
"_tjakal_ _bakal_," combined with them. The natural

right to leadership lay in those families that were
more closely related to the spirits of the village
founders, that is, the true descendants of those
founders. Gradually these "true descendants" became
the hereditary elite of the village, the kentol.
Often the burial ground of a legendary, semi-myth-
ological ancestor (in the eyes of the local inhabitants it was the home of the village's spirit), a
punden, became the common sacred property of the
village. Here general village rituals took place,
and here villagers came with different requests for
blessings before making any kind of important deci-
sions (89, p. 47; 94, p. 323; 99, p. 269).

The organization of the leadership and its division from the basic mass of the population took
place in a situation where ideas on administration
had definitely become interwoven with faith in magic. Inasmuch as the ruling class had formed on account of the isolation of the ruling families or familial hierarchy, which "had risen . . . by the
establishment of religio-administrative control over
the entire community" (43, p. 95), then the traditional prestige and unquestioned authority of this
group, based on faith in its "miracle-creating"
ability, was not only not weakened, but to the contrary was strengthened. The diffusion into the upper strata of society of Hindu culture (in the first
century), putting in the hands of the rulers a special language, Sanscrit, written alphabets and more
developed religio-philosophical ideas promoted this
isolation and transformation of the ruling strata
into its own kind of exclusive caste. Governmental
power and its instruments--the head elite and his
immediate circle of subordinates--were the hereditary aristocracy. The elite-bureaucracy, who had
assumed the special title of prijaji, took on in the
eyes of the peasantry a clearly expressed "miracle-
working, magical" quality. The government inevitably assumed definite theocratic features.

The village, or desa, of the early-governmental
period was a complex social organization. Common
characteristics of its origin could be found in collective work, in the amount of land found in general
use, in work cooperatives, in such general properties as "sacred" objects and ideas, in collective
rituals and magical-religious ideas. The natural

and historical record of societal decay, the isolation of the individual, the severing of the "natural
umbilical cord" connecting him with society, must
have gone through a number of stages: through the
disintegration of ancient, ritualistic, collective
forms of labor, through the reduction in the amount
of public land and the strengthening of individual
landowners, through the loss of the sacred meanings
of ritual, and finally, through the liberation of
the individual from archaic, traditional orientations.

Diverse tendencies were at work in different
areas of the complex structure of these neighboring
communities in the pregovernmental and early-governmental period. A tendency toward the formation of
newer, more individualistic forms of land use appeared, divorced from older, collective forms, and
were seen in adat in the form of labor laws. Village adat permitted two types of assimilation and
appropriation of new land and its subsequent ownership: collective and personal. Accordingly, two
sources of land were formed: collective (or communal) and individual. Individual landownership
created the necessary preconditions for the decay of
communal structures. However, factors related to
collective forms of labor withstood this decay: labor cooperatives, labor obligations, social work for
the benefit of the village or government, work on
so-called public land under village administration.
The spread of individual landownership itself often
accompanied, as several scholars emphasize, the increase of the peasant's work obligations. According
to adat, the members of society received the right
to use land individually only for fulfillment of
definite, clearly defined duties, mostly some form
of labor service (113, p. 4). Finally, individual
appropriation of farmland, woodlands and so forth
had to be sanctioned by a collective majority of the
village through a public ceremony (see 91, pp. 82-
83).

The central Javanese government exerted a great
administrative and political influence on the village and its evolution. This influence was especially strong in the immediate proximity of the ruler's residence, the palace. This part of the

government had a special name, the state sultanate. Here, according to the opinions of several Indonesian scholars, village adat suffered its greatest alterations. All land was declared to be the property of the ruling clique, and village headmen were reduced to simple "rent collectors" (113, p. 3, pp. 9-11).

However, in the territories surrounding the sultanate (subdistricts) the land remained the property of the community (113, p. 6). Governmental or royal power itself saw the village as an inseparable administrative entity, which could impose taxes and duties and had exclusive rights over the village administration. As Haar correctly notes, the ossification of the inner structure of the community only reinforced the rights of administrative chiefs and as a whole reinforced the priorities of the community over the individual (91, pp. 78-79). The presence in the village of a fund of public land, often found in partial redistribution, was the material basis for conservative tendencies. Village administration managed the distribution of public land, which had been formed from the original holdings of the earliest ancestors. The land itself was simultaneously the basis for the preservation of their power and the vitality of all traditional institutions.

The scale of the diffusion of individual landownership had found, in such a way, a reverse dependence on the stability of the community and all of its institutions. This was related in turn to the influence of the government and later to many local conditions, such as rural overpopulation.[5]

Theocratic government exerted a great influence on the most conservative sphere of social struggle, the peasant's social consciousness. Archaic notions about some magical unity which had naturally formed the community (tribe or kin group) had not only

---

[5] So, annual divisions were related to the insufficient quantity of good land and had the goal of managing the economic welfare of all members of society.

transferred to the government the functions of the
village head, but had strengthened it extraordinarily because of personal conflicts over this unity
within its leadership, the princes (the _rajas_, or
ratu). The head of the government, having played an
exceptionally important role in agrarian royal rituals, was idolized, and came to be seen as a reincarnation of one of the gods of the Hindu pantheon,
above all _Vishnu_. He acted as the focus of the magical strength of all the people, as the protector-
patron of the nation. Magical powers also existed
in those in the immediate surroundings of the rulers, such as the aristocracy and the elite-bureaucracy (55, p. 143, pp. 158-159; 99, p. 90; 111, p.
26, 28).

The formation of theocratic government and the
isolation and consolidation of the ruling strata and
administrative apparatus was accompanied by the formation of its own special ideology, elaborating a
philosophical-religious conception of social construction and administration. The ideology essentially nourished old, archaic ideas about society.
We find this ideology in the absolutely domineering
medieval central Javanese government of Mataram
(sixteenth to eighteenth centuries), and in the
post-Mataram period (nineteenth century). Relations
between the people and royalty were expressed in the
formula "_kawulagusti_" ("servant to sir," or more exactly, "man to god"), which had a mystical quality.
Relations between the royalty (or the ruling clique
in general) and submissive subordinates were based
on this idea of the character of personal relations,
on "mutual love and respect," and it was a "model
for social intercourse" (111, p. 15, pp. 21-26).
Material and personal resources that were withdrawn
from rural communities (for the harvest of a _desia-
tina_, mobilization for heavy work, or military service) were primarily interpreted in the peasant mind
as pay for the magical protection of the royal dynasty. One of the clearer examples of this phenomenon could be found in Jogjakarta, where up to the
middle of the twentieth century "an infinite and un-
describable devotion" of the people to the ruler
(the Sultan) was preserved. By tradition "good" objects and policies were seen as "emanating from the
Sultan," from his magical powers. With the prefix

"raja" added to their names, obligatory duties were
seen as honorable achievements in the name of the
prince, and were accordingly articulated in vocabulary. So, cattle were called rajakaya, or "princely
wealth"; values, such as rajasyapen or raja brana,
were "princely values"; natural taxes were rajapun-
dut, or "that which is the prince's property" (123,
p. 20).

Apparently, under the influence of the ideology
of the ruling elites, village society had absorbed
an understanding of "pulung," which designated a
special "political" spirit. The Javanese had "assigned" this spirit to those individuals who were
worthy to be headmen of the village administration.
Such a spirit guaranteed property, harmony and order
in the village (123, p. 26).

Such features of the traditional world view, as
an understanding of the cosmos and social order, interdependence on the Hindu pantheon, the realization
of a universal bond to the created system and the
provision of an unchanging place for each and every
person in this system were strengthened and developed the most during the period of substantial
growth in the Javanese government. The natural
movement of the development of ideas of the "social
order" and the presence of the idea of hierarchy
have put a deep fatalism into the peasant's communal
attitudes: the life and position of a person are
determined from above and are immutable, and a person must submit to fate and patiently proceed down a
predetermined path.

The appearance of the so-called cultural abangan was the result of the blending and symbiosis of
traditional Javanese beliefs and social ideas with
Hindu ideas, and later with several canons of Islam
(from the fourteenth century). Abangan had its
greatest diffusion in the rural areas of central and
portions of eastern Java, regions populated by Javanese. Beliefs in spirits and magic, semi-ritualis-
tic dramas, or selamatans, extensive mythology, in
which the Javanese hero was presented with Hindu
gods and heroes, and finally, the puppet theater,
which was its own kind of moral "instruction for everyone" were components of this native syncretic
culture of the Javanese. As Parnikel emphasizes in

his research, the appearance of the puppet theater, especially its use of shadows, was a form of mysterious education for the peasants to the world of gods and heroes, the empirical manifestation of which was the ruling dynasty (55, p. 125, pp. 160-161). The theater was, in such a way, a powerful means of influence on the feelings, attitudes and entire inner world of the working mass.

The selamatan, primarily a ritualistic common drama, in which both Javanese and spirits participate, occupied a central place in this native culture. The goal of the drama was to strengthen the individual's alarm and anxiety before the spirits, and to allow him to achieve a state of total tranquility, the selamatan state, where "tranquility was a mandatory part of life, which no one considered in any way nonbeneficial" (99, p. 95). In this way, the medieval ideas of the pregovernmental period, as well as later social ideas, were the spiritual heritage of Javanese society.

The colonization of Indonesia by Holland exerted a great influence over the country's socio-economic development. Traditional regions of Java, as our literature has stressed, presented immensely fertile ground for exploitation by colonial governments (66, p. 23). Both the conservation of public land and the bureaucratization of upper-level social groups could be seen in these regions. Traditional familial relations had an almost compulsory character. "The population of the community was divided into five groups, each of which carried the name of a certain day in the five-day Javanese week. . . . Everyone of these groups lived in a particular part of the village. According to its name, every group worked once a week in the service of the colonial power or the rural community. On the remaining days of the week all of the group worked their turn on public land. The groups were led with the special assistance of the village elders" (48, pp. 62-64). As Simoniia stresses, as a result these regions, right up to the beginning of the twentieth century, were characterized by a great retardation in the development of individual land use and the transformation of public institutions and archaic forms of exploitation, which might have led to the

origin of local commercialists and capitalistic
elements (66, pp 25-33).

The preservation of traditional forms of peasant social consciousness was especially evident in
the preservation of traditional public structures in
practically unchanged forms. This was inherent even
in the peasantry of more developed regions of the
island. Traditional peasant orientations were directly reflected in the character of peasant agitation on Java in the nineteenth and early twentieth
centuries. Peasants continued to tie their hopes to
the return of an idyllic pre-colonial era, to the
coming of the messiah. The "prophecy of Jayabaya"
(twelfth century) about the end of the white government and the return of Java to its own beginnings,
its own "children," was popular with the peasantry
(95, pp. 93-95; 123, p. 43). It is not accidental
that the Indonesian researcher Kartodirdjo notes
that peasant actions in the nineteenth century and
beginning of the twentieth century were "expressions
of traditionalism, with its elements of an ancestral
cult, sacred fetishism, ritualism, bond to the land,
kin solidarity and loyalities, and traditional status relations." Tradition itself operated as "one
of the basic values" (96, p. 12).

The work in the village of political organizations of new types--the national organization "Sarekat Islam" since the 1912's and the Communist Party
of Indonesia (PKI) since the 1920's--was the beginning of peasant involvement with a modern form of
social consciousness and political struggle (see
21). It has been shown that such work received its
greatest response in western Java and in those areas
of the island where the community had been disrupted, such as Madiun in central Java. According
to our research we can say that as a consequence of
the age-old forced "closing-off" of society its traditional ideas of "harmony and order" were preserved. The "primitive democracy" of society and
the methods of the central administration, deliber-
ately chosen by the Javanese government, were fused
together on the basis of the ancestor cult. That
is, features were preserved in the public life of
society which actively hindered the establishment of
peasant class self-consciousness and the elaboration
of class antagonisms in the village.

Central Javanese Society in the 1950's: the
Influence of Tradition on Peasant Social Thought

In the middle of the twentieth century the village desa, or the "village complex" of five to eight
of the closest villages, was the lowest link of the
administrative chain. It was called the kelurahan
and had general administrative duties.

Scholarly materials of the first half of the
1950's provide a general impression about the social
peasant of this period. The materials pertain to
the peasantry of several regions of central and east
Java, of territories relatively close to old centers
of Javanese theocratic government.[6]

In the period between the two world wars, four
social groups were usually present in the Javanese
desa:

1) the governing upper elite of society: elders, members of the village council, religious
elites;

2) privileged people[7] with right to the use of
public land, having personal holdings and dwellings,
"aristocrats";

----

[6] We use the materials of the Indonesian researcher
Koentjaraningrat, who had studied two villages not
far from Kebumena in the southern part of central
Java at the end of the 1950's, in which the village Tjelapar was described in detail (98 and 99),
and those of the American researcher Jay relating
primarily to the western part of east Java (Kedi),
in which he described the village complex of Tamansari in the rural areas of Mojokuto (both names
are fictitious) in 1953-1954. Jay published a
seminal monograph (94).

[7] We refer here to the more well-known, diffused
names of privileged aristocrats in the investigated region.

3) semi-aristocrats--persons having at least a personal landholding and dwelling; and

4) _menumpang_ (living off others)--villagers having neither land nor property, the most socially belittled group of the rural population.[8]

Our materials do not allow an even exposition of the social status and economic position of all four of the indicated groups, but do allow the opportunity to illuminate the place and evolution of two of them: societal elites and the privileged aristocrats.

Nearly fifteen people usually worked in village administration.[9] They were directed by elders, the _lurah_. Administrators were appointed by the lurah. Administrators did not receive any kind of remuneration from the elite rulers. Official allotments were their main source of livelihood--traditional gifts, deductions and service. The exploitation of land allotments had the greatest importance and achieved widespread dimensions, especially if we keep in mind how little land there was in the village (94, p. 16).

Koentjaraningrat puts forth the following traditional presents and service of the villagers, or _palagoro_: payment of a predetermined portion of rice annually; deductions for the administration of a small percent from the agreed price according to the nature of the purchase, sale, rent or pawnage; payment to the elders in the case of an exogamous wedding or trip outside the village; work in the

---

[8] Historically between privileged aristocrats and other villagers there were no insurmountable borders. _Setengah gogols_, and especially menumpangs, were usually newcomers for several years after moving into the village. They received public land with the appearance of "free" shares.

[9] Besides the elders this consisted of two elected village headmen, one clerk, two treasurers, two religious leaders, four "military governors" and four messengers (99, p. 273).

domestic village administration for a period (99, p. 273).

The aristocratic landowners participated in the elections of public leaders (also formally in the removal of those having lost faith with the elders) and in discussions of the arrangement of public matters. They had the right to submit applications to the district head.

Their duties were quite widespread. They included work obligations to the village, village administration and rulers (public works), nightwatch in the village and palagoro--the aforementioned rewards and deductions for the administration in natural and monetary form (94, pp. 320-329; 99, pp. 267-268, 273).

At the beginning of the 1950's the landless still did not constitute a majority in the researched regions. They were predominantly peasants having meagre income and holdings. In Tamansari the landless constituted one-third of all households; in Tjelapar also a large number of peasants had scanty landholdings.

The village social structure of the researched regions did not end any of the archaic features inherited from the distant past. So, in Tjelapar a hereditary elite was chosen, the kentol, which large kin groups formed, having decided that their ancestors were the local "sacred personage" or panembhana.

Election to the elders and the possibility of becoming a member of the village administration was directly related to membership in the kentol. Traditional hereditary government was extraordinarily stable, and for that reason the election itself had a rather arbitrary character. This is not counting the elders, who as a rule were chosen for life, and upon their departure only one or two candidates were named. In the researched regions attempts to elect subordinates of the lurah, undertaken after independence was achieved, were unsuccessful (98, p. 269; 99, pp. 93-94).

The prestige of the elders was often strengthened due to the perception of their power as having
a miracle-working quality. Sometimes the lurah were
dukun--magicians and sorcerers--at the same time
(see 94, pp. 195-197 99, p. 272).

There were a number of outer manifestations of
the high social status of members of the kentol:
the size and style of their houses, and the form of
the roofs. The rank and file of the village con-
versed with the members of this group using a special, regulated kind of speech,[10] "high language,"
or kromo. Members entered the village elite via
specific traditional professions having huge prestige. Among these were the guru, or tutor, the men-
tor of traditional Javanese education; the dalang,
the puppeteer of the puppet theater; and finally,
the dukun, or shaman.

In the community council the council of elders,
as a rule, played the role of consultative organ.
This made them experts on adat (99, p. 274). In
several situations the elder himself was a member of
the council of elders. In that case the role of
traditional factors in the management of village affairs grew. The traditional attitude to the village
headman as the "village father" was maintained.
Villagers saw their relation to other members of the
village administration almost like a kin relation;
poor peasants turned to them for emergency food
(usually rice), which they returned without interest, as well as for any other kind of help. In return the peasants usually gave presents either to
all the representatives of the administration, or to
that person they considered their patron (94, pp.
294-295; 98, p. 94).

Traditional norms supported the belief of the
small family that it was "quite important to be economically independent and to fulfill their social
obligations" (94, p. 55). In such a way the ideal

---

[10] In Javanese society there are styles of language
that serve to express socio-structural differences in conversation; among them two are basic:
ngoko, or low, and kromo, or high.

conception of the family domestic economy in the
community in the 1950's had two aspects: economic
independence and the fulfillment of social obligations. Economic independence was understood as work
on personal, all-family[11] or public land, sufficient
for family maintenance; fulfillment of social obligations was seen in participation in various forms
of labor and domestic mutual help, and in village
and family rituals.

Several forms of free, noncompensatory help existed in the village, as did strictly accounted-for
exchanges of labor services. Among these were re-
wang, or "helping anyone" from the nearest kin group
or family, which was noncompensatory; genten, or
"exchange" of labor help, submitted to strict accounting (according to the amount of time spent,
measured from the midday mark), in which all participants were equal; saya, or "all working together,"
which was assistance put together by the peasantry
for field work or home construction (94, pp. 250-
252).

The fulfillment of family obligations had not
only an economic aspect but a large social meaning.
The participants were equal in status in a large
number of the kinds of labor cooperation. The re-
ception to the invitation to such forms of combined
work as the saya was evidence of social acceptance
and was treated more as a right than an obligation;
compensation was a small, insignificant portion of
food (94, p. 227). Finally, this egalitarian aspect
of traditional labor relations was strengthened
still more by the selamatan, where collective work
usually began and which alone affirmed the importance of everyone present.

---

[11] In the region of our research there were many
cases where several families would use inherited
land together. Every family had a share, but at
least one of them had the official document, cer-
tifying property rights for the entire land.
Naturally this member of the group was a privileged aristocrat (98, p. 106; also 94, p. 441).

The incorporation of traditional social
relations had an obligatory character. Consequently, individuals were not to refuse an invitation to
the selamatan or such forms of work as the saya (94,
p. 226).

There were different forms of tenancy and work
for monetary compensation in Javanese villages during the 1950's. The latter were those forms of work
that let the peasant work and make ends meet, but
from the aspect of traditional ideas of equality did
not correspond to the social ideals of the peasantry. Such forms of tenancy as ngedok and mertelon
were regarded as forms of work where the individual
knowingly put himself in an unequal position. The
poorest peasantry found a temporary way out in the
mutual exchange of these forms of labor, which traditionally were seen as lowering social status. The
peasant longed to preserve the possibility of employment primarily for his kin and family; they were
the only ones who had rendered "such service" to
him, and tried to make this "service" mutual, in
order to preserve an appearance of equality. In Tamansari nearly four-fifths of village households,
according to the account of Jay, had recourse to
this form of exchange (94, p. 253, 322).

However, a significant portion of peasants were
not able to maintain themselves on this "slippery
ground." Many peasants were forced more or less
gradually to turn to prosperous landowners as tenants and agricultural workers. As a result a system
of vertical relations arose on an economic basis,
and a relation of patron-client was usually established between landowner and small holding peasant.
In exchange for the material support of the patron,
tenants had to express unconditional respect for him
and do his odd jobs. The fulfillment alone of casu-
al errands, the role of "little boy on errands," had
been judged by village social opinion to be a clearly humiliating position (94, p. 254, 264).

The tenant usually had great interest in a direct relationship with the patron and had to be a
"good client." From the category of "independent"
peasant he would definitively move to the category
of "dependent." The resulting hierarchy largely re-

flected the form of verbal communication; if the
tenant himself had never been hired for work, then
he followed orders in a way that was not favorable
to himself but directly subordinating.

"Dependent" peasants usually were grouped
around a person acting as patron. Often members of
the administration acted as patrons to a particular
family of peasants, especially the most well-to-do.
In Tamansari basically two people acted as patrons:
the village lurah and the most prosperous houseowner
(94, p. 253).

Besides a traditional labor relation, every
family had a ritualistic public relation: distribution of food during family or religious holidays,
participation in festivals being held by families
and so forth. The level of authority a villager had
was in direct relation to the volume of these relations (94, p. 56).

Almost all fixed traditional social bonds were
accompanied by the selamatan. All people were by
tradition considered equal in their rights, and in
such a way it was as if over time the selamatan ab-
rogated the existing social gradation of the peasantry.

We will examine at greater length several peculiarities of the social consciousness of the peasantry. First of all, we must note the presence in
the villager's social consciousness of several levels, from the more archaic to the more modern, existing with a definite mode of cooperation among
each other. The more archaic levels were related to
faith in spirits and the ancestor cult, having been
preserved right up to the 1950's and 1960's in territories where the abangan culture was still widespread. In a village in one of the regions of our
research, faith in the existence of the spirit who
was the patron of the village, and the spirits who
were the founders of the settlement, continued to be
partially maintained. The punden, the place of burial for the "community ancestor," continued to be
important as an overall village sacred object, and
was a place for ritual and pilgrimage for the more
backward peasantry. Such public rituals as "the

village cleansing," the <u>resih</u> <u>desa</u>, were testimony
to the preservation of archaic truths. The village
administration acted as the organizer and leader of
the rituals. Villagers also maintained faith in the
supernatural abilities of the shaman-dukun, and
turned to him in case of sickness or for other reasons (94, p. 323, 326, pp. 339-340; 98, pp. 16-25,
81-111).

At this time a large number of these archaic
ideas were closely interwoven with the social understandings that had been elaborated by the villages
over many centuries. The idea of "pulung" as an attribute of the lurah continued to be maintained in
several rural regions of the southern part of central Java. Members of the kentol considered that,
except for the lurah, pulung could be possessed only
by the high national rulers, who had this pulung in
a significantly greater measure. It was felt, for
example, in the beginning of the 1950's that the
Javanese president had pulung (88, p. 26).

The century-old experience of the joint economic practices and work cooperation of the peasantry,
so necessary in a rice economy, was the basis for
the origin of value systems in the community, the
central categories of which were equality, mutual
aid, collaboration and agreement. These value orientations were consolidated into stereotypes of relations around neighbors. Polite and courteous relations toward one's neighbor were the rule for the
peasantry. Social opinion condemned any violation
of traditional ethics. Neighborly relations in the
Javanese village had been transformed into a powerful regulator of individual social behavior. The
neighborhood, being related to the recognition of
the individual in the community and with a feeling
of mutual support (<u>rukun</u>), compelled the individual
to submit to the value system of rural society,
practically for the extent of the individual's life-
time (88, p. 14; 94, p. 232; 98, p. 94).

The selamatan repeatedly played a large role in
the consolidation of the peasant's value orientations. The following observation by Geertz seems
accurate: "Very short and unpretentious, the selamatan more or less symbolized and occasionally ex-

pressed one of many deeply felt Javanese values: total mutual support and harmony between neighbors. An appeal to this ideal, called rukun by the Javanese, and <u>gotong royong</u> by the Indonesians, compelled them to take the time to consider the other person's well-being, in such a way mitigating the tendency toward social decay to a significant degree . . ." (89, p. 44).

It is even more important to note that the consciousness of the rich groups of the peasantry was identified, as a rule, with the kentol and the village administration, and accordingly, traditional forms of mutual relations were transmitted by them. Relations between rich and poor were treated as patron-client relations, and later on these were understood to take the outward form of relations of older relative to younger one. In such a way, the most powerful traditional control levers of the peasant mass were hereditarily controlled by the decrees of a newly forming class of private rural exploiters.

The very process which had enveloped the "nucleus" of the community (its fully privileged individuals) and its socio-economic differentiation, like the differentiation of "potential antagonists" or class, had still "escaped" the peasant consciousness. In Tamansari, for example, the villagers were not aware or did not want to be aware of the existence in the village of classes or strata: "To the highest possible degree they were inclined to consider their agricultural community as a unified, undifferentiated mass"; "they didn't want to accept the fact that the community was divided into two socially unequal groups" (94, p. 266, 282). Moreover, social divisions into "personal rankings" constantly arose in the course of everyday community life, and the peasantry, as already noted, applied every effort in avoiding the appearance of submission. Here an illusory ideal turned out to be strong in reality. Accordingly, villagers maintained their own kind of "corporativeness," the feeling of belonging to a natural family, through which obligations imposed by these circumstances had to be strictly observed, and an offense committed within village limits was cruelly punished (94, p. 292; see also 98, p. 113).

This traditional type of solidarity supported in every possible way stable norms for the functioning of social mechanisms in the village, especially village assemblies. The essence of these norms was the principle of unity, expressed in such conceptions as the musjawarah, or the joint discussion of questions, and the mufakat, or the unified decision that flowed out from this discussion, for which all participants were considered equally responsible. This decision, as a rule, was a compromise between expressed points of view. Unanimity, mutual respect and the absence of argument were the traditional ideals in the resolution of village affairs. Public differences were to be eliminated at any cost. Researchers note the "deep convictions which had taken hold, that the duty of the village headman and the administrators was to protect village well-being through its indissoluble unity." The fulfillment by the lurah of this role would facilitate this, as he was like the "father" of the village, and it was impossible to contradict him overtly (99, p. 274).

The principles of the musjawarah and the mufakat in the resolution of village affairs were combined with the other principles of social intercourse referred to above, rukun and gotong royong. The acceptance of mutual responsibility of the members of the community between each other and to the entire community in general transformed the village to a unified, cohesive unit of society, based on traditional bonds.

The achievement of independence and the revival of socio-political life in the country, especially in the cities, and the increasing contacts with the city which the peasantry had in the past only observed "from below" undoubtedly strengthened the penetration into the village of new trends. These shattered the traditional structure of social relations and actively influenced the peasant's consciousness.

Governmental politics in the years of independence, from the second half of the 1950's and the beginning of the system called "guided democracy," included a wide-ranging ideological attack on the peasantry. There were a number of factors in this, including official propagandistic slogans and orientations that were favorably received by peasants in especially traditional areas. Age-old dreams about the arrival of a messiah and the return to a "golden age" were in some way rekindled by the achievement of independence and the transition of power into the hands of a national elite. "In the minds of millions the victory over colonialism was personified in most of the leaders who were conspicuous in the national liberation movement. Sukarno was such a leader" (32, p. 157). In the eyes of the masses he was not only the "father of the nation" and government, but had "automatically" become, so necessary for the quality of government leadership, like "manna from heaven" (36, p. 32).

The habitual admiration of the peasants toward local and central government, their concept of the heavenly character of central government, and finally, ancient dreams which were still alive in the remainder of the peasantry--these things in themselves helped produce an environment for the appearance of special traditional orientations in government ideology and the rebirth of several especially archaic features of government. Many of these traditional social appearances, values and ideas which had formed in the distant past and had been part of the official ideology of the medieval Javanese government were present in the doctrine of "Indonesian socialism" created by Sukarno in a renovated but almost unchanged shape. These values and ideals--harmony and order as the basis of society, solidarity and mutual help as the universal and ideal type of social relation (this mutual help on a societal scale was treated as the patronage of the "upper house," the rulers, and the voluntary submission of the "lower house," or the people, above all the peasantry), and finally, unity and solidarity of the nation as its ideal--had accordingly denied the presence of antagonistic classes in society, and had recognized only diverse strata, political trends and "functional groups," who had to coordinate and make their actions agree with the ideals of unity and harmony (32, p. 17, 31; 36, pp. 30-32).

Such a doctrine was clear and understandable by the traditional peasantry of Java. The doctrine itself very nearly objectively regenerated and

strengthened peasant ideas about the magical unity
of society, inasmuch as, according to this analysis,
it was precisely the "center," the leader of the
country and people, that was supposed to decide the
fate of all the people. This invariably weakened
the socio-political activity of class types among
the peasants and reinforced their conformism.

The social politics of the Indonesian elite
were to no small degree inspired by the idea of "archaic collectivism." This was the course for the
consolidation of traditional collective forms of
economic, social and administrative life in the village. This government policy apparently fell on
sufficiently favorable soil.

The material conditions of several neighboring
villages in central and west Java in 1962 revealed
the existence in the village of a rigid administrative structure, encompassing four hierarchically related units. The lowest unit, the neighborhood association, consolidated ten to twenty-five main
families and had its own leader. The remaining
units were the rukun kampong, the grumbul and the
desa.[12] The lurah was the only elected person of the
overall village administration. In all ten villages
of the Banjumas region the lurah were the direct descendants or were the nearest relatives of the
preceding lurah. He himself assigned his two helpers and five to six governors in all the "corners"
of the village (grumbul). In such a way, the entire
administrative upper strata of the village--six to
seven people--were appointed by elders (124, p. 14).

Three governmental organizations were active in
the village: the Javatan Pendidikan Majarakat (Pen
mas--Department of Community Education), Lembago So-
sial Desa (LSD--Village Social Institute, a subdivision of the Ministry for Social Affairs), and the
Pembanguman Masjarakat Desa (PMD--Village Community
Development, a subdivision of the Ministry of

____

[12] The desa included five to six grumbul, or ham-
lets. Each grumbul had two to three rukun kampong. Each of these had four to five rukun tet-
tanga, or neighborhood associations (trans.).

Cooperatives). The Pen mas, in its energetic activity (the drive for the liquidation of illiteracy, courses for preparing leaders for the community and village), proceeded with the goal of "preserving peace" in the village. Still, this arrangement was present in the activity of the LSD, the goal of which was the creation and stimulation of a "climate" of "socially mutual understanding, consciousness and responsibility, directed toward the realization of social well-being in village society," to the realization of a "socio-psychologically satisfactory life" among the peasantry (124, p. 5, 79).

The concrete activity of all three institutions was directed to reinforcement as well as production of traditional forms of mutual help and the practice of free collective work, the only remuneration being food. So the LSD stimulated the collective responsibility of every neighborhood association for the "well-being of every member." Many neighborhood associations had a general supply of rice. On its own initiative the LSD created a food reserve via an account of a small weekly allotment of rice, forthcoming from every family (124, p. 20, 26).[13]

Although according to the plan of activity the LSD should have had to operate through informal, nonadministrative channels, in fact on a number of occasions "functionaries" of the LSD in the lower units of the village structure became administrative personnel--chairmen of neighborhood associations or farmers' cooperatives (124, p. 26).

------

[13] Moreover, in Bodjong village the LSD undertook attempts to organize "neighboring groups," or kelompok, from every five families with daily rotating chairmen. The chairman had to answer for all that was going on that day, mobilize villagers to help in case of someone's death, sickness, or poor harvest, as well as cases of personal or family conflict. However, this attempt was met without enthusiasm and passed away (124, pp. 26-27).

However, it is very likely that the most important unit in the implementation of government policies was the PMD, directed on a number of occasions
toward the reinforcement of community tradition in
industry, construction of infrastructure, living
quarters and so on. A large part of the cooperatives were reorganized along governmental lines but
still included traditional groups' mutual cooperation, combined purchases with payments in rice, combined sales and purchases of necessary peasant goods
and so on (see 94, pp. 365-368; 99, pp. 275-276;
124, p. 20, 27). The transfer into the administrative unit of the mechanics of informal traditional
relations was the result of the process. In the
situation Selosoemardjan described in Bodjong village, after the cooperative was sanctioned by the
rulers (the members of the bureau of the cooperative
were appointed by the lurah), its boundaries were
soon merged with the boundaries of the entire village. Later, the functions of the cooperative also
became part of the village administration, where the
natural form of exchange was replaced by a monetary
one (124, pp. 27-30; see also 17).

Here it is especially important for us to
stress that traditional forms of social control began automatically "to operate" new institutions and
became even more rigid. As Selosoemardjan notes,
social control, which had originated in neighborly
relations, created its own exclusive role: "Social
sanctions were strengthened through the organization
of the farmers' cooperatives and the village administration. Every member who didn't pay his dues to
the cooperative was considered a disrupter of social
norms and an undesirable member of the community.
So not a single person dared to bring upon the re-
sentment of the community for the sake of any devia-
tions from the rule of the cooperative, such as the
LSD" (124, p. 29).

The author of the work came to the conclusion
that the relation of the governing politicians to
their actual work objectively strengthened the "com-
manding position" of the heads of the village; generally every innovation which could have affected
the interests of the lurah was doomed to failure
(124, p. 21, 30).

In such a way, the specifics of the situation which had come together in the regions of Java we researched point to the fact that the authoritative bearers of the traditional heritage of the village were representatives of governmental power and governmental policies. This fact had the following two-sided effect. From one side, in the researched regions a certain rebirth of social relations occurred on a new, national administrative basis, thereby consolidating the authoritative strength of the government. From the other side, as Selosoemardjan notes with total accuracy, it was traditional devotion alone to prominent local figures that determined the success of governmental plans for community development in a given region (124, p. 13).[14]

Apparently, in those regions where traditionally oriented governmental politics found fertile soil, their effect was to strengthen peasant conformism, and as a result, the spontaneous, conscious and forced submission to tradition. This represented a step forward on the path to isolating the individual from society, on the path to his

---

[14] The experience of reform in Jogjakarta at the end of the 1940's, undertaken on the initiative of the Sultan Amangukubuwona IX, testifies very well to this "working in harmony" through the habitual idolization of the "father of the village" in the context of concrete reforms. Exclusively all measures came from above. So-called elected committees were "named," as a rule, by the administrative official from the "more talented people." The new council acted under the "directing guidance" of the Sultan and his old administration, who gave competent guidance as to how the secretariat should be organized, how to carry out procedures and so forth. Even when a decision to reduce administration personnel was made, protests from those who were dismissed were not given much attention. As Selosoemardjan notes, the direct participants in this decision "all knew, that the Sultan's decision was taken in the spirit of national revolution." It was true, though, that whoever was not reelected received a

liberation from the "spiritual plane" of traditional
society, on the path to his independent class self-
orientation in socio-political life.

During the 1950's the activities of the Communist party in the traditional village undoubtedly
stimulated political activity among the poorer peasants to somehow break with their traditional social
values, in the center of which stood "harmony and
order." The weakening of traditional village unity
and the resultant activity of various rival political parties (this rivalry reached a definite culmi-
nation in the 1957 elections) was characteristic for
this period, and led to a weakening role for village
administration (94, p. 38).

The 1950's and 1960's were definitely a turning
point. Sukarno's change of course in 1957-1959 and
the demand for the cooperation of all political parties had a fatal influence on any awakening of political activity among peasants in the traditional
regions. Sukarno's advancement of the slogan Nasa-
kom (a union of nationalists, Muslims and communists), in conditions where peasants in the investigated regions had to a great degree preserved
traditional ideas about norms of social life, was
able to strengthen peasant conformism in its relation to the local administration. This in turn automatically weakened any tendency toward the development of radical forms of struggle by the poor
peasants for their interests. As already discussed,
rapid social changes in the village had the consequence of only a "minimum of social disorganization"
and hardly caused any damage to the relations between members of the village and their ruling elite
(124, p. 13).

In a moment of fervor in the peasant movement
at the end of the 1950's, a vast rural mass from all
the regions in Java was drawn into the struggle.
However, this fact alone cannot be taken as evidence
of a drawing-in of the poorer groups in the village
into the struggle of class types. Because of the

------

living pension in the form of a plot of public
land.

traditional mechanics of leadership and the governing role of the village administration, the role of
the peasantry in any organization was extraordinarily simple--the village administration played the de-
ciding role. In reality often all the villagers
participated in a peasant organization and voted for
a single candidate. The maintenance of the leadership role for the village administration in several
segments of peasant movements invariably weakened
the radicalness of these movements.

Traditional peasant orientations could, evidently, integrate several socialist ideas. However,
these were integrated in accordance with their traditional ideas of collectivism, social welfare and
dogmatic archaic beliefs. They brought into these
movements elements of the ritualistic selamatan,
mystic symbolism and so forth.

It is necessary to keep in mind the role of the
religious leaders. Their prestige was extraordinarily high. In the postwar period on Java in general,
and in central Java in particular, the definite
strength of mystical attitudes and an inclination
toward the "mystical prophet" was seen among some of
the rural masses. Around these charismatic leaders,
particularistic mass movements, basically of a
peaceful character, were formed. Here the objectiv-
ity of the peasant rested on a more archaic basis
--belief in the participation of a many-sided power
in the peasant's fate, and in the exceptional "magical" properties of isolated personalities. These
movements, even though several were supported by the
PKI, invariably reflected to the least degree the
class position of the peasant. Obviously then, the
reorientation or arrest of the leaders in such cases
would have meant the failure of the entire "movement" (see 95, p. 121).

The preservation by the peasants of many traditional features in inner-village relations, in social behavior and in their consciousness, was characteristic for the state of mind of the communal
peasants we have analysed. The "secret" of this
conservatism lies in the inertness of the very community itself, the evolution of which, after the decay of its archaic elements, had in the past re-

tarded the influence of government. The lack of
membership in collectives, the cohesive traditional
mentality and maintenance of traditional features of
consciousness and stereotypes of social behavior remained characteristic for the peasantry. The most
important stereotypes were the conception of the
village (and also the community and government) as a
natural family, the ideals of "harmony and order" in
society, the readiness to submit to the "father" of
the village and government, or, in other words, socio-political conformism.

CHAPTER TWO

TRADITIONAL RURAL PEASANT CASTES
AND PATERNALISTIC SOCIETY (WEST BENGAL)

<u>Some</u> <u>Historical</u> <u>Features</u> <u>of</u> <u>the</u> <u>Formation</u> <u>of</u> <u>Social</u>
<u>Relations</u> <u>in</u> <u>Rural</u> <u>Areas</u> <u>of</u> <u>India</u>

The configuration of the contemporary socio-political situation in Indian villages, the gigantic
diversity and variety of relations of traditional
and new types embracing the rural working mass, the
greatly heterogeneous layers of social consciousness
of this mass--all these were directly related to the
specific historical conditions of the evolution of
this country, and the diversity of its regions.
This included the history of the settlement of the
Indian subcontinent and the very formation of Indian
civilization, with its particular ethnic, political
and economic history, as well as the evolution of
its agrarian structure.

Social strata that were related to the existence in the Indus valley of the diverse Indo-Aryan
civilization, as well as the presence of early-governmental theocratic-type formations wielding arbitrary power, were present at the birth of Indian
civilization (69, pp. 11-13). At the same time of
the Indus civilization there existed a farming tribe
with more or less developed forms of social organization in various parts of the Indian subcontinent:
the Ganges valley, and the valleys, forests and
plains of Deccan. A significant part of the tribe's
activity was consumed in hunting and gathering.

The invasion into northern India by the Indo-
Aryan tribes and their advancement into the farming
regions of the Ganges valley preceded the establishment of a society divided into four groups which
differed at first in their social functions

(Brahmans, or priests; Kshatriyas, or soldiers;
Vaisyas, or farmers and commercialists, and Sudras,
or servants). These groups later came to be based
on the appearance of unequal castes with unequal
rights and the subsequent advancement of separate
caste groups (often the Brahmans) in the eastern and
southern regions of the subcontinent. This laid the
basis for social stratification according to birth,
as well as the cooperation and symbiosis of the
groups within it. The results of this process were
varied and depended on many factors. Particular
features of the social structure which was forming
depended to some degree on the specific proportion
of professional caste members from the foreign Aryan
community on the one hand. On the other hand, the
structural features depended on the form of social
organization of the local people (whether an undeveloped tribal strata, an agricultural village community which could have included early-governmental
structures, or others). We will address only a few
questions having importance for the research of our
topic, not stopping to consider the particulars and
the results of this process in the diverse regions
of India in ancient times, the middle ages, or the
modern era (the religious specifics of the social
processes are examined in our Indian literature:
13; 22; 23).

The division of labor between the bearers of
ritualistic functions (Brahmans) and the military
functions (Kshatriyas), the most inherent feature in
ancient Indian society, often took on the character
of rivalries and sharp clashes between the representatives of the two high castes. On an ideological plane the crux of the rivalry was whether the
management and leadership of the people in their
worldly affairs, as well as the government itself
and its functionaries, was sacriligious or sacred.
The non-worldly sphere, "the world of spirits," remained highly regarded and the Brahmans occupied the
highest place in the hierarchy. The Brahmans were
victors in this ideological debate in ancient India.[15] In accordance with traditional Indian ideas,

---

[15] Apparently, the consolidating role of the Brah-
      mans in ancient India promoted the powerful reli-

worldly activities, including politico-administra-
tive activities, were incompatible with the exalted
activities of the sphere of spirits and were assigned the lowest ranking in their relation with the
latter.

Hinduism, as a powerful and elaborate religious, philosophical and ideological system, still
evolving up to the beginning of the modern era (at
greater length see 39, pp. 174-180), was a multi-
layered formulation. The central theocratic categories of Hinduism, such as its dharma--the moral-religious duty of a person, and the law of karma--the
regeneration of the person's spirit with recompense
for good and bad acts, proved to be the basis for
the formulation not just of value orientations but
of behavioral norms and mores for the laboring mass
of the country. The conception of the absolute and
lofty values of Hinduism was part of an impersonal
worldly spiritual substance--Brahma. Union with him
was the highest goal for an individual. This could
only be the result of the lengthy moral perfection
of the individual for a stretch of several rebirths,
while he fulfilled his own dharma. The fulfillment
of this moral-religious duty in turn was connected
with the maintenance of "purity" and the avoidance
of "impurity," and with a multitude of scrupulous,
petty guidelines, especially numerous for the Brahman. The degree of "purity" and the proximity to
the world of Brahma acted for centuries, in such a
way, as the main ideological criteria, defining the
hierarchy of society and designating the status of
its groups and isolated individuals. Hinduism, ex-
tending and developing the archaic principle of the
sacred hierarchy, of ritualistic "purity" and "impurity," sanctified the division of labor in society
itself in the very same way. In the rural communities, it gave the division of labor an ideological
and theological basis, and promoted the transformation of various social groups (professional, ethnic
and others) into socially unequal castes.

---

gio-cultural legacy of the Indo-Aryan epoch,
leaving an important impression on ancient Indian
mythology, rituals, calendars and culture in general (22, p. 110; 69, pp. 16-33).

Accordingly, the Brahmans occupied the highest spot in the caste hierarchy, and the ones who were "associated with god" were the leaders of ritual. The Kshatriyas were lower rulers and soldiers; still lower were the businessmen and the farmers; and finally, at the very bottom, the Sudras, called upon to serve the higher castes. The further diffusion of Hinduism brought with it the inclusion into caste society of the lowest fundamental link of the caste hierarchy,[16] the low castes and formal outcaste groups (untouchables), and all modern and new ethnic groups and tribes.

Many spheres of personal activity (several aspects of trade, and all agricultural work in a number of regions) were purported to be "impure" and so entire professional and ethnic groups were slighted as "impure."

The advancement of the Indian system of values and the hierarchy of social groups found a constant and systematic expression in religious ceremonies. The Brahmans were the leaders, the representatives of various castes were kept in their clearly marked unequalness by the protocol of place and function, and the untouchables were often generally not allowed to participate in them. The usurpation by the Brahmans of sacred acts and "sacred knowledge" could not restrict access by the middle and lower castes, and particularly the untouchables, to the spiritual achievements of Indian society.[17] It was inevitably

---

[16] An exclusion sometimes was made for elites--those of "princely" birth or of a priestly upper group of autochthonic ethnicity, who could mix with high castes such as Kshatriyas.

[17] At that time the existence in society of intact social strata--Brahmans, Buddhists and Jainists, who could lead practically their whole lives in isolation in monastaries or temples, studying the religious philosophical heritage of different schools, created intense differences over the philosophical identity of India. From here the high level of abstract thought and deep elaboration of concepts were related to the inner-mental

the maintenance by the basic part of the populace of
primitive beliefs and culture that was to a large
degree characteristic of the untouchables and doomed
them to social, religious and cultural isolation.
The existence of a wide cross section of the people
who preserved primitive beliefs and culture exerted
a reverse influence on Hinduism, transforming it
into their own kind of conglomeration of very diverse cultures combined with the formally united
worship of the three central gods of the Hindu pantheon: Brahma, _Shiva_ and Vishnu (see 39, pp. 174-
180).

However, the "pure" or "ideal" model of Hindu
society was not found in real life, because the professional castes, above all, broke with it in a number of regions, and the Brahmans and Kshatriyas were
compelled to cross over to physiocratic, including
agricultural, labor. Conversely, the members of the
lowest castes bettered themselves by virtue of other
means and were able to attain a relatively higher
place in the caste hierarchy in isolated regions.
Nevertheless, the constant reproduction of norms in
ritual form that were enunciated by Hinduism helped
to preserve for many centuries the basic value orientations, moral norms and behavioral arrangements
related to Hinduism and its system of values.

The moral leadership of the Brahmans and the
triumph of Hindu ideology had important meaning for
the process of forming a government in India. The
tendency toward formation of absolute despotic governmental power invariably was present in ancient
and medieval India. The rulers of many regions
tried to use this absolute power and in a number of
unrelated cases achieved this (see, for example, 13,
pp. 115-119). All the same, in general the important idiosyncrasies of the country's history were
the narrowness of the functions of central governmental power, and the relatively self-sufficient

----

makeup of individuals, of logic, psychology and
other disciplines. It should be stressed that
such intensive development promoted a situation
where the philosophical thought of India was of
no real use to the government.

communities and small principalities within the
boundaries of a larger union (see 22, pp. 110- 115).
The prerogatives of the government did not intrude
into the inner life of the community, where relations were regulated by the norms of common law (47,
p. 58).[18]

A few illustrations from the medieval period
will show that administrative organs did not exert
any strong pressure upon the individual (this especially comes to mind from the Chinese traveller).[19]
Corporal punishment was not adopted upon any common
violation of the law. Far more serious were crimes
"against property or justice" and deficiencies of
moral character. The Brahmans enjoyed a special immunity from this.

The absence of a unified central government objectively emphasized the importance for a more free
evolution of local social structures, depending on
conditions. In the early medieval period these
structures could assume varied forms, depending on
the dominant type of landownership (neighbor-commu-
nity, community-clan, individual) and caste

---

[18] "In ancient times," writes an Indian author, "and
in the middle ages the government never issued
edicts or written laws. The rulers did not have
the right to promulgate laws. The king's duty
was to protect justice in accordance with the
Dharma Sastra. The Dharma was the highest law
over kings" (47, pp. 106-107). According to
another author, "Hindu rulers and provincial officials never controlled their subordinates
through the rule of law. They never tried to in-
termingle or administer their rights and obligations, differing in nature, with the help of
laws. The resolution of all societal and familial matters was placed on the shoulders of their
subordinates. People were mainly governed by
their ancient customs and traditions" (47, p.
58).

[19] Administrative power in India was simple--writes
the Chinese traveller Yuan Chwang, who had visited the Indus valley, the central Deccan and

membership in the basic group of landowners (Brahmans, Kshatriyas, farmers-businessmen who were unoc-
cupied with farming, those partially occupied with
it, and Sudras and Vaisyas who were farmers). In
regions where neighboring communities were widely
stratified the decay of social relations and the
formation of partial landownership were part of the
natural evolution of the leadership. Different researchers stress that the diffusion of private landownership was already present in medieval India (see
22, pp. 110-111).

In the medieval period, however, several powerful factors hindered this tendency: the unusual
strength of the role of government, numerous inva-
sions and conquests, and finally, the very organization of castes in the village society working toward
the preservation of the "community state" in the
village as well as the land fund for compensation of
community expenditures.

The Muslim conquest of northern India and parts
of the Deccan in the medieval period had the consequence of greatly strengthening the government role
in the management of the entire land fund of these
and other principalities. It also signified the
"diffusion to the south of Muslim legal ideas, in
particular, ideas about government ownership of all
land" (13, pp. 262-263). In this way, in the medieval period the government itself acted as expropriator for both society and individual peasant
landowners. The tax exploitation of the community
grew with the consolidation of the governmental system. Control of land passed to soldiers and civil
servants who were responsible for tax collection in

southern and eastern India in 630-635--families
were not registered, and villagers were not
forced to submit to compulsory labor. Taxes being collected were slight, and the personal service that was demanded from the people was moder-
ate. Every good citizen had part of their common
property, and everyone worked land for personal
enrichment. As businessmen, merchants were free
to move around and conduct their affairs (40, p.
108).

a defined territory--and sometimes for that territory's protection, considering the weakening of central governmental power in certain regions of northern and southern India. A system of landownership
formed as a result which resembled a European
seignorial system.[20]

Besides a large amount of landownership of a
"feudal type" with its inherent hierarchy of ownership rights, which had developed "in the ruins" of
large government formations for the entire medieval
period, there was an area in the agrarian structure
that was constantly (re)organizing the scale of government landownership. This was related to the wide
diffusion of Brahman and religious landownership in
India.

The extraordinarily high prestige of religious
activity bolstered not only the transfer of important parts of government land to the temples and
Brahmans but the sale of these lands promoted a number of immunities and practically all governmental
prerogatives. These lands created a distinctive
government within the government.[21] More than that,
the existence of autonomous religious territories
was conducive to the emergence of industrial and
commercial centers, little dependent on the government; "the nearby religious settlements filled the
function of cities and had a tendency to end up as
the present cities," as Alaev notes (13, p. 224; 39,
p. 155).

---

[20] The diffusion of landownership to the poligars,
characterized by full private ownership and "the
union of governmental power and private landownership into one hand," resulted in the destruction of imperial Vijayanagar at the end of the
sixteenth-seventeenth centuries (13, pp. 251-
259).

[21] This process was observed in a long historical
period--from the early medieval period up to the
fourteenth century--at least in southern India.

Upon the Muslim conquest of northern India and the submission to Muslim power of significant portions of the Deccan, which promoted an unusual strengthening of government power, temple autonomy was liquidated or restricted in a number of regions (13, pp. 214-219, 223). However, it was preserved in places where a strong central government had not formed and where Muslims had not conquered, particularly in several territories of Kerala.

Brahman landownership played an important role in the consolidation of private landownership in medieval India. The giving of land by the Brahmans, or agrahar (literally this meant, that which is to be given firstly, before others) was considered a god-pleasing act to a large degree, accepted in order to guarantee the prosperity of government. Brahman landownership was still quite dominant. Their land had been acquired, as a rule, with their exemption from all taxation intact. The Brahmans received the eight rights of ownership. The Brahman settlement was a self-sufficient and unified province (13, pp. 225-229; 39, pp. 154-157). Landownership more or less remained a privilege (13, pp. 228-229).

Consequently, for a large part of the pre-colonial period, the tendency toward formation of a strong despotic government, with its ownership of land, which had dealt a powerful blow to the spontaneous emergence of small private landownership, was invariably weakened by exclusion of Brahmans and the temples from government land. It was as if Brahman landownership, with its immunities, was a model for the formation of large, middle and small private landownership, independent from the government and likewise, in some measure, from community relations.

At the same time, the progressive possibilities that had created this tendency to private landownership could not receive full development on these same "Brahman territories." The removal of the Brahmans from physiocratic and in particular agricultural labor (and on a number of occasions from any kind of mundane labor) led to the origin of a system of tenants and subtenants, in which the humble groups of the village were the primary members.

Foreign intervention in the early medieval
period was another factor retarding the natural
process of the decay in community relations. The
northern part of the country, including the Ganges
valley, was exposed to greater influence from outside. In the ninth century northwest India was invaded by groups of Rajputs, Gujars and Jats, who
maintained a clan structure in their settlements.
The consequence of the division of land between them
and the imposition of clan relations on a caste society was the emergence in northern India of a specific kind of community, where landed collectives
acted as a societal and individual exploiter of
landless socially humble groups.

In the territories of northern India with a
high proportion of immigrants having high status in
the caste hierarchy--those in military-farming and
military-governing castes--two varieties of landownership had formed. In Gujarat and Rajasthan, where
members of the military-governing caste were predominant, a system with a "feudal landed gentry," to a
great degree reminiscent of the European medieval
system of landownership, had spread. At that time
the movement of a significant portion of the members
of these castes into farming conditioned the evolution of the agrarian structure of the corresponding
regions toward development of private landownership.
This was limited, however, by clan relations and
caste societal institutions. This tendency to a
still greater degree was seen in territories settled
by Jats and Ahirs, where farming collectives of
privileged aristocrats (members of one clan usually), who in peaceful times had been farmers, were
the core of the society. The collective of landowning aristocrats was a natural "government," not only
through the provision of "public services," but
through the exploitation of a substantial number of
tenants and rural workers (although the individual
renting of land on lease was not excluded). Here,
strong, functioning organs of community self-government existed (both clan and caste).

The power of the Muslim rulers could not destroy the caste basis of rural society. Northern
India, and above all the Ganges valley, became the
cradle for particular forms of Indian society. An
elaborate division of various kinds of labor between

professional caste groups of villagers and a relatively constant contingent of "public servants," including elders, scribes, craftsmen and so forth,[22] received its most complete elaboration in the jajman system (see 44 and 46 about this). Natural forms of compensation for labor was another characteristic of the jajman system. This meant specific principles of remuneration that were not of the service itself, but of "the ability or duty to perform this service" (14, p. 231), the inheritance of a structure of mutual labor relations and relations between families and the absence on both sides of the right to break these relations (14, pp. 224-242; 46).

In other parts of northern India, and particularly in Bengal, landownership approximating large-scale private ownership with some tenancy aspects had greatly developed. The strong power of the Muslim rulers and the distribution of land to the zamindars, or tax collectors, complicated the system of tenancy and subleasing but did not essentially change it. The Brahmans and the members of the other high castes remained the important links in the system of land relations. The very practice of the jajman system in regions where Brahman landownership was widespread had to some degree been transformed, inasmuch as Brahman landowners tried to get "public servants" under their personal control, especially those of them who were necessary for the fulfillment of rituals. Several became the personal servants of Brahmans, and were put to very diverse kinds of work. For this they received compensation, and the relations between Brahmans and "servants" and farm laborers assumed a personal character.

---

[22] Formally, the official functionaries of "public servants" were elders, writers and watchmen who had police functions. This included Brahmans and sometimes musicians, fakirs, etc. Then came the middle layer of artisans, and finally, the low category of servants, usually more numerous, who did the most heavy and unglamorous work (44, p. 6).

After the transformation of India into an English colony the agricultural taxation policy of the
colonizers was in much disrepute. The English engendered two systems of land exploitation, the zamindar and the _ryotwar_ systems, with the aim of regulating tax collection. These two systems in truth
closely approximated two tendencies in the form of
landownership in India. Since the objective goal of
English policy was toward the consolidation of land
rights into private ownership, the policy came to
grief on a number of occasions, especially in regions using the zamindar system, due to the incompleteness of tendencies toward formation of private
landownership and the absence of private landowners
of the European type. The affection and definite
interest of the English to tenants and their rights
found expression in a number of acts in favor of the
tenants. The objective consequence of opposition to
agrarian policy and economic processes that had been
present in the villages since the twentieth century
was the decay of community, including clan, landownership and land use in those places where it had existed, especially in ryotwar regions. Here a great
number of villagers were transformed into middle-
and small-scale producers, partially exploiting
someone else's labor. In zamindar regions the consequence was the growth of private landownership because of the expropriation of the inherited agricultural rights of the peasant tenants.

After the achievement of independence, a number
of tendencies that had been developing widely in Indian villages since the beginning of the twentieth
century all received a new impulse: the strengthening of private landownership, the weakening of traditional Indian society, the replacement of a number
of natural transactions in the village with monetary
ones, a definite shift in the caste composition of
landowners.

Socio-economic processes and the violent nature
of social and political life during the struggle for
independence significantly undermined the position
of Hinduism in different areas of social life. Il-
lustration of this can be found in the legislative
abrogation of caste inequality in 1947. Nevertheless, the place of Hinduism in the system of social

relations of rural society and particularly in the
sphere of social consciousness in the first decade
of independent development was undoubtedly important. The jajman system, although in relic form,
still preserved its semi-ritual importance. This
was especially true in those regions where orthodox
Brahmans were large landowners, had followed the
precepts of Hinduism and had preserved "purity" and
high socio-economic status. Normally they continued
to receive traditional presents from village craftsmen, independent of any need for their products, re-
munerating them as tradition prescribed (see 112,
pp. 143-145). The influence of Hinduism on economic
life to a significant degree came from a traditionally oriented system of values, in which material
value, moneyed wealth and its accumulation were
depreciated. Even in those regions which had been
included in the process of intensifying rural production and where there was a significant number of
small landowners,[23] for the peasantry in the middle
sixties the goal was still the pilgrimage to the
"holy place" and the arrangements for a village holiday on their return. This usually led to the fi-
nancial ruin of the family, however much its social
prestige might be increased. "Superstition remained
a widespread phenomenon; caste cruelty prevailed,"
wrote one author, "and more money was spent on various rituals, related to birth, death and other oc-
currences" (126, p. 27, 44). Hinduism's position
was strongest in the peasant's ideas of the world,
society and personal destiny.

The more general categories, such as dharma,
karma and others, were the steadiest components of
Hinduism. The basic Hindu social hierarchy was
strongly affected by new socio-economic processes.
The appearance of new economic and political ruling
castes, for example in northwestern India, brought
in definite kinds of reformations and the beginning
of religio-political trends that were advocating social equality. Sexism was such a trend, and it
played a large role in the incorporation of new social, economic and political trends.

---

[23] This is in reference to a progressive village in
    Allahabad district in 1964-1966.

Individuals reflected the great influence of
socio-economic relations in their social actions.
One feature of the socio-economic evolution of Indian society was its strong tendency toward the formation of private landownership, and this promoted a
definite erosion of inner-caste solidarity and commercial moneylending castes. We should note some
peculiarities, inherent in the very basis of Hinduism, that were able to exert influence later on.
The concept of karma--eliminating the inherently archaic aspects of the ancestral cult, such as fatalism (an individual's status and all of his suffering
was a result of a previous life), showed the importance and even the necessity of its predominance;
the person could and should improve his future individual karma. This concept, of paramount importance
to the individual and his actions, was unable to
stimulate any definite development of the individual, at least among higher castes.

As a result of any number of these factors, archaic features of traditional village social life,
such as unanimity (at least to the point that con-
troversy was absent), were still dominant in rural
society. Up to the time of independence, clashes
between various groups and leading families of landowners became the stable tradition of many villages.
Hinduism did not produce any special aesthetic
ideology, which might have laid a basis for the
idolization of government power and government representatives, especially central functionaries, by
the peasantry. They were in no way surrounded by
any "holy sanctity" in the eyes of the religious
peasantry. Objectively this created greater potential for freer development of social life and the
social struggle, although these possibilities were
muted by a number of already mentioned features inherent in Hinduism.

It is important to keep in mind that caste society was by no means overcome. On the contrary,
archaic, traditional forms of social mechanics were
preserved in the form of the leading role of the
panchayat, the council of elders. Every local caste
group (not always in every village) had its panchayat which took care of local problems and conflicts.
The panchayat, made up of both elders and the more
prosperous members of the group and established by

both custom and common law, was in this way the authoritative representative of the prosperous traditional base. The local caste hierarchy was reflected in the hierarchy of the caste panchayat, in
which the leading role belonged to the panchayat of
the highest castes or to domination by the sheer
number of middle castes.

The presence in the rural populace of various
caste groups with their own organs of self-government provided favorable ground for the spontaneous
origin of village social conflicts, especially from
the second half of the nineteenth century.

The operation of the country's various socio-
political powers in the village clashed with two
conditions. These were the "habitual" occurrence of
conflicts among villagers and the opposition of various groups, as well as stable "prepared" social relations and forms of consolidation--caste relations.
Both of these conditions retained their significance
and explain to a great degree the violent character
of social life in the Indian village, as well as the
present success of the communists in the agitation
of the agricultural masses in several states.

The most important factor in the rural people's
social consciousness remained the caste. We should
note the following forms of influence on caste consciousness during the 1940-1960's in the social
struggle of the peasantry:[24]

1) The drawing-in of the peasantry was more often a case of everyone in the caste line, through
the utilization of caste relations. Even though a
wide drawing-in of the oppressed masses in the socio-political struggle played a positive role at
first, it is impossible to ignore the negative side
in a given process. Here inclusion into the struggle and even entry into modern peasant organizations
was by far not always an act of personal choice or a
manifestation of a mature individual consciousness.

---

[24] Semenova throws light on this question in a segment devoted to the spontaneous forms of class
   struggle in the village (42, pp. 176-206).

As a rule, this was done on the basis of older,
pre-class forms of consolidation.

2) The feeling of caste hierarchy was not
immediately or always dominant within modern peasant
organizations. The peasantry's caste psychology had
been inculcated in such a way that the peasantry
avoided acting in organizations in which the members
were the representatives of the lower castes and the
untouchables. So, peasant branches of the organization <u>Kisan</u> <u>Sabha</u> in separate states united mainly
rural workers with equal caste status. These were
mainly either the untouchables or the caste peasantry, but neither one together usually.

3) Their own prosperous elite were already
prominent in almost all caste groups, and because it
was exactly these people that acted as the "natural
leaders" of caste groups, this had a great danger
for the further development of the social struggle.
The elite of the caste hierarchy had the capability
to rapidly mobilize the poorer strata for the struggle against the allotment of untouchable land, the
right to the usage of community institutions and so
forth. The leaders who were enriching the elite of
the untouchables in the social arena were able to
play and did play an analogous role.

Nevertheless, the violent socio-political life
of India in the 1950's and 1960's, agrarian and po-
litico-administrative reforms and the intensification of rural opposition, all steadily decayed and
washed away the bulwark of tradition--the caste
structure of India. Additionally, this decay and
erosion went not only at different rates but also in
different directions in the various regions of the
country. By the time of the 1950-1960's, historically formed variations among the regions of the
country in economic forms, in kinds of personal relations within households, in the special functions
of village social mechanics and in tendencies toward
the evolution of caste relations, preserved their
strength. The society that had developed from the
landowning farmers of northwest India (Punjab, western Uttar-Pradesh) now became an arena for the formation of petite bourgeoisie, at least in the aspirations of its peasantry. The rural working mass on

traditional farms (Brahman or a variant therein)
itself remained mainly traditional and caste pa-
triarchical. Finally, the formation of a revolutionary attitude and progress toward activity in the
political struggle of groups of agrarian pre-prole-
tarians from the untouchable caste became possible.

<u>Landless Agrarian Strata in Regions with Wide Caste
Stratification in Paternalistic Systems</u> (West
Bengal)

The historical particularities of the socio-
economic development of Bengal were related to many
factors. Among these none was more important than
the fact that throughout the entire middle ages this
rich agricultural and resource region was not the
center of any kind of large-scale central government. In politico-military relations Bengal was a
buffer zone for the large medieval governments of
northern India. The other peculiarity was the absence of any strong development of commercial and
monetary relations. The absence of strong governmental power was accompanied by the absence of societal unity, even in the eighteenth century. This
apparently furthered the diversity of the ethnic
composition of the people, then a relatively small
number of peasant landowning castes, and the development of commercial-monetary relations. Village
social institutions were preserved in some fashion
to the beginning of the nineteenth century,[25] but in
more developed regions they quickly disappeared.

As already noted, in Bengal there was not a
powerful and large strata of landowning farmers similar to the Jats of Punjab. The economic activity
of the members of the peasant castes--<u>Sadgopes</u>, <u>Ma-
hishyas</u>--developed under the strong influence of the
relatively large-scale landowners of the noneconomic
strata--Brahmans, <u>Kayasthas</u> (scribners) and others.
In eastern Bengal the conversion of a significant

---

[25] "Everywhere carpenters and blacksmiths, the majority of the priests of local gods and spirits,
weighers, money changers, barbers and tanners received many allowances for their expenses," wrote
one English civil servant (16, p. 69).

portion of members of the peasant castes to Islam
evidently helped maintain a group of primarily small
economically self-sufficient peasants with equal social status. In West Bengal peasant landownership
disseminated into the landownership of the noneconomic castes. In conditions of weak governmental
power and weak society, as well as the small number
of productive peasant owners, there was a strong
tendency toward the formation of large-scale landownership in Bengal.

In medieval times the zamindars were masters in
important territories in Bengal. They were free of
the obligation of military service to the rulers,
and they were collecting within "their" territories
a tax, a portion of which was earmarked for themselves. This was always collected, except for the
nonobligatory land tax. Yet the existence in Bengal
society of wealthy commercialists and usurers, even
in the eighteenth century, promoted the transfer of
zamindar rights into their hands (16, p. 81).

The middle and lower zamindars represented a
group in some way reminiscent of the landowners.
The zamindars had "the duty to maintain order," and
often imposed numerous extortions on the people (duties, fines, etc.). The presence of armed police
among the people guaranteed the zamindars full power
(16, pp. 77-78). The middle and lower zamindars
were primarily in conflict with those farmers who
had traditional rights of ownership or were tenants
and farm laborers without such rights. Objectively
in these situations they were able to create and
partially maintain close paternalistic relations between landowner and farmer. However, the varied
composition of the zamindars--civil servants (Brahmans, Kayasthas, Muslims and others), commercialists, usurers (from the Muslim and so-called middle
castes)--that is, primarily people not directly connected with farming and farmers and often not living
in the village, hindered the establishment of paternalistic relations on a number of occasions.

The final conquest of Bengal by the English at
the end of the eighteenth century strengthened the
tendency toward formation of private ownership in
land. The zamindars were the legal owners of land,
which removed the hereditary ownership rights of the

members of the peasant castes, as well as the "public servant" caste. This was accompanied by the
movement of the zamindars into societal-village institutions and the disorganized traditional forms of
economic life in the village in places where these
were still maintained (16, p. 121, pp. 253-255). A
high tax imposed by the zamindars caused much personal possession to be sold in auction, which in
turn promoted the further transfer of these posses-
sions into the hands of those castes already having
moneyed wealth.

Afterward the English endeavored to limit the
rights of the zamindars due to the decay of tenant
rights. However, the rights of the zamindars, who
were only the upper link in the chain of leasers and
leaseholders, were liquidated only after the
achievement of national independence.

The transformation of Calcutta in the colonial
period into a large-scale political and administrative center had great importance regarding the political development of this region. The Bengal intelligentsia were earlier than the intelligentsia of
other regions of the country in beginning to experience European humanistic thought and Western ideas
and value systems, and that made them rather definitively the leaders of modern national liberation
movements which were just beginning to take shape in
nineteenth century India. To some degree this situation influenced the educated circles of "rural society" in Bengal who were closely connected with the
city.

As a result of the division in 1947 of Bengal
into West Bengal, populated mainly by Muslims, the
region was left with a relatively lower percentage
of economically self-sufficient peasants.

Generally, we should note the following specific features of agrarian structures in West Bengal
that existed throughout the twentieth century. The
agrarian overpopulation in the region brought about
exceptionally small limits on landownership. The
caste composition of the landowners had a mixed
character: extensive portions consisted of Brahmans, Kayasthas and other members of high castes;

other parts, members of the middle castes, were
commercialists, usurers, partially skilled craftsmen; finally, several (in some territories quite
substantially) were hereditarily filled by peasants
(Sadgopes, Mahishyas, sometimes Muslims). Predominantly it was economically traditional types,
through which labor and property, or more exactly
labor and ownership rights, that were divided and
set against each other in West Bengal. Landownership stood against socially servile labor. The
presence in the region of a peasant upper elite
helped, in that they were composed of direct producers devoid of land, and were broken down into two
main categories. One of these were the tenants or
bargadars, who as a rule were the only "free" peasant group. The other were the unprivileged farm laborers from the lower castes, untouchables and adhivasi, members of "unregistered tribes" (63, p. 264),
who never owned the land that they worked. Low in-
dices of socio-economic development were characteristic for the state (see 60, pp. 343-344, 349).

Primarily three categories of landless working
peoples were employed on the farms of the region in
the 1950's: periodic farm laborers, daily workers
and bargadars. The main strength of the workers
were the members of the "unclean" castes (for example, Bagdi and Bauri), untouchables (Dom, Muchi) and
adhivasi (particularly Santal).

The greatest part of the landless rural working
people were included under economically traditional
types. This inclusion itself marked their insertion
into the system of traditional relations, often of a
paternalistic nature. Simultaneously subcaste
groups were included under lower, internally cohesive traditional relations.

This important feature--insertion into two systems of relations, having direct significance for
the fate of the social struggle in the village--we
will analyze using the example of the two more numerous lower castes of West Bengal who were involved
in agricultural production: the Bauri (using eight
villages of Hugli district as references) and the
Bagdi (using the village of Ranjana in Midnapore

district as a reference).[26] Both castes were considered "unclean," and their basic occupation was agricultural labor. The overwhelming majority of the Bauri of Hugli were occupied in work such as daily labor (59.04%). Approximately 30% were periodic laborers (seasonal and annual) or _nagas_. Approximately 10% worked land on _metayage_ terms (125, p. 23).

The nagas, or contractual workers, usually were in closer contact with the families of landowners. Often they lived outside the farm, although daily they would go to the farm in the morning for instructions. During the workday they would be fed twice from the farm (82, p. 53).

Contractual work was done in the 1950's and 1960's by the agricultural proletariat because it provided a far better guarantee from privation than other kinds of work. Often the connection of a naga to a particular family of landowners moved from generation to generation, and it was as if he himself became a member of the family. Conversation between the naga and members of the landowning family made great use of kinship terms (uncle, older brother and so forth). The children of the naga were also often pushed toward the housework of the landowners. All this reinforced the paternalistic "familial" character of relations between the landowner and his workers. The paternalistic character of these relations was especially evident in that usually in times of illness or of a natural disaster, the landlord did not make any deductions from his worker's pay (such as rice or the small sum of money at the end of the year), but sometimes helped during these bad times. Often the landowner contributed to the expenses of the farm laborer, and the organization of several typical ceremonial functions--weddings, etc. (see 82, p. 53; 125, pp. 25-26; 95, pp. 230-237).

---

[26] As a historical example we use the research undertaken by the Indian scientist Shasmal in 1962-1965 of the Bauri of Hugli district (125), and for materials characteristic of the Bagdi we use the research of Chattopadhyay in Ranjana village (Midnapore, 1950's) (82).

A significant number of Bauri were daily agricultural workers. Although the bond of such workers to the landowner was less close, here there was evident a direct personal dependence of the worker on the employer, especially as regards indebtedness. Bauri workers, who received only subsistence pay, often required money loans (for conducting religious ceremonies) and rice advances. The way of working off these loans was usually work in the fields at harvest time (125, p. 41).

Only an insignificant portion of Bauri and Bagdi were farm laborers and <u>metayers</u>. Traditionally the farm laborers received half of what was left from the harvest as their families' portion. The formal status of the farm worker assumed a lesser degree of personal dependence on the landowner and was more self-sufficient. Usually metayers contracted little with the employer and daily work was not a requirement.[27]

In "traditional" regions, the turning over of land to the metayers--in conditions of agrarian overpopulation and decay of traditional relations --turned out to be a boon for the landowners. The metayer, formally self-sufficient, was forced in the absence of personal resources to always rely upon the support of the owner in case of natural disaster. Here then was the necessity to constantly cultivate "good relations" with the owner, and to express an undying respect for him. Through such

------

[27] It was not accidental that these relatively independent peasant rural groups made up the basic core of the rural mass movement for agrarian reform. A great part of the bargadars of West Bengal made up that part of the peasant mass who had lost land to the members of the farming-landowning castes. In the 1940's the struggle of the Bengal bargadars led to a more just division of the harvest. This led the elite of West Bengal to undertake legislative action for the bargadars (1950) and land reform (1955). In accordance with this, the wages of the bargadars were 60% of the elite's expenditures for rural work (82,p. 109).

"good relations" between tenant and employer the metayage contract was renewable for an eight to ten
year period (125, p. 234). The threat of termina-
tion of the metayage contract was definitely a means
of political pressure, punishment and blackmail of
the peasantry by the landowners (82, p. 111; see
also 125, p. 232).

The attraction of the metayer to the farms
meant their inclusion into the system of traditional
relations, in which their social position was defined entirely by the landowners.

The acceptance of metayage in traditional areas, such as in Ranjana, often promoted the elimina-
tion of the bargadars and made traditional types of
rural labor more attractive. Later on, however,
older systems went back into effect. Nevertheless,
a definite blow had been dealt to the old system;
persons who had successfully maintained bargadar
status and were the very ones to have received a
guarantee from expulsion could now assume greater
independence from the landowner in the social struggle.

The presence of workers, farm laborers and tenants dependent on landowners raised the latter's
status in rural society. As the author of the work
in Ranjana stresses, such landowners used their respect and acceptance not only among their own metayers and farm laborers but also among "potential
workers" who were employed at a given time in other
occupations (54, p. 53). In such a way, vertical
relations of economic dependence, which had led to
the conditions of traditional society's paternalistic character in the first place, conditioned traditional forms of mobilization for landless groups in
the political struggle. This, naturally, made the
union of the groups based on a program of their own
socio-economic demands of a class character extraordinarily difficult. This conclusion is supported by
one scholar's work in several rural regions of West
Bengal in the 1960's, after intensive farming had
been introduced there. She notes that the nagas
were so dependent on the support of "good relations"
with large landowners (even if they only guaranteed
them a minimum level of subsistence, there were always more workers who could be attracted to their

side) that "efforts to organize agricultural workers
in Burdwan totally collapsed" (87, p. 177).

At this time the landless groups were not a
natural homogeneous mass tied by overall socio-economic and political interests. The caste structure
of society continued to remain the biggest factor in
the consolidation of relatively small groups. Such
groups continued to act in everyday social, cultural
and religious spheres as isolated cells, having
their own tradition, specific forms of organizational worship, etc. We will now look at relations of
this type among the Bauri. The Bauri, like the Bagdi and Dom, occupied a relatively high position
among the "unclean" castes and untouchables. The
Bauri continued to adhere to strict caste endogamy.
They were divided into ten subcaste groups (in the
investigated regions there were six), each having
their own history.[28] The _Meno Bauri_, who had the
highest status, did not accept food or water from
the hands of the members of other subcaste groups
and kept their subcaste endogamy. The lowest place
in the hierarchy was occupied by the _Mulo Bauri_
(125, pp. 51-52).

The unconditional support of caste solidarity
was the absolute demand of any community within society. In such a case, when any Bauri acted as if
his economic interests were higher in value than
that of caste solidarity, he suffered the ostracism
and the boycott of the community (see 125, p. 96).

In the beginning of the 1960's attempts to be-
gin an organizational struggle for a higher place in
the caste hierarchy were seen among Bauri. A Bauri
society in Hugli district ("_Hugli Zilla Bauri Unayan
Samity_") was founded. However, this attempt suffered defeat; it did not find a response from the
majority of Bauri. Possibly this refers to the absence of a prosperous upper elite, who would have
provided an economic basis for this action. The

---

[28] Among the Bauri there was one _gotra_ (called _Kash-
yap_), in which there were traces of totemism and
which traced its origin to one of the totemic ancestors (125, pp. 53-54).

more independent Bauri, especially the hereditary
leaders of the community, tried to give the children
an education that would raise their social status.
They also attempted to utilize to the maximum funds
for the development and education of the members of
the lower castes who were leaders (125, pp. 104-
105).

Centuries of social humiliation and poverty
promoted the entrenchment of the Bauri's entire
world of archaic religious truths, images and ceremonies. In the 1950's and 1960's the majority of
the Bauri were illiterate. In their religion pre-
Hindu worship was interwoven with the Indian pantheon. They believed in the existence not only of
many gods but of mystical strength and spirits, who
could be overcome with the help of magic and sor-
cery. Every local community of Bauri had its own
"specialist on spirits," the gunina.

The Bauri system of values and ideas about a
moral duty was evidence of the deep influence of
Hinduism. So, even though there was belief in gods
and spirits, many Bauri were convinced that "success
and well-being can be achieved through honest and
painstaking labor and acting on the principles of
moral duty." In accordance with the Hindu point of
view, prosperity or well-being of the individual depended on his karma, and prosperity after death depended on proper behavior during life (125, pp.
159-160).[29]

The worship of such gods, like Dharam Devata,
Shasthi, Manasa and Kali, in the form of presents of
fruit, rice and also sacrificial offerings (usually
cocks or goats) was carried out in specific ritual
areas. As a rule, any holiday brought out the entire Bauri community in a given village, and required materials were assembled from other families.

---

[29] So they explained the appearance of epidemics
among the Bauri by the nonfulfillment of a moral
norm. Among the more criminal offenses were the
murder of a person or an animal (especially cattle), matrimonial infidelity, lying, shunning the
gods and so forth (125, pp. 159-160).

Inasmuch as the Brahmans rendered service by religious necessity to the Bauri, the leaders of the religious ceremonies were the heads of those families
who organized the ritual.[30] Many religious holidays
were led by Bauri jointly with other Hindu caste
communities of the village (125, pp. 162-164, 181-
182).

The Bauri preserved their own traditional organs of government: the caste village council, managing "social, ceremonial and religious activities,"
involving moral-existential questions and conflicts
and supporting "peace and order" in the community;
the _sava_, or general meeting of the village Bauri;
the local caste council, which was made up from the
heads of the village caste councils. In the village
caste council, or panchayat, there was a leader, or
moral, his subordinates, the _deko_, several elders,
village religious servants, sorcerers and soldiers.
Although the formal leaders were not legally hereditary ones, more often than not most of them were in-
stalled via inheritance. In elections personal
qualities, economic position and age were all taken
into account. In all of the investigated regions
the leaders of the caste panchayat, the Bauri, had a
comparatively high economic position and were landowners. The services of members of the panchayat
were provided free of charge. The small, almost
symbolic recompense given to the leaders was only
for fulfilling organizational or ritualistic obligations. In several cases the leaders of the panchayat simultaneously fulfilled the functions of the
priest of a particular diety (125, pp. 88-91).

The sphere of action of the Bauri village caste
panchayat in the beginning of the 1960's narrowed
significantly.

---

[30] For example, for the ceremony in honor of Shasthi
in Bhawanipur village in 1968 two rupiahs were
collected from every family (a total of seventy-
two rupiahs) for the purchase of cloth, shells,
paper garlands, paper dishes, fruit and so forth
(125, p. 184).

In the 1950's a more important religious caste
council still existed among the Bauri, the <u>Jati</u> <u>Sab-</u>
<u>ha</u>, which was taking a greater quantity of the vil-
lage work. In the leading organ of this council
were the leaders, the <u>deshmaji</u>, and four of their
subordinates. All five duties were strictly inherited. The members of the council received a slight
monetary recompense only during their meetings. At
the time of this research this council had ceased to
exist (125, pp. 99-100, 103).

The Bagdi were another large group of agricultural laborers. Farming was the inherited activity
of the Bagdi, although in the past traditional activities of significant numbers of Bagdi were thiev-
ery and brigandage.[31] The physiological strength and
warlike morality inherent in the Bagdi were helpful,
in that recently the Bagdi were called upon by the
zamindars to work as guards. This in turn helped to
heighten their caste status. In the 1950's the Bagdi worked in more elevated positions amidst the "unclean" castes. They were admitted into inner rooms
of Brahman households (although they were forbidden
from touching several objects). Their religious
priorities were to serve "lower" Brahmans (82, p.
78; 122, p. 170, 172).

The Bagdi system of religious truths was generally along the ideas of other Hindu castes; they
worshipped the fundamental Hindu gods (not in a temple as much as in separate areas, or altars, where
the gods, Shiva, <u>Sitala</u>, Shasthi and Manasa were em-
bodied in stones) and participated in overall village ceremonies (122, pp. 177-178).

There was not any movement among the Bagdi toward "<u>sanskritism</u>" in the colonial period. At that
time in the regions there was an intensification of
military and political conflicts, such as in Midnapore, and the Bagdi were attracted to the armed
struggle. Starting from the end of the nineteenth

---

[31] The spread of the cult of the god Kali and its
role as the patron of robbers--the <u>Daccata</u> of
Kali--was the outgrowth of such activity (122, p.
170).

century, bargadars working as metayers attempted to increase their share of their production (some bargadars were Bagdi). During this attempt, several local progressive moral leaders, all Brahmans, undertook their first activity to unite the metayers for the struggle against their arbitrary landowners (82, pp. 106-109). In the 1930's, these Brahmans acted in defense of the Bagdi castes, and demanded abolition of their discrimination in religious ceremonies (82, pp. 9-10).

Consequently, albeit to a slight degree, in the researched regions the Bagdi and Bauri were integrated into Hindu society. Before the members of the most humiliated parts of the rural people--the untouchables and adhivasi--there was still the more problematical inclusion into caste society of its two lowest links. Without this inclusion, the possibilities for these two low status groups in farm labor were limited. Repudiation of what was traditionally "unclean" via a caste understanding of occupations was the natural way to remove this condition of humility. The Muchi followed this path in several regions of West Bengal.

The Muchi leather tanners, occupying one of the lower places among the "unclean" castes, and trying to raise their status, remained in their traditional occupations--harvesting and embalming of corpses. In several regions in the 1950's there were already three generations of Muchi occupied exclusively as agricultural laborers. However, in general their social position still remained very low in these states, and usually they were attracted toward agricultural work in later years (see 82, p. 73).

Constantly, the "unclean" occupations went to those groups of rural people who had comparatively not long ago left the tribal groups and begun to live in caste society--Santal, Oraon and others (see 122, p. 167). The Bauri, Bagdi, Muchi and other landless people resisted members of the landowning castes, like the Brahmans and the Kayasthas, as well as Mahishyas, Sadgopes, Goala, Koli and others. Brahmans and Kayasthas, the very groups not working as agricultural laborers, preferred to use the metayage system; Mahishyas, Sadgopes, Goala and Koli, who were directly organizing production, usually hired farm laborers on a contractual basis (125, pp. 38-39). In the regions of West Bengal, the already described close bond of the patron-client type was even closer in those situations where the employers were genuinely productive landowners, and not Brahmans and Kayasthas.

Traditionally a very high place in the caste hierarchy was reserved for Brahmans. A sizeable number of Brahmans, who strongly held back from traditionally ritual directions, occupations and taboos, enjoyed the greatest prestige in rural communities. As a rule, it was just these more independent Brahmans, often having inherited some function at local temples, that were simultaneously included to a large degree in the traditional system of exchange with the services and products of labor that were characteristic of the Indian village. In obligatory fashion they accepted traditional gifts from the members of the skilled castes and other castes, independent from any need for these products, and compensated them with some means of subsistence.[32]

----

[32] Research on various forms of mixed caste relations in West Bengal villages (Midnapore, Murshidabad, western Dinapore), conducted by the scientist Mukhopadhyay in 1961-1963, showed that several villages still preserved traditional relations between established families and public servants (laundrymen, barbers and others), artisans (blacksmiths, potters), boatmen; the labor of all these people was paid for three times a year with grain or other food products. The very character of the form of exchange guaranteed them well-being till the end of the year. On particular days in autumn, as the researcher described, from the outskirts of the village potterers, basket weavers, fisherman, barijibi (who raised betel) came with their products as gifts to the more "influential" families. These gifts were reimbursed by the head of the "leading family" in the village with gifts, grain or straw. Relations of the heads of the Brahman families with members of the artisan and "functional" castes

At this time large numbers of Brahmans had
plots of land that were totally insufficient for
their families' sustenance. Government service,
teaching, religious functions, business, etc., were
historically their basic occupations (82, p. 73).

The Kayasthas blacksmiths were another important group of the higher castes. The Kayasthas, an
educated segment of society in the period of Muslim
government, often were drawn to administrative service and acquired their own land. The rise in their
economic position and in their social status brought
them into a closer collaboration with the Brahmans.
In lower Bengal, such as in Hugli, the Brahmans and
Kayasthas made up a class of "gentlemen"--the bhadroloks. By religious necessity the Kayasthas came
to serve the "higher" Brahmans (122, pp. 168-169).

The Sadgopes had the highest influence among
the landowners. As a rule, they (including the more
independent) directly participated in labor. Among
the Sadgopes there was differentiation according to
the standard of living, isolating rich and poor.
The rich Sadgopes became the patrons in the village.
In Ranjana, four of the richest Sadgopes, in a group
with two Brahmans, were the most important patrons
(82, p. 176).

A large part of Sadgopes having little land (in
Ranjana, for example, an average plot of land for a
Sadgope family was 2.45 acres) were forced to work
as tenants for the entire year (82, p. 76). The
Sadgopes were "clean merchants," but being farmers,
they originally didn't have the right to the service
of their religious needs by any particular category
of Brahmans. However, in the colonial period,
thanks to their relatively prosperous economic position and the process of "sanskritism," the Sadgopes
obtained the inclusion of their caste into the body
of "higher merchants" served by Brahmans (82, p.
207).

---

were even more close, as their services were invariably used during weddings, burials and other
ceremonies (112, p. 143, 145).

     In such a way, the traditional brutality of the
caste hierarchy was broken in regions where landownership had diffused to the Sadgopes, even during the
colonial period. As a result, these regions formed
their own variety of "dual government." At the top
of the social ladder were Brahmans, who concentrated
in their hands the job of village headman, or _morol_,
and were hereditarily ceremonial leaders in the local temple as well as educational leaders (especially in the construction of schools, thanks to their
monetary contributions). Accordingly, the important
means of political, economic, religious and cultural
influence were found in the hands of two to three
Brahman families in the village. At this time members of the castes of the landowning peasantry, the
Sadgopes, had several administrative and political
posts. In Ranjana, where the Sadgopes were numeri-
cally fewer than Bagdi, Sadgopes were represented on
all eight hereditary posts in the overall village
council, the _majlis_ (82, p. 41, 43).

     Agrarian legislative acts, passed by the na-
tional government after the achievement of independence, the revival of the socio-political struggle
in the agricultural areas, the activity of political
parties in the village and other factors all contributed to the definitive collapse of the power of
the majlis. The members of the economically stronger castes advanced to the apex of the village elite,
with Sadgopes occupying the first position. Simultaneously this promoted the movement of the members
of the lower castes into the political struggle, the
majority of which had been totally passive earlier.
Finally, it created the preconditions for intercaste
consolidation within the lines of two basic groups
of the rural populace: the wealthy and the non-
wealthy. The preconditions for such consolidation
were the weakening of brutal caste gradations and
the diffusion of the practice of a ceremonial "fraternization" among the members of various castes.
This invariably led to the disappearance of many
caste taboos[33] from daily life (122, pp. 173-174;

---

[33] The basic forms of ritual fraternization were, as
     a rule, protracted combined work in the field,
     combined pilgrimages, combined studies and so

125, pp. 86-87). This practice was especially widespread among young people.

During the 1950's and 1960's traditional values, ideas and orientations still carried formidable
weight. Brahmans wielded great moral authority. In
daily matters and in questionable situations the
Brahmans usually exercised their preference, and the
insult of a Brahman by anyone was condemned by the
entire village (125, pp. 46-47).

However, with the increasing importance of economic factors in village life and the unusual revival in the role of money in the value system, the
"accentuation" of socio-political ideas was significantly displaced. Wealth gradually became an important criterion of high status (82, p. 49). The duty
of the elders, for example, became the evaluation of
all the villagers primarily according to their access to the village fund, which the elders usually
had individual access to (for example, they could
deposit money and collect interest) (82, p. 45).
The very possibility of achieving an elder's office
or other offices in local organizations was found to
have a direct relation to important economic roles
in the village which potential aspirants played.
For example, on account of the importance of the
rice-milling economy, many landowners were forced to
have "good relations" with those men involved in it
(82, p. 49). The status of Brahmans fluctuated
greatly in new situations, inasmuch as the economic
position of many of them was far from wealthy. Often there began to be situations where their status
was disregarded and where there was agitation for a
specific action to be taken against them (including
action on the basis of false evidence by the Bagdi
and Sadgopes) (125, pp. 46-47).

It was just these criteria of well-being--the
possession of land as wealth or a significant source
of moneyed income--that came to be the important
factors for differentiation in the village. In Ranjana six individuals were the most prosperous and at
the same time acted as the more "important" figures

---

forth (125, pp. 84-85).

in village life. They were: a headman from a group
or "clique" of Sadgopes who were assuming important
positions in local government and institutions primarily related to their business activities; two
Brahman landowners having the necessary attribute of
power--their patronage[34] over the metayers and agricultural workers on their farms; two persons in a
new kind of leadership role, namely that of Brahmans, who had come from poor families but had acquired sufficient funds by working as printers in
Calcutta and were agitating the Bagdi against the
headman; and, finally, a schoolteacher from the
Kshatriyas caste, who had not long ago appeared in
the village and had gained popularity among the lower castes with his democratic appeals (82, pp.
50-51).

At this time the prestige of the newly impover-
ished fell greatly. While in the past they were
very influential families, they stubbornly clung to
orthodox Indian tradition.[35]

In this new period, the socio-political activities of many groups of rural people, members of lower castes and untouchables, in the regions of our
research were still under the dominant influence of
conservative factors. Poverty, lack of education,
low social status, the need to constantly search for
work, economic dependence on the landowners and incorporation into vertical paternalistic systems--all
these defined the low activity of rural workers on
community matters in the village. The most

---

[34] Due to their little land (see 60), the relatively
small dimensions of what they had (seven to eight
acres), and little income, so characteristic in
West Bengal for the large Brahman farm, Brahman
patrons were able to maintain their patronage
only thanks to a constant monetary income unrelated to farming.

[35] Several of such families not only preserved the
importance of the gods but maintained small temples for them. In Ranjana there were two such
Brahman families and one Sadgope family (82, p.
52).

important change in village political life--the social regrouping of the dominant power, the path to
power for the wealthy elite, having, as already
noted, a mixed caste character--little affected the
social behavior of much of the village poor.

The inclusion of the landless into a system of
paternalistic relations was, in the new situation, a
strong impediment to the development of a political
struggle among the village poor. Paternalistic relations found a more full and complete expression in
the form of the village's own "micro-party," the
dhar. The dhar, united across castes and internally
as solid in kin-caste or "friendly" relations as in
relations of economic dependence, acted in the village political arena with a united front. Influential, wealthy families made up the framework of the
dhar. The dhar also included farm laborers, metayers, the workers of landowners and often his "potential" workers. The rural poor renounced involvement in the internecine violence of the important
wealthy families, so much a characteristic of village social life in India (67, pp. 33-42; 85).

Where the caste hierarchy was preserved, and
where paternalistic practices and the dhar were diffused, the introduction of universal suffrage was
not automatically to lead to an adequate expression
of the interests of the numerous poor groups of the
village. This was especially characteristic of the
Bauri. Their large size and representation at general village meetings did not reflect the propor-
tional strength of their voices and did not realize
the advancement of their demands. The example of
the Bauri in Hugli showed that just "as everywhere,
the village council controlled the influential members of the higher castes, and the Bauri voice in
the course of their (the council's) work was very
insignificant. Opinions and demands were usually
ignored" (125, p. 88). Evidently, the attack of the
landowners on the metayers (the refusal to give land
on metayage terms in connection with the introduction of new legislation) did not bring any effective
protest from the Bauri (125, p. 234).

The work of the political parties in the village to some degree affected the passive strata of
the rural people. However, in those areas where

paternalistic relations with the landowners and oppression of the members of lower castes was strong,
then these areas would subsequently, almost automatically, join the National Congress party through
their patron, an "influential person." Even though
the Bauri actively participated in the elections for
the panchayat and in the general elections, "they
were not trying to obtain an electoral mandate, but
wanted to know which groups would give them the most
support in the event of victory. Locally influential individuals," the author continues, "belonged
to diverse political parties, influencing them, agitating hopefully for a promise of support. For this
reason the Bauri looked on individuals as they would
a party and joined sides with them" (125, p. 108).
As a consequence the majority of Bauri supported the
congressmen, who gave a better guarantee of hand-
outs of privileges from the government. These privileges were given through local elected organs, the
majority of whose members joined the Congress party.
The influence of the Communist party in this region
was very weak (125, p. 109).

However, in those regions where socio-economic
differentiation had taken a clearer form and had begun to erode the caste gradation, as in Ranjana,
several other parties were seen in village political
life. As noted above, an important rapproachement
between Brahmans and Sadgopes, which was gaining
strength thanks to the joint management of several
organized and ritualistic functions, had begun to
take shape in the colonial period.[36] This rapproachement continued to consolidate in the 1950's.
This was seen where the Brahmans, as much as the
Sadgopes themselves, tried to hire Sadgopes first
when hiring tenant labor. This was an expression of
the necessity for the Brahmans to strengthen relations with their "allies" in the struggle against
the overwhelming numbers of the politically active
Bagdi caste.

---

[36] Sadgopes, occupying important positions in the
village administration, began "to divide" several
religious functions with the Brahmans, especially
the organization of a number of religious festivals (82, pp. 207-208).

The old mechanisms of power retained their strength here in the 1950's but began to change significantly. After the end of the zamindar system, which had been so much a part of the entire local administrative apparatus, a special law remained only for the heads in the majlis, the morols, who were fulfilling a number of administrative functions and had several privileges, including some related to religious ceremonies. In Ranjana, up to the time of independence, the "leaders" in village socio-political life in the 1950's were Sadgopes, who were a numerous and relatively wealthy caste. All of the members of the village council were Sadgopes. A large number of Sadgopes supported the Congress, which meant, as Chattopadhyay notes, the victory or defeat of the congressional candidate was directly dependent on the strength or weakness of the headman in the village (in 1952 and 1957) (82, p. 56).

We have already noted that the clearer manifestations of socio-economic differentiation in this region had begun to leave their mark on village political life. This was reflected in the socio-political position of the Bagdi and some of the Sadgopes. Even in the colonial period many "traditions" of struggle of tenant versus landowner had formed in some regions. Progressive activities were especially prevalent among the Bagdi with the introduction of universal elections after independence. This began a process toward their unification in the struggle for their own interests. The political power of the wealthy groups was wavering. A large number of Bagdi began to support left-wing candidates. In this region there were also possibilities for the cross-caste unification of the landless strata in the electoral struggle. Consequently, a part of the landless and petty landowning Sadgopes united with the Bagdi for the 1957 election, supporting the candidate of the left-wing party (82, pp. 56-57).[37]

---

[37] After the reelection of the congressmen, "cliques" of morols slowly began to obstruct their adversaries; as a result, many metayers were deprived of the possibility of registering as metayers, in order to receive, according to

Usually during the general elections the polarization between two opposing camps became more apparent. The first group was made up of the members of two "clean" castes, Brahmans and Sadgopes, or bhadroloks. In the second group, or <u>chotolok</u>, there were several landless castes: above all Bagdi, some Sadgopes, Muchi and Santal. During the electoral campaign the process of internal consolidation and unification around a single group of demands was strengthened in both groups (82, p. 41, 45, 47).

However, we must note the following point--the leaders in the movement of the poor groups, especially the candidates from the left-wing parties, continued to act as the representatives of castes with high social status. The dissatisfaction of the poor was often exploited by these leaders in the interests of their own political careers as members of traditional ruling castes.

In such a way, the liberation of the analysed categories of rural workers from the traditional system of relations, orientations and types of leadership in the 1950's and 1960's had still only begun. The political struggle of landless working strata of the village developed along several lines:

1) along the class line; the unification of Bagdi and Sadgope metayers in the political struggle, joint support by them of left-wing party candidates in the elections, the struggle for the realization of guarantees from discrimination;

2) along traditional caste lines; often everyone on the supra-village level; this was a struggle of caste groups for the rise of the status of these groups, the advancement of their own candidates and so forth;

3) along the paternalistic line; the expression of this struggle was the participation of the poor in a politically unified type of dhar in the village, led by influential landlords; here the

the laws of the state, a guarantee from expulsion (82, pp. 56-57).

exploited strata were the direct tools of the rural
exploiters in their personal struggle in the village; and

4) along the intersection of such types; here
the members of a traditionally leading elite such as
the Brahmans were not related directly as gentlemen-
servant to the rural poor, and being interested in
the defeat of the dhar, usurped power, promoted
their own candidates and actively enlisted the poor
in this struggle, which developed mainly within village boundaries.

The social attitude of the peasant population
of India, incorporated into a system of patron-
client relations, was different from any contradic-
toriness or transitoriness. Hinduism was sufficiently strong to support paternalism, giving
patronage "from above" and honest service "from below" a religious and moral basis. Paternalistic relations themselves, taking into account the great
proximity and closer contact between socially unequal groups of the rural people, promoted a definite
weakening of caste brutality, and more appropriate
inclusion of the unprivileged groups into caste society. Objectively, the possibility for the birth
of social self-consciousness of the poor strata was
open here. It was as if two caste groups of farmers, the Bauri and Bagdi, themselves personified two
levels of this process. On the first level, inclusion into the system of paternalistic relations
doomed the peasants to apathy and the absence of
their own voice in village affairs. However, in
contemporary India, when socio-economic processes
"corrode" the traditional foundation of society, but
the work of progressive parties rapidly stimulates
this process in the area of self-consciousness, the
destruction of paternalistic relations and the movement to class orientations in social behavior could
be realized relatively quickly.

THE FAMILIARIZATION OF SOCIALLY SERVILE RURAL CASTE GROUPS WITH MODERN STRUGGLE (KERALA)

<u>Some</u> <u>Features</u> <u>of</u> <u>the</u> <u>Historical</u> <u>Development</u> <u>of</u> <u>Kerala</u>

For centuries Kerala was a very differentiated region of India. The specifics of this region were related to its physical-geographical characteristics and the peculiarities of its population. The territory of lower Kerala[38] was a narrow belt of fertile land along the southwestern seacoast of the Deccan, relatively isolated by mountains. In the middle ages, and at least at the beginning of the modern era, it was a region of intensive maritime commerce. The farming tribes of the region were the aborigines. Apparently they were newcomers from the earlier settled and assimilated regions of the Deccan and were found at the borderline of our era at various levels of their evolution. In Kerala territory, for example, in northern Travancore, there were traces of the government of an aborigine farming society which subsequently became one of the more unprivileged castes of farmers, the <u>Pulayas</u>. There were traces of the organs of communal self-government (the duties of the <u>valluvan</u>--a societal headman and six of his subordinates) (79, pp. 90-91). Simultaneously, the tribes of the foothills, relatively isolated from the coast, were inherently at a

____

[38] After the administrative-political reforms of 1956 the territories in the existing principalities of Travancore and Cochin in the south and Malabar region in the north, which had earlier been in Madras province, entered into the state of Kerala.

more primitive degree of societal development.

The important moment in the formation of this system of social relations, which existed up to the beginning of the twentieth century, and in a deformed mode up to the middle of the twentieth century, was the "colonization," or in other words, the settlement of Kerala territory by Brahman Nambudiri, who came from the northern regions of India in the first century. In the course of events, a significant portion of cultivatable land was parcelled out among Brahman communities (at first, according to tradition, there were sixty-four such villages) (118, p. 240). Local farmers were forced to cultivate their fields. Tradition maintains that the Sudra Nayars appeared together with the Brahman Nambudiri in Kerala. It is possible that the Nayars were in reality a privileged class from the indigenous early-governmental formation.

Starting with ancient times and continuing right up to modern times in Kerala there were two relatively autonomous social structures: the early-governmental formations and the Brahman (and religious) territories. Within the government structure the industrial sector possessed substantial independence, on the basis of which relatively autonomous Christian and Muslim societies subsequently grew up.

The residences and land of elites originated in the first structure. A substantial segment of the population were Nayars, a less privileged rural people. A portion of royal land, the personal property of the rulers themselves, was cultivated by tenants. Nayar society owned large tracts of land through inheritance.

The elite exercised control over their lands (mostly in Travancore and Cochin) and administrative control of the entire national population (except for the Brahmans and the persons supporting them) through the Nayars, who were unified in a network of matrilineal and matrilocal groups. The lowest unit of this social structure was the Nayar village--the tara, which often represented a settlement of one or several large matrilineal families, the taravad (13, p. 295; 118, p. 250).

These taras preserved the features of south
Indian society (diffused especially in Tamilnad)
with its inherited "servile personality," and with
its collective forms of religious life. The tara
was the basis for the administrative structure of
the state. The meeting of the Nayar representatives, especially their overall caste assembly, the
kuttam, could at times remove the elite (118, pp.
25-26, 251).

A great part of the governing body of Kerala
did not achieve the stability of the central government. The economic and political conditions of the
region--the absence of the necessity of large-scale
irrigation works, the presence of "international"
commerce, the power of the Brahmans and the relative
independence of the Nayar military class--checked
any tendency in the governing body of an evolution
toward despotism. This in turn promoted the maintenance of an exclusively political partitioning of
the region right up to the appearance of the Europe-
ans here in the sixteenth century (see 118, pp. 61-
73, 250-251 and others).

The special physical and geographical conditions of the region promoted, even in ancient times
and in the early medieval period, an intensified development of indigenous industry, the export of specific agricultural products, the disassociation and
independence of the numerous early-governmental formations as well as distinct economic entities. Kerala, and above all Malabar, did not form villages as
such; homes were arranged at intervals, one from the
other, like a khutor, or separated farm (13, pp.
291-292).

Among the specific peculiarities, so numerous
in Kerala, we should note the following: the basic
military class, the Nayars, had great political
strength, did not pay taxes and were obligated only
to military service. The fundamental source of income for the elite was commercial customs--income
from commercial monopolies, duties, etc. (13, p.
302).

The most important function of the elite was
military, and in some cases religious as well, as in
Calicut. A portion of royal land, as already

indicated, was elite property (normally of an elite
"family") and tilled by the tenants. This kind of
land tended to expand according to the degree of
governmental consolidation.

The population of cities and coastal zones came
from the commercial sector: merchants, industrialists, skilled handicrafters. Later on, according to
the extent that immigrant commercialists acquired
land, the economy of the seacoast became dominated
by the immigrant elements of this sector.

The substantial landholdings of the Brahmans
and the temples was another fundamental aspect of
the social structure of Kerala. During both medieval and modern times Brahmans were the most important group of large landowners, a powerful social
force in rural localities and in society in general.
The Brahman hereditary system promoted the preservation of large-scale ownership.[39] In substantial territories of Kerala, above all in Malabar, the "Brahman territories" maintained practically full
autonomy from governmental power. Up to the second
half of the eighteenth century (up to the invasion
of Mysore by Malabar), a large portion of Kerala
land was not assessed any national taxes[40] (13, pp.
300-304; 74, pp. 15-118, 261).

The leading role of the Brahmans in the societal and religious life of Kerala was strengthened
extraordinarily in the ninth century and was related
to the "triumphal march" through India of the teach-
ings of a native of Kerala, Sankara, the founder of
advaito _vedanto_. The construction of temples as a
rule formed the basis for an autonomous structure of
education, or _devaswan_ (literally, the property of
god), and for their own kind of "theocratical

---

[39] According to this system, which was preserved in
full strength till the 1930's, all land was inherited by the oldest son of the Brahmans; he
also was the only one who entered into legal marriage with Brahman women and had legal Brahman
children (74, p. 10).

[40] Travancore was an exception.

government" within a government. Brahman land that
was grouped around the temple often was part of temple territory. The Brahmans, having transferred
their land to the temple, became members of the collective leadership of the temple as an autonomous
religio-political institution. The more important
temples possessed special rights, or <u>sanketan</u>, which
presupposed absolute jurisdiction. Interference of
the elite in temple matters could lead to a serious
"governmental crisis" (118, p. 343). The temples
hired, as a rule, Nayars or other people for the
economic and administrative management of temple
lands, through which these lands were successful in
farming and could be sold.

A large number of Brahmans maintained individual ownership. These Brahmans joined forces in the
village as the <u>grama</u> with elected leaders. The total economic and political independence of the Brahmans and the exclusively high social status of these
more authoritative bearers of Hinduism and caste
consciousness in Kerala promoted notions of caste
cleanliness and hierarchy that were accepted in a
refined form and conserved for centuries.

The special economic conditions of Kerala--the
abundance of water resources and the absence of any
real necessity to cooperate efforts for irrigation
(such as in Madras) (106)--conditioned the diffusion
of individual landownership and land use, for Brahmans and others. "Brahman society" did not become a
unified economic entity. The weaknesses of cooperative labor in the rural localities and the very absence of a village class society as such opened up
great possibilities for the economic liberation of
the individual, which made the wide diffusion of
commercial and monetary relations in Kerala much
easier.

As Alaev notes, in general "private ownership
of land undoubtedly was dominant" in Kerala. This
was especially a characteristic of Malabar, where it
was recorded in one of the tax journals: "With the
exception of some estates which had broken out in
revolt, it seems there were no governmental lands at
all" (13, p. 301). In Kerala a form of unconditional private ownership, <u>jajnma</u> ownership, free of all
government taxes and vassalage status, was

widespread. The _jajnmi_, owners of jajnma, "had full
judioial immunity in their ownership; tribes living
on their land were considered dependent on them"
(13, pp. 305-306).[41]

Inasmuch as a jajnma could be the object of
purchase by merchants, ownership of jajnma gradually
spread from the Brahman Nambudiri category to the
Nayars as well as the Muslim _Moplahs_ (13, pp. 305-
307). Jajnma-type property, while not legally limited and outside the boundaries of government, was
nevertheless to some degree limited by tradition,
that is, by traditional norms of land exploitation.

A tendency toward private landownership was
clearly manifest on the Malabar seacoast. Up to the
end of the eighteenth century and beginning of the
nineteenth century, according to Alaev: "There
wasn't any land which belonged to the whole village,
nor any establishment of village servants and
skilled handicraft workers being paid by the collectivity. . . . There generally didn't even exist a
threshing floor for the village" (13, p. 294).
"Community property," wrote an English civil servant, "or common right to land was unknown; every
law or privilege related to it was found in the
hands of individuals, nothing but a collectivity of
individuals" (13, pp. 294-295).

Tendencies toward formation of distinct economic cells independent from each other was inherent in
those regions where the Nayar taravad was dominant;
"productive relations between taravad did not exist," although the taravad itself remained formally
unified (13, p. 295).

---

[41] It was evident that during reform in the principalities of private landownership, "governmental
land" itself had a tendency to form like private
land; for example, in Cochin, a great part of
tilled land belonged to the raja "essentially under those conditions of private landownership
(jajnma), and other lands belonged to Brahman
Nambudiri" (13, pp. 300-301) and could be sold.

Even in the middle ages religious diversity was obvious. Large landowners were numerous in the northern sector of Malabar. Formation of a centralized government and the consolidation of a governmental monopoly on land and commerce was more strongly manifested in the southern part of the region, in Travancore (especially in the eighteenth century) and Cochin. Accordingly, there was a rather large stock of royal land here and less diffusion of large-scale individual landownership. This region was characterized more by rural communities of Nayars as economic and administrative units subordinate to the government (13, pp. 296-297).

The sources of income for Nayars in service were work wages or, more rarely, land grants. The land was tilled by tenants and personal laborers. A large group of Nayars also acted as kanamdars, or tenants, on Brahman land. The kanam tenant system resembled land mortgages. The kanamdar put up a traditionally fixed advance payment to the Brahman, and then rented the land to a direct producer, or verympattamdar, who paid a fixed rent (13, pp. 310-311).

Commerce, strong because of the very absence of any centralized despotic government, was wearing down for many centuries a great number of archaic social relations. It was to a definite degree building new relations outside of typical caste relations. Such relations grew in the cities and seacoast regions and were part of the new "industrial" culture. As already noted, foreign commercialists (Christians, Muslims and Jews) had long ago settled on the Kerala seacoast. The timeless existence in Kerala of autonomous sectors or territories in the form of the temple holdings and the Brahman settlements served as models for the communities of incoming businessmen, who possessed substantial monetary resources. The elites of some principalities, having attracted foreign businessmen, gave them high status and a number of privileges, such as the status of "well-born." Analogous to Brahman societies, several features of autonomy, or sanketan, prevailed in immigrant communities of Muslims, Jews and Christians (118, p. 72, 242; 119, p. 16). New privileged groups of foreigners appeared. Large settlements of

Christians formed in southern Travancore and Cochin,
Muslim Moplahs in Malabar.

The presence in Kerala of immigrants from regions with other features of socio-economic development, having their own religion, culture and value
system, had great importance. Many of them became
landowners and attracted to their estates members of
the untouchable castes. Caste, social and cultural
barriers were in these situations so much weakened
that it objectively opened up the possibility for
the assimilation of the untouchables into new norms,
customs and value systems (121, p. 38). Such assimilation especially promoted the conversion of untouchables to Christianity or Islam.

The spread of slaveholders in the eighteenth
and nineteenth centuries was directly related to the
intensification of trade. Kerala's far-flung trade
relations could not protect it from the slave trade
and slaveowners. The slave institution, imported
possibly as a commercial system of exploitation, was
imposed here as a brutal caste system and took on
very extreme forms. A substantial number of untouchables, above all Pulayas in Travancore and Cochin and the <u>Cherumas</u> in Malabar, became the "objects" of servility.

Numerous materials that date to all periods of
the nineteenth century draw an image of the "agricultural" slavery in the region. Slaves were the
full property of the master. They could be sold,
leased and pawned like land itself, cattle or other
things (121, p. 375). The personal and ceremonial
expenses of the slave were paid by the master, yet
their subsistence was wretched. The social position
of the slaves was extraordinarily poor and their
very presence was thought profane. A minimal distance to be kept from them was strictly fixed; this
included the Pulayas, <u>Parayi</u> and other untouchables
from the Brahmans, Nayars, <u>Izhavas</u> and others. From
1865, all Pulayas, including women, were forbidden,
for example, from exposing the upper half of their
bodies and their legs below the knees, to wear new
and clean clothes, to use shoes or silver jewelry.
In conversations with the members of higher castes
the Pulayas were to refer to themselves as slaves.

They should cover their mouth with their hands and
their entire demeanor should express obedience. The
name Pulaya itself became, according to the research
of Alexander, "a concrete symbol of uncleanliness,
of low status and everything that aroused disgust"
(76, p. 46, pp. 48-50; 121, p. 380).

Slavery, an unusually strong "institution of
the untouchables" was not able to wipe out caste
hierarchical gradations even among the slaves. A
hierarchy among the slaves--Pulayas, Vettovans, Parayi and those who were still below slave status,
like Nayadi--was preserved. The Pulayas, somehow
ending up with the generally "lower" untouchable
work, were required to perform a purifying abolition
and began to observe a ritualistic distance (121, p.
382).

It is important to note that slave castes had
several rights and privileges, participated in a
number of agrarian rituals and had fixed rights and
duties for religious holidays in the temples (121,
p. 384).

Slavery, in such a way, was strengthening the
worst features of the caste system, and for a long
time stifled the social progress of substantial portions of the humble rural peoples of Kerala. Slavery was abolished in Kerala in 1830. However, up to
the beginning of the twentieth century a large number of the untouchables continued to remain both
formally and practically in the position of slaves.

The transformation of India under English colonialism and the submission of Kerala to the English
at first did not bring any significant changes in
the functioning of the two most important structures
of society in this region. The intrusion of the
government into the autonomous sphere of the Brahman
settlements had the most importance for the agrarian
sector: a definite strengthening (and legal registration) of the "supreme" Brahman rights on land,
and an effort toward legislative regulation of lease
relations. The English organization of the new administrative apparatus had great import for social
progress in that it enlisted educated members of all
the castes, including the low castes.

A large number of Nayars who lived in Brahman
cities, and to whom a brutal system of inheritance
closed off any chance of landownership, experienced
the strong influence of these ideas toward the end
of the nineteenth century, and European culture and
social thought at the beginning of the twentieth
century.

The end of the nineteenth and the first decade
of the twentieth century was a time of significant
redistribution of land within the lines of the upper, middle and partially of the lower estates.
Many Brahmans lost land, and some went into agricultural labor. A substantial number of Nayars turned
out to be large-, middle- and small-scale owners and
peasant leaseholders. A great number of Izhavas[42]
also became owners of land in basically unirrigated,
arid valleys. In this way a segment of the peasant
types in Kerala--smallholders and tenants--were basically Nayars and Izhavas (45, pp. 304-310).[43] In
Cochin in 1941, for example, agricultural workers
were 27.6% Izhavas and 12.3% Nayars (45, pp. 304-
305).

Progress at the end of the nineteenth and the
first decade of the twentieth century--the loss of
traditional sources of wealth and decline in the
standard of living for an important number of the
members of the high castes, which was accelerating
socio-economic differentiation among the Nayars,
along with the diffusion of monetary forms for the
payment of labor, above all in Malabar--prepared the
path for the development of antagonistic classes in
the rural localities of several regions of Kerala.

---

[42] On the Izhava caste (Ilavan, Tiija) see below for
detail.

[43] In Travancore in 1931, of the landowners and tenants tilling land 68.4% were worked by Nayars and
31.6% were worked by Izhavas; in Cochin in 1941,
43.2% were Nayars and 20.9% were Izhavas. In
Travancore in 1931 of the working owners tilling
land 42% were Brahmans, 51.2 % were Nayars, 13.2%
were Izhavas and only .3% were untouchables [sic]
(45, pp. 304-305).

The diffusion of ideas about class protest was related to changes in the system of traditional relations about the world, society and social arrangements, fundamentally among the members of such
castes as the Nayars, Brahmans and Izhavas.

<u>Progress in the Social Consciousness of the Hindu
People of Kerala in the First Half of the Twentieth
Century</u>

The relatively quick radicalization of important groups of the Keralian people at all levels of
their stratification represented an exceptional case
for India. Radical tendencies which were developing
among the members of the socially dominating castes
of Hindu society--Brahmans and Nayars--played a
leading role in the development of revolutionary potential in Kerala.

Radical action among the Nayars began at the
end of the nineteenth century. This was related to
the fact that Nayar men, employed in administrative
services and in municipal businesses, were much less
dependent on the matriarchal family. Action directed against the archaic system of marriage and
inheritance produced the legislative acceptance of
the small family (1896). Struggle ensued for the
division of large family holdings.

Struggle flared up among Nayars and large numbers of Nambudiri closely related to the Nayar community, due as much to a special system of marriage
relations as the fact that both groups worked together in the administrative apparatus up to the end
of the nineteenth century. The marriage system and
the heritage the Nambudiri had left behind gave the
majority of the young men of this caste the chance
to have families and inherit land. The <u>yogakshema</u>
movement for many social reforms and for the study
of the English language began among the young men of
the Nambudiri in 1908 (93, p. 1847). As a result of
the so-called Nambudiri revolution of 1917--the action of a young, radically oriented generation--new
schools were opened for Nambudiri as well as a score
of other reforms. It was just this generation, who
were beginning the struggle against archaic traditions and religious dogma, that turned out to be

more receptive to the progressive Marxian ideology.
A number of young Nambudiri leaders, selfless ideal-
istic champions who broke all family ties, emerged
to help the downtrodden and unprivileged groups of
Kerala. This tradition remained up to the middle of
the twentieth century (54, p. 120; 107, pp.
191-193).

Consequently, we can say that of the several
specific forms of functioning caste structures in
Kerala, the very conservativeness of these forms
conditioned their "falling out" from this system,
from the highest link of the entire hierarchy, and
their subsequent transformation to a contemporary
form of ideology.[44]

The socially humble groups of Kerala faced
still more difficulty on the socialization path to
the class struggle. Progress in the political development of groups of the Keralian rural mass where
a brutal caste system still existed invariably took
one of two forms. First would be the attempt to
change its social caste status within the limits of
the existing system on the way to "sanskritism,"
i.e., a definite change in the image of life and
forms of religious direction in accordance with the
strict dogma of Hinduism. Another form is a "departure" from Hindu society and is the acceptance of a
new religion. The movement to contemporary forms of
consciousness and struggle for concrete socio-economic interests can obviously arise only in the modern era, and in a situation where a social group's
caste humility could be advanced.

The first step in the improvement of the situation of servile groups in Kerala with regard to
their caste exploitation goes back to the medieval
period. It is related to the attempt to depart from
the limits of Hindu society and to enter into other
religious modes which at least formally guaranteed
the equality of all its members.

---

[44] This paradoxical interrelation was emphasized in
the research of the Nambudiri by Mencher (see
107, p. 193).

More often all the members of the lower castes
in the coastal areas--fishermen, netmakers and oth-
ers--turned to Christianity and Islam. It was not
uncommon for the members of the very low "agricultural" castes, such as the Pulayas, to find a place
in these religions.

Although the economic position of these people
in such a case changed little and caste discrimination was only reduced and did not disappear completely, nonetheless the move to Islam and Christianity promoted changes in the social consciousness
of the converted, and objectively provided the distinct possibility for their members to make progress
toward ending their caste servility.

There existed then, even in medieval times,
alongside a hierarchically structured caste society,
a formally egalitarian religious society with less
regulated norms of social intercourse, advocating
the equality of all "before god." This undoubtedly
had the effect of destroying the appearance of an
orthodox Hindu society, especially its ideological
basis. The organizational principles of the bu-
reaucratic apparatus and the system of education
which took after the model of English government in
the nineteenth century also moved in the direction
of weakening Hindu dogma. From here, the appearance
of social reformist tendencies were an inevitability
in the strongly Hindu community of Kerala.[45]

The struggle of the Izhavas for a raise in
their caste status was more important for further
elaboration of the state's socio-political development. By no means was it accidental that a segment

---

[45] Reformist sects that proclaimed the equality of
all "before god," and which were inherently Hindu
from ancient times gradually and consistently attracted people from the exploited strata. However, only in 1920-1930 did objective conditions
become ripe for religious-caste reforms to
incorporate socio-political struggle. This latter
development ended, in the movement led by Ghandi,
with significant changes in the entire caste system.

of the rural population who were traditionally tied
up with the agricultural culture of the littoral regions turned out to be more prepared to struggle for
a change in their social status. The manufacture of
vodka from palm juice was the traditional occupation
of the Izhava caste.[46] From that time on, caste members were characterized by the birth of self-consciousness and the onset of a fight for the elimina-
tion of caste discrimination.

The considerable disorganization of the Keralian economic structure at the end of the eighteenth
and beginning of the nineteenth century due to the
invasion of Mysore by Malabar (which accompanied the
forced Islamization of the people and the flight of
the Brahmans from their region in the south) and
English expansionism was the socio-economic precondition for the Izhavas' struggle. The miserable position of a huge number of Nayars, a substantial
number of whom had left Brahman families, put them
on an equal economic basis with the Izhavas, especially in urban and suburban areas. Under conditions of life in an old, disorganized economic system, the penetration of new European views about the
individual and a new value system, and the development of new possibilities for a rise in status
through education and work, a substantial number of
Izhavas were successful in improving their material
positions, in acquiring land, in business ventures
and so forth. The change in their economic position
stimulated a fight for a change in their place in
the caste hierarchy.

The struggle of the Izhavas began in the middle
to the end of the nineteenth century. The spiritual
leader of the movement was Sri Narayana Guru, born
in 1854, who advocated "a single caste of a single
god for all." The organization that great numbers
of Izhavas and Nayars became part of repudiated
caste hierarchy, demanded monogamy and the

____

[46] Tiija is the old name for castes that are now
   present primarily in Malabar district (see 71, p.
   115). Izhavas, Izhuvan, Irava and Ilavan are
   various transcriptions of modern names for these
   castes.

repudiation of any sacrifices of living beings and
other archaic rites from its members, and adopted
Hindu ceremonies, for which special temples were
built (92, p. 367; 119, p. 160). The Izhavas who
were joining the movement and trying to reject the
existing hierarchical relationship in the village
endeavored to limit to a minimum ties of economic
dependence with the landowners, as well as contact
with the low castes. Up to the 1930's, the Izhavas
of Malabar were successful in overcoming to a significant degree the more archaic and fictitious truths
and getting accustomed with Hindu religion, ceremonies and philosophy.

The movement played a great part in weakening
segregation of the Izhava caste and in obliterating
the caste isolation between Nayars and Izhavas in
particular. Consequently, this was at least one
instance of the movement of one of the very many
groups of landless rural peoples, the Izhavas, from
the ranks of the untouchables into the ranks of the
low castes.

A change in social status for such a large
group of the Keralian people as the Izhavas had
great social and political importance. Objectively
this was the basis for a freer socialization to the
modern socio-political class struggle--people with
no land or Nayars with little land, without ties to
any caste discrimination, and isolated from other
important groups of the rural population.

The worsening of the socio-economic position of
those groups of Izhavas who were tenants on the
farms of large landowners had already begun in the
colonial period. For centuries the large landowners, jajnmi, were greatly limited in their prerogatives, their rights to the control of their land and
the fate of their tenants, not from "above," not by
government, but from "below," by tradition itself,
which dictated the conditions of rent, terms of payment and so forth. After the East India Company
declared the large landowners absolute property owners, landowners began to be more arbitrary. There
was more frequent turnover of tenants and an increase in their personal dependence on the landowners.

Modern political movements, which regard
socio-economic demands as of the utmost importance,
spread in Kerala in the 1920's. Socio-economic conditions in several regions of Kerala were favorable
to the development of class antagonisms in rural localities. In Malabar relatively large landlords
were often absentee landlords: Brahmans, Nayars
working as municipal workers, businessmen and so
forth. Landless Nayars and Izhavas were the primary
tenants under these landlords. It was among just
these tenants, less liable to caste segregation, who
were related to the monetary economy, the cities and
the new ideological beliefs, that a widely felt dissatisfaction with their economic position and the
prolongation of individual dependence on the large
landlords spread among in the 1920's. In the
1930's, it was just these regions of Malabar that
became a more favorable area for the enlarging influence of left-wing congressmen, who were then developing an active campaign for the reduction of
rental terms and for the abolition of medieval customs, such as the jurisdictional prerogatives of the
owners in their relations with all who were living
on their land. This category of tenants entered
into the peasant union Karshaka Sangam in the 1930's
(93, p. 369). The movement of left-wing congressmen
allied with the Communist Party of India (CPI) into
the local leadership meant a new orientation of the
peasant masses toward support for the CPI.

At this time we must take two circumstances
into account. First, up to the 1930's, the consciousness of a great part of the Izhavas remained
significantly caste based. As several Indian researchers stress, the caste leaders of the Izhavas
were leaders of a charismatic type, but the forms of
agitation were often an appeal to caste pride and
honesty (75, p. 12). Secondly, a substantial number
of Izhavas who were living in the isolated regions
of Kerala remained unprepared for the class battle
that was unfolding.

The socio-political development of those segments of the rural working mass who had been untouchables or slaves in the not too distant past was
far more advanced in the 1910-1930's. At this time
in many territories of Kerala, above all in the cen-

tral and southern regions such as Cochin and
Travancore, the land of the large, middle and small
landholders was worked by permanent laborers "attached" to the farm, by daily farmhands and by agricultural workers from the untouchables: Pulayas,
Parayi and Cherumas (45, p. 304). Workers who were
"attached" to the landholder continued to carry full
slave status. At the beginning of the 1920's the
practice of the slave being sold with the land, or
"rented," remained among the Cherumas of Cochin (who
made up 50% of all agricultural workers) (74, p.
79).

It should be noted that in those regions where
slave labor was widespread the members of the higher
castes, such as Izhavas who were employed as agricultural workers, suffered more social discrimination (74, pp. 92-93).

Massive social movements in defense of the socially servile groups that were taking place in India in the 1920-1940's did not pass Kerala by. In
1932 Ghandi organized the "Union of the Servants for
Harijans," and in the 1930's formed the "All Indian
Organization of Untouchables" under the leadership
of Ambedkar. The proclamation for free entrance
into temples for all Hindus, independent of their
caste affiliation (in Travancore and Malabar) was
the result of this overall national struggle. These
were the times of the first attempts to form a colony for the untouchables.[47] These events, however,
did not mark any important change in the social position, social activity and social consciousness of
the overwhelming majority of untouchables of Kerala:
the Pulayas, Parayi, Nayadi and others. Although a
portion of the members of the castes were converted
to Christianity and Islam (that invariably weakened
but did not eradicate their social servility), nevertheless the overwhelming majority of untouchables
remained in the religious caste system of Hinduism
and experienced increasing social discrimination.

---

[47] The colony of untouchables in Kurichi (Kottayam
district) was an example. It was founded in 1938
with the goal of creating a new social milieu for
them (79, pp. 81-82).

The natural legacy of the slaves was, at least
in the 1920's, their oppression and their indiffer-
ence to any perspective toward changes in their
lives. The right to use public roads and bazaars on
a level with that of the members of the high castes
stood in the center of their demands. Any increase
in their income, notes the observer of a Cochin village, "invariably found its way to religious service
and to public shops." Many centuries of social discrimination and socio-cultural isolation as "non-
people" and slaves conditioned the preservation of
many archaic customs and more primitive truths in
their lives.

In this way, up to the time of independence and
to the 1950's, a period of an accelerating socio-political struggle in the state, diverse segments of
the rural Kerala mass were found at various levels
of social evolution.

Basic Groups of the Keralian Rural Mass in the
1950-1960's: Social Consciousness and Social
Struggle

At the end of the 1940-1950's, the agrarian
structure of Kerala basically maintained those components that had been taking shape for centuries in
the pre-colonial and colonial period. Some indica-
tions of this were the dominant forms of landownership, land usage, tenancy, hiring, forms of work
payment and others. Although the general features
of this structure have been touched upon in our literature, here we stop short of such questions as the
mutual dependence of caste and landownership, religious differences within state boundaries and others
(52, pp. 85-86).

In 1960 the Hindu population of Kerala was 61%,
Christians were 23% and Muslims were 16%. Among the
Hindus the Brahman Nambudiri made up 8%, the Nayars
25.3%, the Izhavas 44.4% and other castes 20.4%
[sic] (54, p. 120; 93, p. 184). Land usage was
generally characterized by wide use of leasing,
which included three to four hierarchically related
units: the landowner of the existing jajnma, tenants as middlemen (kanamdars), tenants as direct
producers or as direct organizers of production

(verympattamdars)[48] and finally, agricultural workers and farmhands (52, p. 86; 105, pp. 80-82; 108,
p. 41). Within the lines of this general scheme we
can draw out three variants of the union of direct
producers with the land.

In the 1950's the first variant was present in
the rice-producing regions and generally in the regions of food production. The owner, for example
the Brahman, Nambudiri or Nayar, cultivated his own
land, or more exactly a portion of his land, "directly" with the help of dependent farmhands attached to the landowner--Pulayas, Parayi and others.
The labor of these workers was paid for in natural
form, rice and some of the necessities of life. The
presence of a category of permanent "attached" workers from the socially humble groups, the personal
character of the relation between the workers and
the landowner, and the preservation of several paternalistic practices were the components of this
management scheme (87, p. 135; 105, pp. 96-97).

In the second variant, the owner gave a portion
of the ownership to the kanamdars,[49] often mostly
Nayars, who transferred a small strip to the verympattamdars (often all Izhavas or Moplahs) for one
year, or in accordance with traditional norms, for
five to twelve years. The verympattamdars either
tilled it themselves or hired farmhands like the Pulayas or Cherumas. The verympattamdars were also
often personally dependent on the landowner (87, p.
129).

Finally, in the third variant, common in regions of commercial production such as northern Malabar, the landowners "cultivated" their land,

---

[48] Traditional forms of tenancy in Kerala were reminiscent to some extent of mortgages, and the
"tenant" almost always had to pay in advance a
significant sum of money with the property owner
or intermediary (105, pp. 80-81).

[49] During agrarian reform in the 1960's the rights
of the jajnmi were ended and the kanamdars became
property owners.

attracting either tenants as direct farmers (Nayars,
Izhavas and sometimes Pulayas), or "free" agricultural workers from these three castes (105, pp.
85-97).

It was as if in the first and second variants
socio-economic gradations reflected and retrenched
the caste hierarchy, then in the third a class "wa-
tershed" passed "through" the caste--Nayars and Iz-
havas--cutting and influencing its internal caste
relations. The first two variants were more characteristic of Travancore, Cochin (although in Travancore Nayar landownership was widespread, but the
forms of labor organization remained traditional)
and the southern part of Malabar (Chunangrad, Erima-
jur) (105, pp. 96-97). The third was more characteristic of northern Malabar and the littoral regions in general.

Finally, the agrarian sector of Kerala included
a substantial number of the small farms of independent owners and farmers. These farms were formed
from a fraction of the large property of the Nambudiri, joint ownership of Nayar taravads and the
transfer of strips of land into the hands of Izhavas, Moplahs and even, in northern Malabar, of Pulayas (105, p. 97).

Accordingly, the caste composition of the rural
working groups was as follows:

1) property-owning peasants (Hindus) were primarily Nayars, less often Izhavas, and in very rare
cases Pulayas;

2) peasant tenants were represented by the Nayars, Izhavas, more rarely (in the north) Pulayas;
more substantial numbers of tenants were concentrated in Malabar;

3) "free" agricultural workers, a category more
characteristic of the northern part of the state,
was filled by Izhavas and Nayars, and some Pulayas
in the north; here were members of the isolated

mountain tribes,[50] cut off from littoral territories; and

4) "attached," personally dependent agricultural workers and farmhands, represented by slave
castes such as Pulayas, Parayi and Cherumas, characteristic for Travancore and Cochin.

At the beginning of independence all Keralian
society remained deeply religious in its world view.
The worship of gods, and the division of these gods
into higher or lower categories, retained importance
among a majority of Hindus. God worship was accom-
plished through ritual dancing and sacred offerings
of living things and flowers (119, p. 145). Simultaneously, there was no definitive discarding of belief in the spirits living in the village, or, in
the minds of a wide stratum of the people, ancestral
worship (this retained a special strength among the
Nayars) and serpent worship, characteristic of all
groups in the population--from adhivasi (members of
"unregistered" tribes) to Brahman Nambudiri (119,
pp. 147-149). Religion was an important feature of
life for the members of the two highest castes, the
Brahmans and the Nayars, and their observation of
numerous rules, rituals and so forth testified to
this. The important role of the temples as the sole
center of social life and religious holidays was evidence of the high level of religiosity (119, pp.
143-144, 151-156).

The struggle for national independence and the
victory of the Indian people in this struggle, which
increased political activity among almost all the
groups in the national population, was essential for
the development of the revolutionary process in Kerala. Above all it should be noted that in this region of India the struggle of segments of the peasant population for their class interests proceeded
simultaneously with the national liberation movement. The 1950-1960's was a period where a greater

---

[50] In the north, for example in Bayanad, the granary
of Malabar, there were farming tribes of Kurichi:
<u>Kurumabas</u>, <u>Adiyan</u>, <u>Chetti</u> and others. In the
south there were hunter-gatherers, Nayadi.

and greater number of rural workers were recruited
to the class struggle. The process proceeded, however, in an extraordinarily unequal manner. Regional characteristics, which had left an important imprint on the forms of agricultural production and
types of relations, had an effect upon the level of
social consciousness of the rural working mass in
different districts of Kerala.

We can discern three levels of the rural working people according to their level of social consciousness: the property-owning peasantry with a
persistent caste form of consciousness; the tenant
groups, who approximated the class form of consciousness; the landless, socially humble groups
from the untouchables.

The middle and small landowners of Travancore
and Cochin, fundamentally Nayars and some Izhavas,
came under the first group. In the 1950-1960's this
peasantry was under the influence of the caste organizations of the Nayars and Izhavas, a kind that
were particularly strong. One example was the "Society for the Preservation of Nayars." These groups
and their organizations in the political arena basically supported the Congress (54, p. 120).

The rural working groups who came under the
second and third groups are of greater interest to
us. The existing hereditary tenants of Malabar, Izhavas and Nayars, were the leading members of the
second group. They worked on the rather large estates of the local landowners, and as already noted,
were starting down the path of class struggle even
in the 1930's. In the 1940's, when the struggle for
national liberation had come to fruition, it had
taken place in Kerala simultaneously with an unusual
strengthening of the class demands of the rural
groups. At that time the Communist party in Kerala
came out with slogans for an end to caste discrimination, the organization of the large estates and an
increase in the work pay of agricultural workers.
In 1946 the union of Karshaka Sangam resumed activity in Kerala. In 1946-1948 the struggle of a more
politically active and organized portion of peasant-
ry--the tenants of the large farms--reached an intense point. The tenants, following the national
policies conducted by the CPI, refused to give up a

share of the harvest to the landowners, divided up
the harvest among themselves, and entered into
fierce encounters with the police. These often cul-
minated in bloody reprisals against the leaders of
the tenants (42; 92, p. 369).

However, in the 1940's this rural avant-garde,
who were actively putting the CPI line into practice, found themselves essentially isolated. A substantial portion of this vanguard, above all Izhavas, beyond the borders of Malabar were still
politically passive and either registered their reservations about any social fighting or were drawn
into the fight along caste dimensions. Even in Malabar the majority of the working landless people
were still isolated from the programs and slogans of
the CPI. Often the rural peoples were actually a
great number of reserved, inwardly cohesive subcaste
groups (108, p. 42). The communist supporters from
the Nayars and Izhavas, who were demonstratively re-
pudiating caste organizations in their daily relations, often were isolated, and suffered the condem-
nation and attacks of the inhabitants of the village
(92, p. 367). There did exist, however, an important group that was "passively" sympathetic to the
CPI--the so-called anubhavis.

At the end of the 1940's a switch of a substantial mass of Izhavas from caste orientations to the
orientations of class and the CPI began to emerge.
In this at first a great number of them were only
passively sympathetic to the communists.

The decisive movement in the political situation of the state occurred in the second half of the
1950's. Agrarian reforms in the middle of the
1950's, comprehensive social action, the growth of
education among the unprivileged groups,[51] dependence among the landowners and their tenants and
farmhands--all this significantly changed the social
situation. These changes developed even more clearly in the northern part of Kerala, particularly

---

[51] We should note the extraordinarily high level of
literacy in the state: 60% in 1971, with the
all-Indian index near 29% (54, p. 119).

northern Malabar. After the acceptance of a state
act to defend tenancy in 1955, many existing tenants
became agricultural workers. The deterioration of
economic standards accelerated the growth of radical
moods. It should be noted that these rural prole-
tarians were not estranged from the hired workers in
the city and suburbs, because the agricultural workers themselves seized every chance to earn extra
money in the city and because lineal and caste relations between those who settled in the city and
those who remained in rural localities were preserved.

The participation of tenant Izhavas and Nayars
in class action invariably influenced intercaste relations. Even though caste gradations were dominant
here in the 1950's, there were still genuinely close
relations between members of different castes. Here
class antagonisms assumed more brutal forms. According to the observations of one of the Indian researchers who was visiting a village of northern
Malabar in the second half of the 1950's, the social
role of the landowners fell and the transformation
of land relations "from ethics to business" occurred. In 1957 he observed that relations between
basic categories of rural peoples (kanamdars, landowners and actual farmers) achieved the state of a
"cold war" (75, p. 77).

The second half of the 1950's and the beginning
of the 1960's was marked by the movement of the majority of rural people of the second segment of
peasantry to a position of active political struggle. This process was related to the introduction
of a universal system of elections and the manifest
activity of the communists in the rural localities
of India. The first elections of the local organs
of government, the panchayat, which were held in
1952, had showed that a substantial number of the
tenant rural mass, especially in Malabar, supported
the communists. These panchayats, the majority of
which were made up of communists, oriented their
daily work (material assistance, organization of social labor, construction of village facilities and
so forth) to the landless groups of society. The
work of the communists in attracting the rural poor
to the struggle for their demands was crowned with
great success in the elections for the state

legislature in 1957; only the communists enjoyed
success against the elite. The CPI received 33.59%
of the vote in the rural regions, and in regions
where tenants and rural workers were predominant
they received 42.84% of the vote (for more detail
see 52, p. 92, 100; 54, p. 122). The elite began to
undertake steps toward radical agrarian reform. The
initiation by the government of mass discussion on
new agrarian bills and the debate of various points
of view on the agrarian question were for a significant part of the rural poor the first familiariza-
tion they had to the fight for their own interests.
An important division among the radical-minded landless mass was revealed in the course of discussions
at provincial conferences. These conferences were
pushing a demand for the creation of a ceiling on
landownership at ten acres. The work of the more
radical elites of the leading communists during the
debate on the Indian Law on Agrarian Relations in
1959 and the vigorous work of the communists in the
panchayat helped consolidate their base among the
masses in the 1950-1960's. In regions with predominant non-propertied working groups (tenants, agricultural workers), candidates for the Communist party polled 50% of the electorate in 1960 (and 43.8%
overall in the state) (52, p. 100; 54, p. 125).

At this time a process of transformation of the
very composition of researched groups of tenants
into agricultural workers continued. The comparatively passive "reserves" of the Communist party,
sympathetic to the "anubhavis," i.e., tenants and
agricultural workers, Izhavas and members of the
poor skilled castes in regions of southern Malabar,
moved to a more active political stance in the
struggle (92, p. 371).

At the beginning of the 1960's, these segments
of the rural mass of Kerala, even though maintaining
in their world view many religious features and a
sustained caste consciousness, crossed into an active political struggle of a class nature.[52]

---

[52] We must note that the "backward steps," that is,
the retreat from a class position to a caste one
in the socio-political struggle, did not include

Religious and caste-oriented consciousness itself
was substantially changed and reformed in this process. The violent economic, social and political
processes which were developing in the state at the
time of independence directly, if not indirectly,
dealt a substantial blow to orthodox Hinduism.

In the middle to the end of the 1950's there
were departures from the religious necessity of carrying out a number of Hindu ceremonies by the Brahmans and Nayars. This was seen in their uncoopera-
tiveness in fulfilling their official duties (119,
p. 150). Inasmuch as it was the members of these
high castes that had acted as reference groups for a
substantial part of the rural mass, then the success
of these changes had great importance for the weakening of religious-caste dogma, at least among those
members of the low castes who were in relatively
close contact with Brahmans and Nayars.

The rural mass entered into the class struggle
through leaders who, as already noted, were often
entirely drawn from among the Brahmans and Nayars,
repudiated religious-caste dogma, and accepted Marxist ideology.

The third segment of Keralian peasants was made
up of socially humble groups of the landless rural
peoples, or untouchables. The overwhelming majority
of these people had, in the rather recent past,
throughout the 1920-1930's, been found in different
forms of a wholly slave-like personal dependence on
the landowners, the members of the high castes. In
the 1950-1960's there were radical, sudden changes
in the social behavior of these groups. In an extraordinarily short time they were incorporated into
a political struggle which had serious consequences
for the fate of the entire socio-political process
in Kerala. We will now examine several features of
the evolution of the social consciousness of these
groups in the indicated period from the example of
one of the more numerous castes of untouchables, the
Pulayas.

----

the Nayars or Izhavas, who were usually allied
with the Communist party (54, p. 124).

The basic mass of Pulayas were concentrated in the central and southern portions of Kerala, on territories where more conservative forms of social relations were maintained. The majority of Pulayas were personally dependent, "attached" workers of large- and middle-scale farms, or farmhands being employed more or less regularly on the farms. Many Pulayas did not have even a plot of land to build their homes on. Such a plot would have made them a landowning employee, and that would have strengthened even more relations of personal dependence. In a number of situations the Pulayas lived in a series of small settlements, called <u>cheris</u>.

As already observed, the very conditions of social discrimination, religious-caste organization of society and cultural isolation doomed the lower castes of Keralian society to many centuries of socio-cultural stagnation. At the end of the 1940's and beginning of the 1950's the Pulayas maintained many features of socio-familial relations in their social organizations. Among the Pulayas there were six subdivisions with diverse social status, every one of which was divided into several exogamous branches, one-half with inheritance along the matrilineal line. Organs of traditional social leadership preserved their strength. Every locality had its own headman, or valluvan, having five assistants, three for socio-administrative problems and two for ritualistic questions (79, p. 91).

The basic mass of Pulayas followed their traditional archaic-religious truths and worshiped their own gods and the god Kali as ruler of the entire multidimensional world. The Pulayas believed in the existence of evil spirits and demons and worshiped them in special sacred places, the altars of <u>kavu</u> (the demons). Belief in ancestral spirits was maintained. In contrast to orthodox Hindus Pulayas performed blood sacrifices. Belief in black magic, to which they turned to in times of illness, danger and so on, was widespread among them. During the time when they were under the influence of Hinduism, strengthened thanks to contacts with high castes, particularly Nayars, the Pulayas began to worship the central gods of the Hindu pantheon, Vishnu and Shiva, to include several restrictions on their

diet, and to perform ceremonies prescribed by
Hinduism (76, pp. 91-98).

Many centuries of the influence of caste ideology had its effect on widely held legends in Pulaya
history concerning their origin. According to now
accepted versions, one branch of Pulaya had a higher
status than another, because the first were descendants of the slaves of the Pandavas (conquerors in
the legendary struggle for Kurukshetra) and a second
were descendants of the slaves of Duryodhana.

In the first years of Indian independence the
basic mass of Pulayas remained oppressed and politically inert.

The middle of the 1950's, the time of active
socio-political struggle which invariably found some
expression even in the stagnant corners of the
state, marked the beginning of sudden changes in the
social consciousness of the Pulayas. Their social
activity was directed above all into traditional
channels. The idea of advancement in caste status
through "sanskritism" became popular among the Pulayas, and this meant both a repudiation of more ancient administrative and fetishistic truths and ceremonies and a more strict observance of Hindu norms.
The Pulaya leaders, developing their tactics with
the goal of improving the spiritual behavior of
their caste members, including their familial relations and economic activities, came to power on just
this path. Caste political organizations such as
the "Pulaya Maha Sabha" arose as well, and pushed
for education and "sanskritism" among the Pulayas,
their inclusion into the political struggle, into
electoral campaigns and so forth.

The activities of these organizations had a
definite affect. The material situation of the Pulaya colony in Kurichi (Travancore) showed a change
for the better in 1961 that was beginning to effect
the social consciousness of the Pulayas in these
relatively prosperous conditions. The traditional
organs of leadership in Pulaya society, the valluvan

and his assistants,[53] lost their strength in the
colony (79, p. 91). The influence of Hinduism--the
worship of Brahma, Shiva, Mehesvar and especially
Rama--was more clearly seen in the social consciousness of the Pulayas, in view of the puja, prayer
reading in the evenings, collective singing of Hindu
hymns at regular Saturday meetings and the pilgrimage to holy places. They turned to their own gods
only in those situations when, according to their
beliefs, black magic had a place. Belief in evil
spirits and in dead spirits which could carry evil
had still not been overcome, so these spirits could
be used in the puja, for the special tasks that ceremony performed (79, p. 91).

The situation of the Pulayas in Travancore in
the middle 1960's showed that different local groups
of Pulayas could be found at different levels of
evolution in their social consciousness. There were
substantial numbers of Pulayas living in a more traditional and closed type of rural society (for example, the rice-producing regions to the southwest of
Alleppey) who lacked any notions of the reasons for
class discrimination. The more oppressed groups of
Pulayas were oriented to the preservation of traditional images of life and did not consider the possibility of any improvement in their condition (76,
pp. 82-83). However, they were not very numerous.

The awakening of social self-consciousness
touched even the most oppressed groups to some degree. The most decisive influence for most Pulayas
was a negative attitude to physical labor that was
mostly inherent for traditional Indian society.
There was a place here for aspirations toward
white-collar labor. The leaders undertook efforts
toward a change in the traditional professions of
Pulayas (79% of the researched Pulayas were illegal
agricultural workers, coolies) through an organization of local leather and textile enterprises. But
even in those regions where traditional landowners
such as Brahmans and Nayars were the reference

----

[53] However, in neighboring settlements of Pulayas
the position of the valluvan was preserved (79,
p. 91).

group, the Pulayas had already ceased to believe in
the divine origin of the caste system and conceived
of different explanations for the origin of the high
castes (76, pp. 81-82, 176, 177). At this time Pulayas, now in closer contact with the city, with
Christian people and especially by living in cities
such as Trivandrum, had developed a greatly transitional self-consciousness--from caste to class.
They related untouchability and its low status to
the seizure of land by the Aryans, to the needs of
other exploited groups of society, with their own
dependency on others, and with any inborn inferior
quality they might have, as if they were escaping
from a previous birth (76, p. 187). Here was a gen-
uine desire to improve their position, to become
like others and not to work like slaves. It is important to underline that this improvement was tied
into ownership of the means of production: land,
animals, etc. Many Pulayas saw the path to change
in their position in the redistribution of land,
thinking that the elite should give them land, forests or the land of other landowners as well as the
means for the cultivation of these lands. However,
the debate was not always about land, but often
about economic position or work: "Where there is
money, caste differences disappear automatically"
(76, pp. 83-84, 171-172).

But even in these more complex regions most efforts were directed toward receiving an education,
which, as the thinking went, was the best means of
advancement. Caste organizations widely propagan-
dized the training of children and adults. Even
young educated Pulayas were chosen for responsible
posts in caste organizations. A great number of ordinary, educated Pulayas in the developed regions
rejected their despondent agricultural work and
strove to acquire their own homes or to become independent tenants (76, pp. 187-190).

In the researched period, the mid-1960's, the
basic mass of Pulayas remained religious, but there
were important variations in the level of this religiosity among the various groups of Pulayas. So, in
one region characterized by total apathy, the cults

of the god Kali and demon[54] and ancestral spirit
worship retained their full strength. There the recently organized government of the colony erected
altars, or kavu, where ceremonies were regularly
carried out and living sacrifices were practiced.[55]
There was a clear turn to "sanskritism" and to the
Hindu religion. This process had only begun there,
and in spite of the former rule of free entry to
Hindu temples, a great proportion of plain-living
Pulayas did not enter there, afraid to soil the temple and anger the gods (76, p. 113).

In the traditional regions, where the orthodox
Brahmans and Nayars were the reference groups for
the Pulayas, the wide reach of the practices of the
higher Hindu castes spread among them (puja in the
temple, the pilgrimage, reading of puranas, food
fasts and so on). To some degree, this transformed
the worship of traditional divinities, such as Kali,
and led to an almost total rejection of demon worship. The social distance between them and the members of the high castes shortened, and the deviation
of some of the Brahmans and Nayars, especially the
young generation, from many of the demands of Hinduism exerted a progressive influence on the Pulayas
(76, pp. 99-108).

Significant changes in the social consciousness
of the Pulayas took place in the regions with a high
proportion of Christians and Protestants. Here the
practices of the ancestor and demon cults were absent, and the Pulayas adopted the Hindu practices of
the upper castes. Besides the Hindu temples, caste
homes, built in every region, became religious centers. At that time many Pulayas rejected Hindu conceptions of reincarnation, dharma and karma, and

---

[54] 90% of the interviewed Pulayas turned to "the
graces of the demons for relief from illness"
(76, p. 109).

[55] Several Pulayas abandoned the colony, explaining
that the demons disturbed them there, and that
they could not go there to pray to the spirits of
the ancestors, and for three years they had not
given any presents (76, pp. 110-111).

like the Nayars did not observe food fasts and several other ceremonies (76, pp. 117-122).

Finally, only the educated elite of the Pulayas situated in the large city of Trivandrum had an inherently more modern view of religion and other kinds of beliefs. Only they withdrew from so widespread a practice as the pilgrimage to holy places, showed a lack of piety in their relations to Brahmans during any sacred service (expressed by the rule; "who knows ritual should perform it") and ignored food fasts and other taboos (76, pp. 123-125).

In the 1950's, when the Communist party had begun the great effort toward the advancement of social protest and political activity in the rural areas of Kerala, a large number of the rural poor had still not come to grips with the problem of their inclusion into Indian society on an equal basis with others. This problem was not just a formal one. "Noninclusion" itself meant not only the preservation of groups with more archaic administrative and fetishistic ideas and customs, but of social passivity, related to centuries-old social humility and the absence of an ideological class framework and practices of political struggle. The difficulty of the situation in Kerala was that all the problems relating to the phases of various groups of society and of segments of the peasantry all stood on the agenda at the same time.

Meanwhile the state's socio-political process further accelerated incorporation of various groups of untouchables into political life. This process was related to the struggle for agrarian reform that had been elaborated by the communists since the beginning of the 1950's. A mass movement had been alive since 1953. It took very different forms: rallies, seminars, the dissemination of literature, the elucidation of the position of CPI and so forth. Although the slogan "land for land users" was advanced by the congressional committee on agrarian relations as early as 1935, the concrete slogans of the masses started to approach this appeal only in the beginning and middle years of the 1960's. The demands advanced in 1954 and 1956 by Karshaka Sangam touched upon the cessation of the efforts of the isolationists, for an inventory of landownership, for the freezing of the duties of agricultural workers and so forth (114, p. 1975). In the final analysis the greater part of legislative acts, adopted or proposed in 1947-1956, were not implemented due to strong opposition, as much on the legislative level as on the implementation level. The period 1957-1969 was characterized by a quantity of radical legislation and active, spontaneous movements. In this period the communists were in power in the state for a total of five years and were the initiators of a series of radical agrarian reforms. In the periods when communists were barred from power they led mass movements (114).

Agrarian reforms in the 1950-1960's were accompanied by covert uprooting not only of tenants but of "attached" workers also. The mass of recently oppressed and unprivileged rural workers, who felt out of the system of traditional relations with landowners, flowed into the pre-proletarian segment of the rural masses. Dissatisfaction with their position, as researcher Gough, who had visited several regions of Kerala in 1964, stressed, had seized a great number of landless Pulayas, who half a decade earlier had been in a deep state of apathy. A most obvious reason, in spite of the definite growth of take-home wages in later years, was the constant threat of unemployment. The demands and expectations of this group and the dissatisfaction with their employers, according to Gough, "grew extraordinarily" (92, p. 363).

The overwhelming majority of those who in the past were the most underprivileged groups supported the communists, who were advocating a radical change in the social system (54, p. 129; 76, p. 84). The influx of these "newly awakened" masses to political life, with their expectations and hopes, invariably brought into the communist movement itself an element of radicalism and leftist extremism. It is possible that the very presence in Kerala of this comparatively new, politically immature segment of the rural pre-proletariat was an objective precondition for a split in the communist movement in Kerala and the birth of an extraordinarily strong and radical "left-wing" communist movement in the state [56]

In the first half of the 1970's, when the state government was under the direction of the CPI, a mass radical movement--"left-wing" communism, the CPI (M)--the tempo of agrarian transformation accelerated extraordinarily.[57] As a result, a policy was implemented which brought changes in the class structure of rural society. In essence, any change in traditional landownership, not involving the organization of the means of production, went in favor of the "propertied-farmers" who employed workers. Existing dependent workers became agricultural workers, tied to their employers through concrete relations. Changes also took place in the composition of the movement itself. Tenants and other intermediate elements who had been changed into proprietary landowners were included in the process of embourgeoisement, and they now manifested a powerful opposition to the rural poor (114, pp. 1583-1584).

In general, when interpreting the path of the social struggle in Kerala, it is possible to say that even in a region of very active class struggle by the rural masses the social attitude of the rural workers contained a number of traditional features. The poor rural groups who were either not exposed to caste discrimination or managed to overcome it for one to two decades within the researched period constituted more favorable surroundings for the formation of a class attitude. The absence of discrimination and a weaker intracaste unity facilitated socio-economic and class differentiation within defined caste groups. Although in this situation the

---

[56] It was not accidental, apparently, that the more outgoing "leftist" leaders of the Kerala communists made special use of their large influence among the landless rural workers and plantation workers of the more isolated regions in Kerala, Travancore and Cochin (54, p. 129).

[57] The CPI (Marxist) was formed by leftists who broke off from the main body of the CPI in 1964. They were committed to mass movement tactics (trans.).

landless rural masses had still not rejected their
religious forms of consciousness, their caste psychology and their traditional forms of leadership,
nonetheless the fundamental manifestations of their
social behavior to a great degree began to carry a
class character.

By far the greatest obstacles to the growth of
a class attitude were those met by the socially humble groups, since for centuries the natural model
for these outcasts was the caste organized society,
with its ideology, value system and regulated forms
of life. The upper castes were their reference
groups. Conforming to Hinduism and the example of
the upper castes provided the only possibility to
join society, and this invariably brought orthodox
and conservative-religious orientations into the social struggle. At the same time, the ideological
underpinnings of caste society had collapsed, and
the socio-political situation itself had opened up a
wide path for political activity by untouchables.
For several years some of them made do with this
path, on which members of other castes had traveled
for decades, while others adopted more radical at-
tudes.

CHAPTER FOUR

OVERCOMING CASTE CONSCIOUSNESS AND
DEVELOPING A BOURGEOISIE ATTITUDE (PUNJAB)

In general, the development of economically independent peasants into a petite bourgeoisie rarely
gathers much momentum. Although agrarian reforms in
several countries created definite conditions for
the development of a peasant petite bourgeoisie and
rural bourgeoisie, a number of historical and contemporary economic factors greatly limited the evolution of the peasant economy into a capitalist
economy or a modern farming economy, as were characteristic for Western countries. Such factors, on
the one hand, were land scarcity, limited possibilities for accumulation, the dominance of village usurers and the pressure of traditional relations and
orientations. On the other hand, governments often
set limits to economic growth and accumulation in
peasant economies when they developed political
goals and policies.

It is true that in many regions of Asia, from
early times to the present, commercial and monetary
relations had developed greatly. However, on account of a number of historical circumstances we
rarely find in past eras farming that was independent from community, clan, caste and other relations, not to mention government exploitation. Accordingly, some of the most important features of
the social consciousness and the socio-psychological
attitude of the petite bourgeoisie, like the development of a feeling for ownership and the search for
economic advantage, although they were invariably
produced by economic conditions, were very rarely
dominant or prevailing in the minds of the peasants.
Apparently, we could say that in a majority of Asian
countries a widespread, stable and powerful strata

113

of such peasantry, primarily petite bourgeoisie in
their social consciousness, had still not formed up
to the middle of the twentieth century.

Obviously, then, the peasantry could establish
a close bond with the market--a high level of industrial production, a "free market" of agricultural
products--only when the achievement of economic advantage was the key to its survival. Preconditions
of this kind were present only in the most recent
decades, in the time of encroaching scientific and
technical innovation in agrarian production, during
the so-called green revolution.

In several countries agrarian reforms were intended to create a widespread group of small farmers
and government subsidized peasants. However, the
experience of many countries of Asia showed that to
create such groups through unilateral governmental
means was in fact impossible, since one of the main
conditions--a free economy and a free market--re-
mained absent.

As a matter of fact, we primarily find peasants
of the petite bourgeoisie type in those countries of
Asia where historically there was a widespread group
of relatively economically independent (independent
from the government and landowners) farmers. The
green revolution and the intensification of agricultural production greatly accelerated their evolution
into "farmers." The path of such a transformation,
even though it was slow and nowhere complete, was
nevertheless transforming traditional features of
the social consciousness of the peasantry. In this
chapter we examine this process in Indian Punjab.

No one has any doubts today about the special
place the green revolution had during the 1950's and
1960's in India. It showed that India was one of
only a few regions that was relatively ready for a
process of "capitalistic" (with all the weaknesses
of that term) agricultural production and apparently
had maintained in its socio-economic structure the
potential for such a possibility.

Cultural features specific to Punjab included
its numerous bonds with the historic past of this

region, particularly its ethnic and caste composition, system of landownership and land use, with forms of religious movements mixed in. In the final analysis, the specifics of the development of the region came down to one important circumstance: the domination of a substantial territory of the state by members of the farming (in the past military-farming) castes of the Jats.

Large indigenous unified clans of Jats appeared in northwestern India in the early medieval age. Captured territory became the property of clans who settled the land and formed a clan-familial society consisting of a widely stratified group of military-farmers, all of whom had equal rights. The Muslim invasion wasn't able to destroy this widespread group, but did reduce the Jat settlement into a tributary state, and the inhabitants into taxpayers of the Muslim government. The preservation of traditional rights of landownership by Jat clan society proved to be fertile soil for the diffusion of the religious ideology of Sikhism.

Even though Hinduism with its ideas of caste inequality and hierarchy influenced Jat society, it nevertheless ran counter to the socio-economic experience of the society's equal-status military-farmers. The fundamental principles of Islam, with its declaration of equality, was in somewhat greater accord with this experience.

Sikhism, which arose in the sixteenth century, and which exerted a strong influence on Hinduism and Islam, better expressed the socio-economic experience and the political problems of the Jat soldier-farmer community.

At first Sikhism rejected the idea of armed struggle, but in the seventeenth century, using the religio-political ideology of the Jats and soldier-farmer societies, and being exploited by the Muslim government, it took on an offensive character. At the very end of the seventeenth century a sect of Sikhs was transformed into a religious society, Khalsa--a society of equals. Much of Sikhism had a democratic and egalitarian character. The need for protection from the coercion of the Muslim rulers

115

promoted its offensive character, since Sikh society
was of necessity transformed into a military organization. The future fate of a great number of Jats
was tied to a government created by the Sikhs.

From the 1760's to the middle of the nineteenth
century government's role was only to help form a
widespread and relatively unified strata of economically independent members in this part of India,
comparatively little exploited by the government.
There were relatively restricted possibilities for
the origin of feudal landlords in their midst (65,
p. 29, pp. 52-54). Simultaneously, tendencies toward commercial agricultural production did not
greatly develop in Jat villages. The Jat economy
was primarily natural. The influence of caste society and Hinduism had combined stability in clan relations and the preservation of organs of clan community self-government with a functionally "nirva-
nic" Sikh society. This included high expenditure
for religious necessities, above all for ceremonies
related to the life cycle. The Jat community had to
a large extent become a secluded and religiously
oriented society.

The English assumption of power in Punjab legally preserved independent peasant landholdings and
eliminated a number of different kinds of extortion.
Primarily, it reduced tax rates and included more
peasants in market relations (65, p. 149, 162, pp.
167-168).

In the 1920's the Jat was known in India not
only as the largest landowner, but as an individual
who combined within one person the "landowner, set-
tler, emigrant and soldier" (84, p. 36). Caste ideology could not overcome such old Jat peasant features as love of land and farming. The Jats were
famous for their ability to till the soil. They
were proud of their affiliation to their caste and
referred to themselves as zamindars. Their inherent
occupation found its way into their folk proverbs
and sayings. For example: "The Jat baby, instead
of a toy, has a grip from a plow" (65, p. 3). Char-
acteristically, such Jat features as their attention
to the market and to their inclination to exploit
market conjectures, as well as opportunities for

116

business expansion, distinguished the Jat from other
Indians at the close of the 1920's (84, p. 35, 43,
67).

Nevertheless, the influence of traditional Indian society was manifest in many forms of Jat life.
Consequently, extremely large sums, often incurring
indebtedness, were spent on weddings and funerals
(80, p. 43, 48, pp. 57-59). The influence of Hinduism was reflected strongly in the peasants' value
orientations. This was evident in the value attached to the sense of well-being. Usually they
valued its moral-aesthetic consequences negatively
(84, p. 147, 225).

The traditional system for the maintenance and
payment of the small number of village servants invariably remained. Workers from the lower castes
and untouchables were always employed in the economy
(60, p. 409).

Right up to the achievement of national independence, and in the first decade afterwards, Punjab
villages retained their own kind of "duality." The
tendency toward formation of Jat petite bourgeoisie
and bourgeoisie was far from complete. Traditional
relations obstructed such a completion in two ways:
one more ancient and strong--caste (or clan) community, and another less old--paternal relations between Jat landowners and their workers from socially
inferior castes. Relations of the first type were
manifest in life in clan villages that were princi-
pally isolated and self-governing. So, within the
limits of these villages there existed inner exogamous elements, or _patti_, often having their own
counsils, or panchayat, meeting places, shops and
places for religious ceremonies (128, pp. 148-149).

Relations of the second kind--paternal relations of the patron-client type--were especially
characteristic for those territories of Punjab where
large landholdings were widespread, and where large
numbers of untouchables became laborers. Here there
was a "thoroughly elaborated system of land rights,
responsibilities and duties." The characteristic
feature of the economy was the "responsibility of
the family head for the guarantee of food, shelter

117

and clothing for all who worked on his fields . . .
the inalienable right of the landless to cattle and
to collect feed for their breeding pens, the inherent responsibility of the landholders for support
and practically no-interest loans" (83, pp. 460-
462). The worker's salary was invariably paid
through a definite annual amount of wheat.

Just as the natural form of labor payment had
preserved for generations the "friendly relations"
between the landowner and his regular workers, it
was also characteristic for all Punjab in the period
of the 1950's and objectively was indicative of the
weakness of the development of capitalistic relations in the state (80, p. 61).

Hinduism and the traditional system of orientation around a powerful godhead influenced economic
expenditure. As the analysis of the debts[58] of the
inhabitants of Kuran village (Ferozepore district)
done in 1962 showed, if "domestic necessities" were
included under the rubric "payment of old debts,"
these came to 43%. Then there were those necessities connected with family and caste ceremonies,
which came to 29.1%. All other necessities taken
together, including construction and the upkeep of
cattle, were 27.9% of the entire debt total (80, p.
104).

On the other hand, the socialistic aspects of
the Punjab peasant Jat, which had brought about his
economic self-sufficiency and the weak character of
the inner-village hierarchy, often times dominated
neighboring relations between landowners (Jats and
Ahirs) in their own caste. They left an imprint on
socio-political processes in the village. The Punjab peasants were comparatively active participants
in state political life, as politics was character-
istically tied up with direct economic and social
interests (128, p. 150, pp. 158-159). Even in the
1950's there was a definite change in the norms of
intracaste and intercaste relations under the influence of new, socio-economic factors: the

---

[58] The analysis was made to identify the sums appro-
priated.

concentration of power into the hands of the rulers
of the various castes, the union of common interests, as well as changes in the very criteria of
leadership (127, pp. 16-17).

As has already been noted in research in Soviet
economics, after India achieved independence in agricultural production, an all-accelerating process
began in Punjab of the inclusion of the economy in
market relations and renewal of its technical base.
This provided a leading role to the state due to the
level of socio-economic development (60, p. 200,
341, 345). This process was by far not immediately
reflected in the social relations of the village.
However, beginning in the mid-1960's the more developed regions of Punjab were already showing substantial social changes. The green revolution provided
a strong impulse for progressive social change. To
explain the crux of this matter, at least from the
period since the introduction of the green revolution in Punjab villages, we must refer to the masses
of Punjab peasants as if they were petite bourgeoisie, although with important reservations.

As is known, the green revolution did not develop spontaneously but was planned out. The essence of it was an active stimulation of governmental reconstruction of the agrarian structure and the
intensification and commercialization of agricultural production. This was seen in the widespread sub-
sidization of such construction in infrastructure
and irrigation systems, in advantageous tax policies, in the encouragement of cooperative movements
and in the information provided on new kinds of food
grains and new methods of cultivation (see 61). In
Punjab such a course found fertile ground and transformed significant numbers of Punjab workers to
something closer to farmers. Changes appeared in
the type of technical equipment in the economy, in
cultivation of large parts of land with new high-
yielding varieties of wheat, in wide applications of
fertilizer and so forth. A tendency toward a transformation of large, middle and small farmers into
modern farmers appeared in such districts of central
Punjab as Ludhiana, Jalandhar and Ferozepore. Above
all, this tendency seemed present among the middle
and wealthy peasants who had at least ten acres of
irrigated land.

119

However, the social and socio-psychological
consequences affected the entire Punjab peasantry in
general. The biggest change of all was the new economic relations. As the author of the study on the
Ludhiana village at the end of the 1960's noted,
"for landowners with ten to twenty or more acres of
irrigated land the increasing of production and making money became new ways of life" (101, p. a-75).
This new relation to money was shown above all in
the change to scrupulous accounting of expenses,
which was followed by the rational division of resources in the economy.

The change to the accounting of expenses in
conditions of grain's high value, low taxes and extraordinarily advantageous economies of scale made
the question of payment for the extra workers, who
for many decades had been coming into the economy,
of paramount importance. The traditional form of
payment, namely natural payment of a portion of the
harvest, was the existing element of paternal relations and practices on all farms, above all the
large ones. Economic gain turned out to completely
ruin the ancient relations between landowners and
their workers from the socially inferior castes.
The landowners began to switch to a monetary form of
payment for labor. This change in traditional practices was enough for the "amiable and natural" system to become upset. Untouchable farm laborers responded to the innovation with boycotts, but in
response to this landowners for the first time in
many centuries forbade them the use of the pastures
and cattle on their land (83, pp. 460-461).

In a number of regions, however, the Jats did
not manage to change to a monetary form of payment,
not on account of tradition and paternalism but because of the development of the agricultural worker's standard of living. In regions of intensified
agricultural production the demand and the wages for
labor power were high. So, their wages in the second half of the 1960's grew two-fold, consisting in
monetary terms of nearly five rupiahs a day in
1968-1969 to nearly eight rupiahs a day in 1972 (77,
p. a-102; 87, p. 36; 101, p. a-77). Only in certain
conditions did rural workers carry on a fight for
the preservation of the natural payment of labor
wages. As Frankel, who had done research in the

Ludhiana district, noted, thanks to pressure by the workers this share constituted one-thirtieth of the gross yield of grain. However, the landowners took revenge, depriving the workers of traditional privileges--the right to a corn yield for their cattle with a no-interest loan (87, pp. 36-37).

Nevertheless, the reorganization of wages in a large part of the Punjab economy in the beginning of the 1970's did not generally occur. The daily meals of workers, for example, continued to enter into the figuring of labor wages for both annual and seasonal workers (77, p. a-101, a-107).

The high level of labor wages was circumstantial, depending little on the better disposition of the capitalist landowners. Attempts to expose the interdependence between "progressive" economics and the level of labor wages by Blanckenburg led him to an inference about such interdependence (77, p. a-102). As other materials have shown, and as already mentioned above in research on Ludhiana, often it was "progressiveness" alone, seen in the intensification of production on the most enterprising farms, that lowered the possibilities for a minimum labor rate for domestic workers such as women. So, women occupied in preparing cauliflower for shipment in intensive vegetable gardening on fifty-acre plots received as "payment" only what was remaining from the surplus vegetables (101, p. a-79).

It is important to note the active character of the operation of new, modern farming. In Punjab the expansion of the modern economy adopted such a pace to keep improving the scales of production that it pushed smallholders having two to four acres into tenancy (87, p. 34).

Due to the relatively high level of wages for agricultural labor through natural form of payment in Punjab, the steady exclusion of hired labor, both technical and domestic, had begun. Long-standing relations between landowners and workers were thereby ruptured.

However, if paternalistic relations under the pressures of the new economic situation were destroyed rather quickly, then traditional clan-caste

relations became significantly stronger. It is necessary to keep in mind, on account of the relative
self-sufficiency of a significant number of Jats and
the predominance over them of landowning groups,
that at first the green revolution did not become an
issue of the day as regards the sharp stratification
among Jats. A large group of landowners benefited,
if not directly from the intensification of agricultural production, then from advantages in tax policies and the high value of wheat. Even though economic differences and variations in the benefits to
large and small landowners (in Punjab small-scale
farms were those up to 7.5 acres) sharply grew as a
result of the green revolution, these did not assume
the character of sharp socio-economic differentiation and contrasts of the class type (see 101, p.
a-81; 120, p. a-146). Caste relations did not suf-
fer any damage.

Severe weakening of the traditional caste relations among the Jats occurred more indirectly, in
ideological areas such as traditional orientations
and the traditional system of values. Attempts to
not only survive, but to benefit, and to not only
receive material benefits, but to maximize these,
put a definite strain on traditional practices for
the division of the means of production. This was
evident in a significant amount of "shady" income
(on large farms above 40% of the entire sum of expenses) that began to make its way into productive
necessities and into the expansion of economic oper-
ations (120, p. a-146).

Traditional law had apparently been disrupted
first. This was evident where the growth of incomes
was invariably accompanied by the growth of expenditures on socio-religious necessities. Expenses for
weddings and so forth had remained extraordinarily
high--not much less than a third of the entire expense sum.[59] These expenses, however, were very

---

[59] We are using the materials of the research of 135
farms of Ludhiana, conducted by Deb and Agarwal
in 1969 and 1970. The ratio of expenditures for
production to socio-religious necessities based
on the lowest square margin of farm groups (up to

clearly set apart by some farms from living expenses, and apparently began to seem like an obligation they were stuck with from outside. Blanckenburg showed that for the new group of agricultural
barons the traditional forms of the enrichment of
social status through the organization of lavish
holidays and such lost their attractiveness and
meaning. Pressures to replace the demonstrative and
generous expenditure for public necessities, which
were to a large degree ceremonious, came on the one
hand from the need for capital investment in the
economy. It also came from investment in new, tangible symbols of wealth, already carrying a particularly ostentatious character, albeit in new private
modern villas (77, p. a-102).

The new type of economic existence influenced
the plans for future farms. According to Blanckenburg's research, in plans for future farms--real and
hypothetical (large monetary sums for grains, for
example), Punjab farms put purchase of land and investment in agricultural production and technology
first (77, pp. a-109--a-111). Another researcher
notes that Punjab farmers dreamed of more modern
tractors and acquisition of self-propelled combines
that worked electronically, which would make them
independent from hired labor (101, p. a-79).

New orientations found fertile soil in the new
leadership systems in the village. In the traditional leadership system, the following were the
more important factors (ranked according to decreasing importance): caste system, landownership,
wealth, family reputation, age, genealogy and other
qualities, right down to the number of family members (127, p. 13, 15). Such demands on the leadership were characteristic of Punjab in the 1950's.
However, in the first half of the 1960's, progressive methods of running farms, the greater significance of an education and personal, individual

---

fifteen acres) was 29.18 or 32%, in a middle margin (sixteen to twenty-seven acres) 30.3 and
26.9%, at the highest (above twenty-seven acres)
36.9 and 29.6%, accordingly (fractions rounded
off to nearest tenth) [sic] (86, p. 4).

qualities all began to operate as criteria for leadership on Punjab farms.[60]

With the introduction of the green revolution into Punjab villages and the placing of a high value on the personal knowledge needed in running a farm, an understanding of good management and the concept of a "better farmer" came into agricultural society. In the villages Blanckenburg researched the majority of farmers had a clear understanding of who were the "better farmers" and, as the author stressed, attentively took note of what occurred on the farms of these men. The overwhelming number of the author's informants considered the influence of the "best farmers" significant (77, p. a-14). In such a way, the green revolution greatly strengthened the importance of managerial, economic criteria (in their modern meanings) and, it should be noted, "anti-bourgeoisied the criteria of leadership."

Changes in the structure of government in the villages connected with strengthening the petite bourgeoisie and bourgeoisie orientations in the Punjab peasantry did not have a latent effect. Inasmuch as this preorientation affected the practices of all or almost all of the landowning peasants, with large landowners acting as the leaders during the process of capitalization, then this subsequently would give them a leading role in the organs of power. According to Blanckenburg, progressive farmers, and above all large farmers, occupied a strong position in various organs and institutions of the village. However, the following observation is of extreme importance from the viewpoint of changes in the social psychology of the bourgeoisie group in the village: in Punjab villages the number of progressive farmers in the government was much smaller than in Mysore--29% to 48% respectively. The author went on to note that the progressive farmers worried little about their social positions in the village; they preferred to concentrate their efforts on improving their personal property. This let these farmers change from social to personal interests,

---

[60] We are using material from research done in Mohali village in 1963-1964 (127).

from concern about position in the social hierarchy
to interest in personal economic achievements (77,
pp. a-104--a-105).

In this way there was a tendency, totally alien
to traditional rural Indian society, where prestig-
ious positions and the right to act as the "leader
of the village" was a possible stimulus to a struggle between various castes and inner-caste groups of
a village.

This new tendency, however, was not widespread.
General caste interests which encouraged the development of the peasantry into a bourgeoisie were not
so much overpowering as intrinsic within the caste
and its members and, in a sense, inevitable. It was
not the prestige of castes as much as caste economic
interests that became of paramount importance in the
psychology of Jat-farmers. Changes were not, then,
full or complete. They did not lead into changes in
caste requirements or orientations.[61]

The political situation in Punjab was experi-
encing the influence of changes in the socio-economic situation and social orientations of the Punjab

---

[61] Materials from the 1950-1960's on the traditional
caste organs of the Jats from other nearby regions of India, including western Uttar-Pradesh,
show that in modern conditions these organs not
only grew and became stronger but became the
spokesmen and regulators of new, proto-bourgeoi-
sie tendencies. So, the religious conference of
Jats (Sarv-Khap) of Muzaffarnagara in 1950 accepted a resolution limiting expenditures in marriage ceremonies, in order for more economic use
to be made of the money that was directed toward
education and religious necessities. The conference (Sarv-Khap) in 1956 reflected this tendency
of the birth of solidarity between members of all
propertied, landowning castes. The Rajput, as
members of parliament, called for a conference
for a "union of all Jats, Gujars, Rajputs and
Ahirs, who had one cultural and ethnic basis,"
and also acted against Western democracy, and for
Indian custom (15, pp. 48-49).

125

peasants. Most important was the decline in the influence of the communal parties "Akali" and "Jan
Sangh" in the state. Inasmuch as the ruling party
in the National Congress acted as the initiator of
reform in the villages, and its local representatives had acted as the workers of that apparatus,
through which measures for the intensification of
agricultural production were carried out and material means were disbursed, then economic interests
conditioned the orientations of a large number of
Jats in the National Congress.

Within this same Congress the Punjab farmers
acted as the national initiators for socio-economic
demands, which included a number of elite privileges
and strengthened the role of Punjab as the leader of
the green revolution. Even though class stratification was undeveloped among the Jats, they acted with
a unified front on such questions as resistance to
the increased tax on irrigated land and overall
electrical and land taxes.

Blanckenburg refers particulary to the undeveloped process of socio-economic differentiation among
the farmers who had been affected by the intensification of agricultural production in his research
into the circumstances surrounding social repression
in various regions. In the opinion of the same in-
formant farmers, such repression had been reduced
for the past decade (77, p. a-107).

Simultaneously all Punjab landowners unanimous-
ly acted against agrarian reforms in the state. The
economically clever Punjab elite were politically
clever enough to prevent the realization of agrarian
reform and to defend the position of the landowners.

To some extent the pre-bourgeoisie orientation
of the small holding peasantry was testified to by
the fact that the peasants, acting through the organization "Kisan Sabha," persistently campaigned
for an increase in an artificially high value for
wheat, but not for all the benefits such an increase
could bring. According to reviews of the newspaper
this indicated the pro-kulak tendency inherent in
peasant organizations (104, p. 19).

The experience of Punjab's green revolution
shows that the evolution of caste consciousness
toward a petite bourgeoisie one is possible given
the presence of many favorable factors. At this
point it is obvious that at some time this evolution
occurred without a radical destruction (on a massive
scale) of inner-caste solidarity and without overcoming several important features of caste consciousness.

CHAPTER FIVE

THE PEASANT'S CLASS ATTITUDE IN REGIONS
WITHOUT PATERNALISM BUT WITH LANDLORDISM (IRAN)

Iran is one of those countries where right up
to the beginning and middle of the 1960's large private landownership was the basic form of landownership. The overwhelming number of peasants were
sharecroppers on the landlord's estate. The 1950's,
a time of democratic convulsions in Iran, was at the
same time a period of numerous movements by the
peasants against the landlords in different regions
of the country. For the purposes of this research
our interests lie in the wide swing to anti-landlord
feelings in the country, as well as the historical
preconditions of this situation.

_Several Features of the Formation of Agrarian
Relations and Social Outlook of the Peasantry_

The agrarian structure of Iran at the middle of
the twentieth century was the result of a long evolution. A peculiarity of Iran was the presence,
right up to the time of our research, of a large
portion of territory under tribal law, which exerted
influence on every aspect of social life. However,
in a given period we are above all interested in regions with typical estate landownership. On these
territories we can consider the clan settlement, a
basic unit of social structure, as the starting
point in the evolution of agrarian structure. The
final step of this evolution was characterized by
dependence on the village landlord and the development of communities of peasant tenants who were not
connected to each other by durable neighborly bonds.

For one thousand years the basic social building block in agricultural localities was the village. In these settlements, the peasants, who were

both the workers and the basic taxpayers, "built"
the governmental apparatus. Simultaneously the exploiters of the peasants were their rulers (often
from foreign ethnic groups) and also large owners of
government land, with more or less independence from
the central government. There were villages whose
forms of organization and structure remained essentially unchanged. At the same time the composition
of village inhabitants was changed rather often by
numerous wars, devastation and natural calamities.
A sustained destruction of the more archaic type of
relations ensued. The chasm existing between villagers and representatives of the governmental class
and the partial change in the composition of the
villagers hindered the installation of the traditional hereditary elite in these villages.[62] It promoted the preservation of many ancient democratic
institutions. The main principle of organization of
the Iranian village as a working entity was the
equalization of shares, both of land and of water,
between villagers (102, p. 3). The right to the use
of village land, the use of straw for cattle and so
forth was related to adherence to shares, or _joft_.

The influence of ancient despotic Persian governments, in spite of their many archaic features,
promoted the preservation of the village as a uni-
tary administrative entity. Villagers had collective responsibility for crimes which had occurred
within village limits, taxes and labor conscription
which were figured into the joft accounts. This
system remained unchanged for many centuries, except
for military-political intrusions, which have punc-
tuated Iran's entire history. However, the composition of the rulers and the direct exploitation of
the peasantry had changed.

---

[62] The formation of such a type of elite had begun
in the time of the first large ancient Persian
governments in Iran in the person of the head of
the village, the _dihgan_, having hereditary administrative power in the village, rights to land
and responsibility for collection of taxes (102,
pp. 13-14). However, the numerous military inva-
sions did not allow them to definitively take
shape and consolidate.

In the period preceding the invasion of Iran by the Arabs and their Islam, the country was ruled for several centuries by ethnically foreign elements who had replaced the Persian elite, which greatly strengthened the exploitation of common rural producers. Peasants under these foreign rulers organized on a clan basis and were totally without rights and defenseless (102, pp. 13-14).

Old beliefs and ideas, transformed by the Zoroastrians to some degree, were preserved by the peasantry in these conditions. Ancient Persian government itself had promoted the foundation of the cult of the idealized king, while ancestor worship also remained strong (73, p. 57, 274). Political turmoil and a partial changeover in elites promoted a revitalization of more primitive beliefs.

Important changes in Iran's agrarian structure began with the Arab invasion. Arabs, who had appeared here in the seventh century under the banner of Islam, had already learned relatively developed juridical and legal norms. They had invaded Mesopotamia and other territories with different formations of governmental apparatus and commercial relations. Islam itself, which propounded the formal idea of autocratic, sacred government, had already exerted a considerable influence on these norms and principles.

From the point of view of Muslim jurisprudence, as Petrushevskii stresses, "social ideals were theocratic, which meant the union of spiritual and political power in the hands of religious leaders. However, even though during the reign of the Umayyad dynasty the theocracy was maintained in theory, in reality it was transformed into a function of the secular government. The Shariah, Muslim law, was inherently a mixture of religious and legal understandings" (57, pp. 146-148). Especially under Sunnism, the ruling doctrine in Iran after the sixteenth century, the secular-in-practice principle had become rather clear.

The interpretation by only the legalistic Sunni order of the caliph, the "deputy" to Mohammed in the tenth and eleventh centuries, and even the accept-

ance of an "indigenous" choice of a more desirable
method of filling the post of caliph (57, p. 150),
shows how far from preceding theocracy the theory of
Muslim government had come. "The caliph was not
considered the bearer of sacred well-being. . . . He
was not the indisputable arbitrator on religious
questions. . . . He was only a secular supporter of
the Shariah" (57, p. 156). Relations between the
caliph and Muslim society were seen as a "two-sided
question, in which both sides assumed definite responsibilities" and through "the people" (Muslim society) they were able to eject any caliph who was
not fulfilling his duties (57, pp. 152-158).

Forming and changing in the process of conquest
and government of invaded territories, Muslim law
had already begun in the fourteenth to sixteenth
centuries to reflect the notion of strong government
(57, p. 158).

Even if some of the basic dogmatism of the Muslim legal order had undergone changes through implementation, orthodoxy still remained in areas such as
landownership. From the very beginning, in principle Muslim law contained two diverse but clearly
outlined laws on landownership. On the one hand,
private landownership was not only accepted but declared immutable. On the other hand, water, pasture
and part of the land's acquired money and wealth was
considered the property of all Muslim society (102,
p. 16). The presence of two forms of landownership
at first propelled the masses into violent encounters within the occupied territories of Iran. Several categories of land assumed different taxation
policies, including categories such as public and
private lands, as well as waqf land[63] (56, pp.
284-285; 102, p. 20).

---

[63] Primarily this was unsellable land, the property
of the conquerors, who had relinquished their
right to it for the benefit of all society. Later on, as waqf land had been taken and formed,
it was "sanctified," that is, it became a "sacred
object" (57, p. 162; 102, p. 27).

The existence of different categories of land
had one clearly expressed tendency--the transfer of
large portions of land, including those intended for
the public use of Muslim society, into private
hands.

The conquest of Iran by the Arabs promoted the
conversion of the peasantry to Islam. It is important to stress that, compared to the powers of despotic government, this conversion presented wider
possibilities of legal power to the peasantry. The
recognition, albeit in theory, that all members of
Muslim society were equal before the Prophet to some
degree promoted the freeing of the peasant consciousness from its humility before despotic power.
Under Muslim law the category of ". . . serf or feudal dependence of the peasant that was not seen as
personal dependence" (57, p. 163) was absent. However, peculiarities which were deeply ingrained into
the country's agrarian structure did not promote the
development of these new elements of consciousness.
The widespread presence of large private landownership kept the peasantry in a dependent state. Peasants often could work only as holders of governmental land, waqf land, <u>iqta</u> land and so forth (57, p.
163).

Here a type of rather developed social relation
was found, one where relations on the basis of land
were basic for all other kinds of relations.

The appearance on a massive scale of such forms
of landownership as iqta was related to changes in
the composition of rulers in the country, namely, to
the establishment from the eleventh century on of
the power of members of nomadic tribes--the <u>Seljuq
Turks</u>. With the destruction present in the country,
the Seljuq Turks tried to adjust the functioning
taxation system in the distribution of administration or in the number of compensations for service
in certain territories.[64] Stressing the difference

---

[64] According to the customary law of the roaming
tribes, the country was viewed as the personal
property of the aristocrats, being run by them in
the name of the people. This was used in the di-

of the iqta system from the feudal West European
system, Lambton notes that the muqta (people receiving iqta) originally had no kind of military obligation before the elite. Furthermore, muqta more often lived in the cities and not on their holdings
(102, p. 54).

The legal and economic self-sufficiency of the
peasants, related to the iqta system, had varied
significantly depending on what kind of land they
lived on--untilled or cultivated (102, p. 29). In
the first case, the power of the landowner over
those peasants he ruled was much stronger and absolute. In the second kind, the power of the muqta
was weaker, as peasant collectives resisted him,
having traditional landowning rights and related social interests.

Because of the weakening of the central government, a larger portion of public services were taken
over by the government of the muqta, and the people
were compelled to resort to the protection of the
strong muqta. The iqta system in the "dark" times,
and there were many in Iran's history, began to grow
into a system of patronage and of paternalistic relations between landowner and peasant. A tendency
toward formation of hereditary ownership continued
to take shape during the period of Mongol domination
(thirteenth to sixteenth centuries). The Mongols
inflicted widespread destruction and dispatched soldiers to organize the use of land, for which the
peasants not only had to pay taxes but perform services for these officials, not the government, and
had to remain attached to their land (102, p. 90).

In the thirteenth to fourteenth centuries, as
Petrushevskii notes, large feudal landownership exercised complete sway in the north; it had combined
within it small peasant land usage. A plot of

-----

vision of the country into governmental districts
(primarily nonhereditary) headed by the nearest
branch of the ruling family. This practice was
carried forth in Iran. The influence of Muslim
law grew in that government gradually came to be
associated with landownership.

arable land that a peasant received at the start of
his tenancy, either through the rural community or
his own initiative, was an unexpected bonus. Often
community land had not undergone any redistribution
and plots were found in constant use by the peasants. Pasture was in common use (56, pp. 284-289).

Where peasants were defenseless before holders
of government land who controlled the organs of law
and violence, the community was a form of consolidation for the peasantry. As Petrushevskii notes, in
isolated mountainous regions peasant communities often vigorously resisted attempts to impose new obligations on them.

In several periods of Iran's history from the
sixteenth to the eighteenth centuries, and from the
establishment of the Safavid dynasty, the central
monarchy grew stronger. However, a reverse tendency
toward some preferential order of land, to formation
of private landownership, was too weak. Military
action, raids and devastation often desolated the
land, and led to the transfer of occupied land into
the hands of the ruling family or the government,
with eventual distribution as holdings. In peaceful
times these holdings[65] were changed into a variety
of types of private ownership.

In this way, the basic tendency in the development of landownership, dating at least from the
fourteenth century, was the gradual displacement of
the idea of government-communal ownership of land,
supported by Islam, to a conception of full private
landownership. Even from the end of the fifteenth
century, it is clear that large land estates often
received full immunity and were guaranteed no interference from civil servants, tax collectors and so
on (102, pp. 102-103).

The spread of actual private landownership was
especially strong at the end of the nineteenth and
beginning of the twentieth century. This was the
result of the sale of the government lands of the

____

[65] In the Qajar dynasty, which existed up to the
twentieth century, they were called tuyul.

ruling dynasty of Qajar. Since 1843 attempts toward
a European form of private ownership had been initiated. Practically this formulation of the "right to
unconditional private property on land and water"
had begun in 1923-1927 and marked the consolidation
of landlord rights to land (30, pp. 23-24, 70-72).

The sum total of the socio-economic and political history of Iran at the beginning of the twentieth century was the formation in rural localities of
a "royal" feudal order. It was comparatively independent from the central government, practically not
only having formed the right to landed property, but
having managed law and order on its own property.
The invariable result of the defenseless peasantry
before the tax robbers, oppressive landlords and
raids of nomadic tribes was the peasantry's involu-
tion, preservation of archaic beliefs and orientations toward a hope of older times, "an ideological
layer" understood through Islam. At the same time,
the existence in several regions of a communal peasantry with hereditary landownerhip rights, preserving its unity and solidarity while suffering the
cruel yoke of the landlords, sheltered neither
through religion, nor caste, nor other covers, and
the weak expression of paternalistic relations between landlords and peasants, promoted formation of
class consciousness in the peasantry.

The growth and final victory of Shiism was tied
to the spontaneous approval of the peasants. Widespread education in Islam could naturally not promote any kind of radical transformation of ancient
beliefs. After the formal conversion to Islam,
there remained, untouched, a deep layer of a popular, archaic world view: worship of fire via a sacred tree and source, belief in spirits and so
forth. One doctrine of Islam in which these beliefs
found great support was Sufism, a belief in Muslim
mysticism. The activity of Sufis was carried out in
village fraternities. The sheiks were tutors of
Sufism, respected as holy possessors of a gift that
could work wonders and revive the dead (57, pp.
235-236). The holy cults which were taught by Sufis
gradually became part of all Islam, and a pilgrimage
to the holy tombs was one of the sacred duties. The
places of ancient cults--the mythical dieties,
agrarian cults and sacred trees and

springs--gradually came to be seen as sacred groves
(57, pp. 237-239).

Shiism accepted many ideas, inculcated Sufism,
and was also guided by more archaic social ideas of
the people. So, in Shiism the law of imamat (the
"office" of the Imams) was directly related not to
personal features or other people, but to a blood
relation with Mohammed and his son-in-law Ali. According to Shiite theory the Imam was the bearer of
sacred well-being or religious manifestations. He
alone, not a consensual idea among the religious
community, was the highest religious authority for
Shiites. In the end part of the dogma became accepted as truth in the return of the twelfth Imam of
Mohammed, Mahdi, who rehabilitates "the restored
theocracy with the Sunni caliphs, filling the world
with truth and justice," and "eliminating tyrants
and tyranny" (57, pp. 264-265, 267).

The death of the first three Shiite Imams
showed one aspect of Shiism--the cult of martyrdom
as "the direct path to paradise" and as "the highest
service before god" (57, p. 242, 258).

Belief in spirits, in the imminent arrival of
the true ruler and creation of a "prince" of justice, the possibility of overcoming death through
the martyrdom cult--all this did nothing to give
Shiism an active or decisive nature.

In the ninth to fifteenth centuries Sunnism remained the official ideology of the government. If
up to the ninth century peasant protest action had
developed under a non-Muslim guise, then Shiism
gradually became an ideological cover for national
protest. Shiism was more widespread in rural localities than in the cities, and under conditions where
Sunnism was the governmental religious ideology Shiism became a sign of anti-elite propaganda. The
center of the uprising of the peasant underground
was under the sign of Islam. This was particularly
true in those regions of Iran near the Caspian,
where a self-governing paternalistic society was established and pagan beliefs were more diffuse (57,
p. 24, 350).

The Mongol invasion, which at first was
directly felt by both sects, strengthened the position of Shiism. However, Sunnism remained the official religious ideology in the fourteenth and fifteenth centuries.

In the fourteenth century the first local government formed by Shiites took shape. Thanks to the
widespread participation of the peasants in the formation of these governments, which were formally
theocratic, the democratic tendencies in them, which
were toward an equal distribution of well-being and
social equality, were expressed rather clearly (57,
pp. 356-358). The result was a general strengthening of Shiism in Iran. It was just this situation
that prepared the ground for the transformation of
Shiism into the official religious doctrine of the
Safavid dynasty in the sixteenth century.

The victory of Shiism could in a definite sense
be seen as evidence of the strength of domiciled religious beliefs in the mass and the political importance of the peasantry itself, who up to the very
moment of Shiism's victory had been enslaved by the
government.

The wide diffusion of large private landownership in Iran was noted above. Toward the end of the
nineteenth century villages with _arbabi_ landlords
were more widespread. Behind them were the villages
of peasant landowners, or _kordah malaki_. Next were
villages on the territories of land users, or tu-
yuls, including government land and villages on waqf
land. There were also villages founded by tribal
groups or aristocrats. Finally, there were villages
led by some of the religious leaders (57, p. 155).

In the landlord villages the practice of redistribution was still observed--the redistribution of
shares to the peasants, in which some of the landlords did some interesting things. In some cases,
where the village inhabitants had tilled the land
from time immemorial, as in several districts of
Iran's Azerbaiyan region, the peasant's right, at
least in the first quarter of the nineteenth century, was clearly indicated, and societal institutions were clearly stabilized. Landlords did not
have the right to expel the peasantry for only

138

non-payment of rent. Landlords generally had almost
no contact with villagers, and all village matters
were decided by a council of elders. Questions on
the shares of land distribution were also decided by
a council of elders, and the rights of the individual were always limited (102, p. 172).

However, at the end of the nineteenth century,
the practices of authoritarian management of farms,
compulsory labor for peasants and the prohibition of
travel from the estate became more characteristic
for landlords everywhere. The intermediaries between the landlord and the peasant were the village
elders, the kadkhuda, entirely appointed by the
landlords. According to the rate of absenteeism,
always a characteristic feature of these regions,
the villages were transferred into the hands of managers who wrung out of the peasants the maximum
product of labor they could.

The borderline of the nineteenth and twentieth
centuries, the revolution of 1905-1911, giving Iran
its first constitution, and the reforms of Reza Shah
marked the entry of the country into the modern age.
In the area of agrarian relations the existence of
change meant, as already noted, a strengthening and
formulation of private ownership on primarily landlord property. However, a group of economically independent peasants, kordah malaki, endeavored to increase their numbers (30, p. 74).

Measures toward legislation regulating tenant
relations were passed in the thirties, but under the
conditions of the absolute power of the landlords
these remained in effect only on paper. Collection
of taxes, sometimes accompanied even by torture,
forced the peasantry to look for protection from the
landlords and, accordingly, to accept these very undesirable living standards, as Demin notes (30, p.
29).

However, historical conditions had formed two
basic classes in rural localities, related to each
other not so much by natural obligations as much as
by opposition to each other. Large landowners were
not hereditary aristocrats with traditional rights
and obligations, did not have deep ties with the
village, and often did not even live in the village.

They did not have the correct ethnic, clan or paternalistic relations with the tenant peasants. The
right of the landlords to decide the life or death
of the peasantry was not a law handed down by tradition. It was the law of the strong over the weak.[66]
Under these conditions, personal characteristics
like individual development, well-being and cooperation between peasant and landlord were not developed.

However, the peasantry's relations with the
large landowners was not the only factor forming its
social consciousness. Downtrodden and oppressed
peasants remained deeply religious. The priesthood,
and in a number of cases the local hereditary aristocrats and nobility, had an enormous influence on
them (30, p. 53, 56). This was clearly present in
the anti-imperialist struggle, which took the form
of a pan-Islamic movement in the northern part of
the country in 1915-1918. The organizers of
speeches and militant groups--groups of _mujtahids_
--were often large landowners and local aristocrats
(35, pp. 16-18). Religious slogans, as well as
anti-colonial ones dressed up in religious form,
were an effective means for mobilizing the peasant
mass by members of the exploitive elite right up to
the 1920's. As the gifted researcher Osetrova
showed, up to the beginning of the 1920's revolutionary action had "almost left the peasantry unaf-
fected." The Iranian peasants "became an additional
political factor and began to assume their class
identity" only after the revolutionary situation in
Gilan in 1920-1921 (38, p. 49). Actually, in the

---

[66] We should note that several other characteristics
were relevant in the relations of tribes who had
moved into permanent settlements and landownership; here the tribal apex, the aristocrats, were
related to the working mass and preserved ethnic
self-consciousness, ethnocentrism and simple traditional relations. Finally, in the year Reza
Shah took power a new type of landownership appeared, hereditarily reserved for civil servants,
military men and businessmen. The form of exploitation in these conditions was, as a rule,
softened (102, p. 262).

Gilan movement, led by Kuchek Khan, the anti-landlord attitude of the peasantry appeared rather
clearly. The peasants reduced the amount of rent
payment and duties to the landlord. Many landlords
fled the region (35, p. 29, 85). But even then, so
close to the Russian revolution, the leader of the
movement, Kuchek Khan, appealed to the precepts of
the Koran, to the Shariah and to a peasantry inherently blinded by religion (37, p. 57, 61).

The general democratic development of the country, particularly in Iranian Azerbaiyan and northern
Kurdistan in 1945-1946, was a new step forward on
the path to the elaboration of class demands for a
number of Iran's peasants. The rulers of Azerbaiyan
had seized a portion of land of the more radical
landlords. In a number of regions, especially to
the north, anti-landlord movements were seen, with
the peasants refusing to pay the landlord a portion
of the harvest and so forth (18, pp. 103-105). National leaders made the decision to increase the
peasant's share of the harvest to 15% (64, p. 136).
However, at this time the anti-imperialistic struggle, which spread quickly in the peasantry, was
strongly tinged with religious fanaticism and was
united with the _jihad_, or of struggle with the "un-
faithful." At the head of a more massive campaign,
one for the nationalization of oil production, stood
the reactionary religious figure Hassam--proponent
for the idea of pan-Islamism and Shiite jingoism
(31, pp. 94-100).

In general we can say that the peasants of
Iran, insofar as they were openly oppressed by the
landlords to the middle of the twentieth century,
were not able to free themselves from their religious orientations, and only in isolated regions
could assume a class position in the social struggle.

<u>Iran's Peasant Tenants in the 1950's to Beginning of
the 1960's: Social Consciousness and Social
Struggle</u>

In the pre-reform period of the 1950's, landless and small holding peasantry, both agricultural
workers and tenants constituted an overwhelming ma-

jority (over 80%) of Iran's peasantry (18, p 37;
39, p. 86). The typical and more interesting one
for analysis was the peasant tenant. The economic
position of the Iranian peasant tenant and conditions of tenant leasing in the 1940's and 1950's
have been repeatedly described in our literature
(18; 29; 64). Here we can only note a few high-
lights. Very different forms of leasing were used
in the villages, and these defined the basis for local traditions (18, pp. 47-51; 64, pp. 66-90). It
is important to stress that a single principle was
the basis for the distribution of the harvest. This
was one's share of helping with material expenditures, coming under five elements, which were seen
to have equal value: land, water, working cattle
(and implements), family and labor. The personal
dependence of the peasant on the landlord was often
defined by just economic factors, depending on who
controlled the third and fourth elements (64, p.
53). This principle of accounting for expenditures
through the distribution of the harvest was usually
observed everywhere. Increasing exploitation went,
as a rule, above and beyond this accounting.

Decreases of the peasant's share had two
sources: the first was related to the omnipotent
landlords, the second to the stability of traditional forms of organization of village life.

As already noted, the transfer to the government of their prerogatives through the "deputy" or
"leader" meant the passage into law of compulsory
labor for peasants, the collection of extortions,
means for maintaining an administrative apparatus on
the local level and so forth. This practice was
preserved right up to the middle of twentieth century in peasant obligations. It is of no small importance to note that relations between landlords
and peasants took shape as a contract between two
parties, and obligations such as labor were stipulated by the landlords in the contract (64, p. 97).

The volume of obligations was usually greater
in regions of larger landowners--Iranian Azerbaiyan,
Kurdistan, Khorasan, Fars, Kerman (102, p. 331).
Obligations included unpaid conveyance of the landlord's share of the harvest to the threshing floor

in the granary, unpaid labor to the landlord from a
few days to a few dozens of days in the year, including work on and maintenance of irrigation channels and so forth (18, pp. 71-76; 64, p. 98; 102,
pp. 330-334). Natural duties were seen as obligatory delivery to the landlord of a number of products (grain, meal and eggs). A share of land, either joft or domicile, was given either as an
obligation or an extortion. Often the peasants were
obliged to give presents to the landlord and pay
visits to the village of the mubashir or collector
of rent payment (64, p. 102).[67]

The extent of the landlord's power over the
peasant and the conditions of tenancy were to some
degree limited by local traditions and economic conditions. In several regions historical conditions
were on the peasants' side (they had maintained
hereditary landownership rights). We should note
that the Shariah confirmed the hereditary ownership
rights of the peasantry, the so-called institutution
of rih se (64, p. 64). However, this institution
was maintained to the middle of the twentieth century only in isolated districts, and then only in
residual form. In many territories of Iranian Azerbaiyan the land rights of the haqqi-jivar were preserved, as well as the priority given to the care of
the peasant's land on the estate, which really only
meant rehabilitating wasted plots of land. In case
the rental agreement was rejected the landlord had
to pay compensation to the peasant, and upon sale of
the land the new landlord did not have the right to
drive the peasant off. Sometimes, according to local custom, the peasant could transfer his landowning right by way of succession and even sell it. In
several regions the landlord was obliged to buy his
land from others, due to its rejection in the rental
agreement by a peasant who had both home and garden
on the property. Landlords fought this tradition,
most frequently by redistribution and forbidding the

[67] The latter custom was so established, that in
several of those cases where mubashirs were members of the government they continued to receive
a share of the peasant harvest for their sustenance (102,p. 335).

143

peasants to till gardens (64, p. 65; 102, pp. 296-
297, 302). The remainder of land rights were not
stipulated. However, the idea (albeit not absolute)
of the peasants cultivating their own plots of land
was nurtured by elders and stipulated in the Shariah. The landlords acted in such a system as violent
usurpers of peasant rights and uprooters of tradition.

Generally, the availability of a fund of free
land to some extent objectively limited the all-pow-
erful landlords and the practices of extortion (102,
p. 304).

As research on the pre-reform Iranian village
of the 1950's shows, relations between landlord and
peasant usually were free of paternalistic, particularistic nuances and had a tendency to assume clear
forms of antagonism. Lambton provided the basic
conclusion of the field of research in this period.
Between landlords, as a class independent since
birth, and peasants there was a deep abyss. They
did not to the slightest extent have a feeling of
collaboration or participation. Their relations in
general, although not without exceptions, were characterized by mutual distrust. Landowners usually
saw peasants as a means solely intended to supply
their income. If relations with them were without
cruelty, they could shove their own duties off onto
the peasants. Any improvement in the peasantry's
position the landlords saw as a symptom of a weakening of their own power (102, p. 263).

However, the landlord was opposed not by an
isolated peasant or individual. He often confronted
the village with its indigenous forms of social organization. Village land was usually divided into
shares, or joft (102, pp. 4-5), where periodic redistribution often occurred, in which landlords usually had much at stake. Some tenants formed the
right of "perpetual tenure"--their land was not subject to partitioning (18, p. 57; 64, p. 65; 102, pp.
298-299). Villages had an administrative and service staff: the elders (kadkhuda); the pakars,
their assistants; the dashtbans, the watchmen of the
fields; the murabs or water overseers, shepherds,
blacksmiths, carpenters and others. All of these

were paid entirely by a traditionally defined sum of
the harvest, up to 26% of the crops (29, p. 30).
Yet in regions where landlords dominated most of the
land the elders were the representatives of the
landlords, and submitted to them in managing their
property, or often paid their helpers from the peasant share of the harvest. The dashtbans were chosen
by the peasants, and their pay--a share of the har-
vest--was divided up either from the distribution of
the harvest or from the peasants' share. Village
blacksmiths and carpenters, and sometimes bath-house
attendants and barbers, were paid independent of
their output of work. This was a defined quantity
of grain from every portion of wheat from the harvest (102, pp. 338-339, 345-348). It is necessary,
however, to keep in mind that these practices of
paying village personnel, which were leading to significant losses in the peasant economy, were not religiously motivated.

According to old custom, the peasants had to
contribute a portion of the harvest to the religious
leaders. By the 1950's this practice had disappeared. However, the same forms of payment for _mul-
lahs_ and rural teachers, both natural and monetary,
were retained (29, p. 30; 102, p. 348).

The peasant's attachment to his own plot of
land and his interest in its retention was greatly
weakened by frequent redistribution, as already
discussed. At this time many factors strengthened
the solidarity of the peasant. Besides living entirely in the village and participating in village
affairs, the very forms of labor organization--in a
hot climate the necessity of organized irrigation
--increased their solidarity and cooperation. Many
peasants, particularly those not owning cattle, were
forced into joining work groups and drawing up a
contract for a designated kind of work. This practice was rather widespread.

In areas where landlords were especially arbitrary or cruel such groups were able to act in anything but a strong fashion. Village land was divided into distinct "parcels," or _sahra_, which were
tilled by "field groups," headed by the _salar_ or
sar-salar, named by the elders. Territories under

the sahra were redistributed yearly. The salar and
sar-salar had the right to one day's unpaid labor
from every member of the group. As Lambton notes,
such organizational systems of labor under the management of the elders converted the peasants into a
single undifferentiated working force (102, pp.
298-299).

The economic position of an overwhelming majority of peasants was characterized by generally acute
poverty and indebtedness, as a rule, to local rural
moneylenders.

Labor cooperation as well as the constant opposition of the peasants to the landlord formed the
basis for the peasantry's strong solidarity in socio-political life. On the side of the peasantry
were the ancient practices of relative economic
self-sufficiency (especially where the peasant had a
family and farm implements), which helped form a
tradition of cooperation and solidarity. On the
landlord's side were the means of economic and administrative pressure and military power.

As should be clear, objectively there were important prerequisites for the emergence of the peasantry's class interests and its transformation into
a very active, fighting anti-landlord class. Among
those factors weakening the full effect of these
prerequisites, besides the power of the landlords,
we should note the traditional world view of the
peasantry. Horrific poverty, hunger, almost complete illiteracy and defenselessness before the
landlord's personal power did nothing but strengthen
the remaining features of the peasantry's consciousness, its religiosity and fatalism.[68] Actually, during the time of our research, Iran's peasantry retained its deep religiousity, to the point of being
"fanatical believers" (31, p. 6). Even the very
special nature of Shiism, as discussed, preserved
many features of an archaic world view in the

---

[68] "Among the peasants," wrote one village researcher, "fatalistic spirits continue to roam, without
which . . . it would be impossible for them to
live in such conditions" (30, p. 93).

faithful. Islam's theory of an inseparable spiritual and worldly power, applied to the day to day life
of Iran, was seen by the peasantry as the priority
of spiritual power over secular, of the spiritual
person over the civil person. For centuries the
Shiite priesthood controlled the Shariah courts,
played a role in the original legislative organs and
was the highest sanction for civil legislators (30,
p. 54; 31, p. 35). Between the nineteenth and twentieth centuries the "priesthood exerted a larger influence on the people than the official representatives of Persia" (30, p. 54).

Although the reforms of Reza Shah led to the
first tangible limitations on the Shiite priesthood,
their position in the economic and political life of
the country remained well fortified, as seen by how
during much of the reform, from the 1920's to the
1960's, the priesthood led an extremely reactionary
life on the social scene.[69] Mullahs and pishnamaz
acted as advocates of Shiite truth in the village.
The mosque remained right up to the 1960's the center of both religious and political life in the village (31, p. 57; 109, p. 490). The ritualistic life
of the peasantry was quite regulated. Five times a
day Shiite peasants performed the namaz (the prayers
of Allah), and on Fridays participated in a solemn
prayer service at the mosque. During the Muslim
holidays they took part in religious rituals and
listened to sermons. Religious events, such as weddings, divorces and burials, occupied a huge part of
the peasant's life and inculcated a high degeee of
unproductive character.

For centuries, right up to the time of our research, the notion that all situations were the realization of the will of Allah, and of the necessity
of submitting to this will, or fate, was fixed in
the peasant's consciousness. Simultaneously the notion to oppose the enemies of Islam, and of readiness to go to war for truth--jihad--was intensively

---

[69] Consult the work of Doroshenko (31) about the
    makeup of the Shiite spiritual hierarchy and
    their economic and legal position in the politi-
    cal struggle.

ingrained in the mass consciousness. Several religious traditions of Shiism (such as mourning the
deaths of Hassam and Hossein during funeral proces-
sions), as Doroshenko shows, exerted a deep psychological influence on the believing. In this state
the naive, believing multitide never entertained the
thought that the religious leadership would use them
for political ends (31, pp. 52-53). Any periodic
"heating-up" of religious feelings strengthened the
fanatical, impatient attitude toward the "unfaith-
ful" and remained an explosive area for religious
strife (31, pp. 53-54, 58-60).

According to tradition, every Muslim had to
perform the pilgrimage to Mecca, the hajj. The pilgrimage to the holy Shiite tomb, the burial place of
the great Imam and other "holy ones" was a religious
duty. Massive visitation of "holy places" during
the Muslim holidays was also a religious objective
of the peasantry, and sometimes served a political
propagandistic end (31, pp. 53-54, 58-60).

One object of the peasantry's deep respect and
even superstitious worship, regardless of any
thought of personal welfare, was the Sayyids, descendants of the great Imams. In those cases where
the peasant traced his origins from the Sayyids, a
direct lineal relation was often maintained.[70]

The religious practices of orthodox Islam, as
well as the presence of the officially unrecognized
Sufi priesthood, Sufi sheiks and dervish, with their
"miracles," dominated the peasant's mind (31, pp.
31-32),[71] and did nothing to assist him in getting

---

[70] The investigator of one mountain village (1947),
the inhabitants of which considered themselves
the descendants of two Sayyids, noted that all
the inhabitants (100 families, 460 people) considered themselves related, and called each other
first cousins and vowed to their ancestors and so
forth (33, pp. 107-108).

[71] As noted in the research of Doroshenko, it was
just the possibility that the individual could
reach god without intermediaries, without a mul-

rid of his archaic, paganistic and magical ideas.
These archaic aspects of the peasant consciousness
led to the need to experience the pilgrimage, to
have faith in the amulets of the Koran, in a superstitious attitude to the Sayyids and so forth (31,
p. 20, 55; 109, p. 491).

Islam consolidated in the peasantry its deeply
conservative line and suspicious attitude to every
new idea--the same features, as already noted, which
were present in the Iranian village in the 1950's
and beginning of the 1960's.

In such a way, if socio-economic practices
pushed the peasantry toward realizing class antagonisms and class protest, then religious practices
and religious ideas in general oriented peasant behavior in another direction.

The socio-political situation in the rural localities of Iran in the 1950's and beginning of the
1960's was influenced primarily by the relation between two opposing factors: on the great power of
the landlord in certain places, on the one hand, and
on the degree the peasants overcame their apathy and
religious antagonism on the other, augmented by the
presence of any who might have had experience in the
anti-landlord fight. The weakening of the first
factor and the strengthening of the second greatly
determined the level of influence of progressive urban ideology in a given rural location.[72]

lah and frivolous rituals--the path to perfection
through his own nature--that could not be accepted by most of the rural mass. However, the
asceticism of the Sufis and the equality of its
membership could not demand respect and sympathy
from the peasants. Their "miracles" made a special impression on the people (31, pp. 25-26,
30-32).

[72] Inasmuch as we are referring here to the peasantry of the landlord regions, then such important
factors of the peasant's social behavior as ethnic and tribal relations on tribal territories,
and clan relations, also, based on the principle

149

An important aspect of social life in those rural locations where the landlords retained full power and control over the situation was factionalism --struggle and rivalry of groups being led by large landowners and "larger figures." As Lambton notes, this struggle was often a continuation of rivalry which had begun in the cities, such as between various estates. The peasants endured a double sacrifice in these struggles. On the one hand, the landlords as the active participants in the rivalry gave them everything important they might need, that is, the administrative apparatus level was made up from their subordinates. In this way the apparatus was transformed into the simple tool of a hostile camp. The defeat of the landlords in the civil struggle was often accompanied by an open attack by the hostile groups on their enemies' villages and their destruction. Finally, factionalism often functioned within village limits. The peasantry, including those economically independent, turned out to split up into hostile camps not along class lines but along membership in groups headed by landlords. For example, in a significant portion of Kurd territory from the end of the nineteenth century right up to the 1950's and 1960's (the time of Lambton's research), the social struggle involving the peasantry was played out between two large factions (102, pp. 264-266).

In a number of regions in the first half of the 1950's, as much research has indicated, class hostility between landlords and peasants assumed an open character, and it was this that determined the basic line of social behavior for both peasant and landed. So, many landlords resorted to intimidation of the peasants, from corporal punishment to torture and fines for late back payments, for "disobedience" in reading the paper, even for the peasants conversing in their native (Azerbaiyan) tongue. Besides the civil ban on violence many landlords had special prisons built for peasants (18, pp. 113-115; 64, p. 120, 121, 130).

of blood ties to many outlying, mountainous isolated regions, remain as the parameters for the research (see source 33).

The very inclusion of the peasantry into the
internecine struggle of large landowners for power
could not have occurred, apparently, without men-
tions of "whips" and threats.[73]

In conditions of utter povery and hunger the
peasant's forms of protests often were escape from
landlords, urban riots and the plunder of shops (18,
pp. 112-115; 64, pp. 131-135).

However, in a number of regions the peasants
were sufficiently strong and diffused to struggle
openly against the landlords. It is important to
stress that this struggle was a definite manifestation of two peasant ideas: the realization of its
class hostility to landlords and deep religiousity.
Peasant socio-economic demands included the fulfillment of the 1946 law on increasing the peasant's
share of the harvest, changes in duties and obligations and redistribution of land. Peasants organized demonstrations at the homes of the landlords,
refused to pay the landlords their share of the harvest and made their situation unprofitable. Usually
such action was accompanied by internécine feuding,
where the death of a peasant was often followed by
the death of one of a landlord's henchmen (64, pp.
147-152).

Even the first peasant agitation in 1950 had
made the agrarian question real. The Shah acted
with new agrarian legislation (64, pp. 137-148).
Furthermore, peasant action developed into a wide
discussion of the country's agrarian problems. Invariably, this stimulated the activity of peasants
in a number of regions. Peasants responded with appeals to the ministry's premier concerning oppression by the aristocrats, made complaints to administrative centers, made collective demands on the

---

[73] The following fact, although dating back to 1946,
is true. According to reports of a free press,
peasants who had refused to participate in the
landlords' organization, the ruling party of
"Democratic Iran," were evicted from the village;
moreover, they were threatened with the death
penalty (18, p. 59, 106).

landowners and organized strikes (64, pp. 149-150).

These actions make clear that the solidarity of the Iranian peasantry was real, as well as the readiness of all to stand for the defense of arrested comrades. Forms of such solidarity were the declaration of <u>bast</u>, or a "sitting strike," protests and riots (64, p. 150, 152; also 18, p. 105).

In several more developed regions, closer to urban centers, after having mobilized their progressive strength, the peasants were able to exert much influence on local elections for deputy, advocating a program of socio-economic change in the village (64, pp. 152-153).

At the same time the consciousness of the subjugated majority of peasants continued to remain deeply religious. Even though in our research of peasant action the peasant consciousness wasn't given much attention, its religiosity shines through in the description of the concrete actions of the peasant: in the slogans of protesting peasants,[74] in the forms of protest (for example, sitting in bast, in places which were inviolable to Islam) and finally, in the very things the peasant did trying to understand his membership in the progressive party--such actions were often made understandable to peasants when they vowed to the truth that is contained in the Koran, thus making it their reference for living (a fact dating back to the 1940's) (18; 64; p. 135, pp. 149-150).

Generally, the peasant struggle at the beginning of the 1950's did not extend beyond local action and did not form a united front. However, it gave a jolt to agrarian reform which resulted in legislation in 1952 on abolishing extortions, on "internment" in farming and on the creation of local

---

[74] We quote an excerpt from the work of Seidov: "The paper 'Dad' stated that on April 9, 1950, 500 unemployed people, among whom there were many peasants, with the cry '<u>Ya</u> Hossein! Ya Hossein!' made an assault on the bazaar in Zanjan and on the food warehouses" (64, p. 135).

councils for village public construction. Although
due to the great power of the landlords these reforms could not be realized, they nonetheless stimulated peasant action to new directions. This situation continued into the 1950's and 1960's. There
were a series of new laws which were not implemented. In reality, the peasants were occupied fully in submitting to the will of the landlord--right
up to delivery to the landlord of a written promise
of a "voluntary repudiation" of the guaranteed legislation (29, p. 188, pp. 194-199; 64, p. 183). In
places where they were stronger they responded with
protests and agitation. Generally the peasants did
not turn out in force to overthrow the landlords'
power, in spite of the support of those circles who
were interested in the country's capitalistic development.

The "white revolution" was more radical in the
regions of estate landownership, since it gave land
to the farmers. The tenant peasantry of Iran, as we
have shown, was historically, socially and by class
origin prepared for the transformation to an independent stance. However, it had to deal with other
economic problems, especially with the extension of
credit.

The very path of agrarian reforms[75] confirmed
the primarily antagonistic character of relations
between peasant and landlord. The landlords[76] attempted in every possible way to obfuscate new legislation, and they continued to use torture and extortion. The peasants attempted to secure
implementation of the new laws. Peasant lawsuits
against landlords and the refusal of peasants to pay
rent became characteristic features of regions

---

[75] On the high and lows of agrarian reform, the
steps taken and their results, see 30, pp. 114-
177 for detail.

[76] It is necessary we keep in mind, however, that "a
group of peasants were so taken in by the landlords, and especially the tribal aristocrats, in
the 'agrarian chaos,' that they were turned
against reform" (30, p. 113, pp. 131-132).

implementing reforms (30, p. 217; 103, pp. 100-101,
172-174). It turned out that even such "normal"
procedures as land inventories stimulated peasant
protest. Several peasant tenants put down the cultivated portions under their names and declared that
once they paid the tax to the government then the
landlord no longer had any say over the land. Proposed reforms strengthened class attitudes so much
that the landlords rarely dared to appear on their
estates without being accompanied by armed guards.
Through the use of force they were able to redefine
their share of the harvest (103, p. 100). The fact
that the rulers were forced to take measures in order to suppress "the encroachment of the peasant on
the home and estates of the landlord" underlined the
situation (30, p. 123).

The reforms essentially changed agrarian relations in the village, transforming the overwhelming
majority of tenants into relatively independent
farmers. In the process of the green revolution 2.3
million peasant tenants became property owners (30,
pp. 125-126, 160). Tenant rent was practically
eliminated and in a number of cases long-term rents
were fictitiously substituted.

Invariably, the situation of reform was a more
stimulating influence on the emergence of the peasant's class interest. However, a fundamental change
in the peasant's consciousness was far from complete.

In isolated rural localities a change in estate
landownership was accompanied first by the definite
revival of traditional norms of social life and the
strengthening of the power of local elders. Research on a village in Khamseh in 1963-1964 can
serve as an example. Here reforms liquidating existing landlord boundaries and attacking poverty essentially hastened socio-economic differentiation;
poor families became the credit-receiving poor.
Village social structures were essentially hierarchical at the time of research. The "elite" constituted two families who had the greater quantity of
land at their disposal; three to four families were
considered "closest" to the elite and directly in
their favor (109, pp. 487-488).

Agrarian reform and administrative
reorganization put power in the hands of the council
of elders, in which were found the "leaders" (that
is, members from more well-to-do families) of all
the "segments" of the village,[77] the _dangs_. Smallholders and the landless were not represented on it.
There was essentially no election of people to the
organs of power. Here the peasants remained timid,
oppressed, deeply religious and conservative in
their attitudes to new ideas (109, pp. 488-496).

However, for the peasants of more developed regions having a relatively clear class orientation,
social movements in the village were a step forward
in the path to the foundation of class consciousness. Peasant expressions about reform testified to
this: "we remained slaves, only changed owners" or
"to have become productive is economic, but freedom
is dearer than money" (103, p. 230).

The activity in the village of "Organs of En-
lightenment" or "Organs of Public Service" had definite import for the uplifting of the village cultural level, the widening of its horizons and the
transformation of its conservatism (30, pp. 162-
174). However, socio-cultural reform in the country
had a local character.

At the start of the 1970's the historically
formed class self-consciousness of the Iranian peasantry had begun a strong offensive, due to "_pehlev-
ism_," an "ideological doctrine being spread by the
powerful propagandistic elements of the ruling circles" (31, p. 118). According to this doctrine "the
Shah was the reflection of god on earth. Islam was
the highest progressive religion," and Iran was the
country being called upon to raise the banner of
pan-Islam (31, pp. 119-121). Invariably, this governmental religious doctrine (especially propagan-
dizing "the body of truth"; this had been at work in
the village since 1971) was directed at weakening
the class position of the peasantry in its relations

---

[77] A dang is actually one-sixth of the village land.
   The largest landowner of each dang is a _sar-dang_,
   head of a one-sixth of the village (trans.).

with the government. Simultaneously, the deep religiousity of the peasant was allowed to express itself throughout the country--this posed a less immediate danger to the elite.

In any event, it was beyond doubt that the more
developed portions of the Iranian peasantry showed
themselves in the 1940-1960's to be an active anti-
landlord class, and had provided an important con-
tribution to the reform of the agrarian strata of
the country.

CHAPTER SIX

THE PEASANTRY'S CLASS ATTITUDE WHERE
TRADITIONAL RELATIONS ARE WEAK (CENTRAL LUZON)

The peasant movements in several territories of the Philippines are a type that is relatively rare in Asia. There, peasant actions in a particular historical period, basically in the 1940's, acted as an independent force on the social struggle, activating and organizing political strength on a class basis. This process took place in a region of total tenancy, central Luzon. Such provinces of central Luzon as Nueva-Ecija, Bulacan and Pangasinan were teritories with relatively weak forms of personal dependence of the peasants on large landowners, but the province of Pampanga serves as an example of clearly expressed class hostility (the majority of writing on this period is on the peasant struggle). Even though the radical mass movement was defeated on Luzon in the 1940-1950's, the subsequent fate of struggles in the village put the peasantry of central Luzon in a position of relative maturity among the class-oriented segments of peasants in Asia.

<u>Some</u> <u>Historical</u> <u>Preconditions</u> <u>of</u> <u>the</u> <u>Development</u> <u>of</u> <u>the</u> <u>Peasant</u> <u>Movement</u> <u>on</u> <u>Central</u> <u>Luzon</u>

The earliest history of the Philippines, and particularly Luzon, contains a number of features not inherent in other corresponding regions of South and Southeast Asia. More exactly, it simply did not have several features inherent in other regions. Above all this concerns the formation of an indigenous government. The conception of government in Asia, the rate and direction of the evolution of early-governmental systems in the villages of that time, in the natural-historical conditions (with relatively little interference from outside) was closely related, as in other regions of the East, to

ecological conditions Here we refer to the research of Deopik, who has analysed the prerequisites
of social evolution in various <u>Malaccan</u> communities.
As shown in his research (28; also 28-a), the Philippines' ecological conditions in a particular historical period, the end of the bronze age, had
helped start the "falling behind time" of the Philippines compared to other parts of Malaccan society.
At that time other Malaccan peoples, particularly of
southern Indonesia, had formed governments based on
the development of irrigated land and the elaboration of social relations. As Deopik notes, there
were no large forests or valleys in the Philippines
for the formation of an agrarian complex on the model of Java, nor was there a natural center; all
agrarian regions were endowed with equal natural resources. Here there was no stimulation for the acceleration of socio-political centralization or the
origin of government. At a time when new forms of
economic contact between large population centers
and governments were taking shape, the Philippines
turned to one side. The rudimentary forms of government in the pre-Islam period (from the eighth to
the thirteenth centuries) have no entry in the history of Malaccan society. Philippine society moved
to the level of class society and government only
when Islam and Catholicism appeared, sweeping away
traditional religious forms. At that moment, as
Deopik notes, a definitive difference between the
Philippines and other countries of the area had tak-
en place (28).

The absence of the development of a centralized
government on the Eastern model with such attributes
as a complex governmental apparatus, an elite-bureaucracy, an archaic-ethical ideology and conservative ancient religious ideas, along with its invariable results, such as preservation of archaic social
forms of labor and property, had enormous consequences for the subsequent socio-political history
of the country. Invading in the sixteenth century,
the Spaniards found an ancient system of isolated
communities or <u>barangays</u>, whose members were related
to the community by birth. In practice the barangay
preserved many features from the time when migration
to the islands first took place. Such communities
numbered from thirty to one hundred families. At
the head of the barangay stood the ruler, the <u>datu</u>.

Besides the rulers, several other groups were active
in the barangay: the maharlikas, or noblemen, who
assisted the datu in defense matters, hunting and so
forth; the timags, who were free people enjoying
status close to that of maharlikas; alipins, or un-
free, inherently dependent tenant farmers; namama-
hays, or "slaves" who paid half of the harvest as
rent; and sagigilids (basically slaves), a category
of people with less rights. As land had been dis-
covered, it had gone into individual ownership. In
several barangays land began to be transferred into
the hands of the rulers (20, pp. 5-8). The absence
of a central government in this system of landownership conditioned the instability and inflexibility
of class differences, such as the transfer of land
from a single owner to others. In the barangays,
where archaic-religious beliefs dominated the inhabitants, an important part of social life was "contact with the gods and spirits" through rituals,
practically stabilizing the status of the datu,
thanks to their functions in the rituals, as Sturtevant notes in his research (130, pp. 23-25).

The invading Spaniards attempted to create a
unified governmental system. The barangays became
administrative units, so-called barrios, where the
Spaniards tried to introduce elections for the head
of the barrio. Later, the introduction of a poll
tax and the organization of a civil militia and civil courts created a strong impetus for public law
(130, p. 36).

The Christianization of the population had
great significance. The archaic religious orientations of the rural mass and the absence of any kind
of meaningful religious system was fertile ground
for the inculcation of the Christian religion. As
several researchers have noted, the very invasion of
the Philippines by the Spaniards facilitated this,
for one sacred duty went forth with the invasion;
one form of religious leadership replaced another
(130, p. 26). In the process of Christianization
the religious orientations of the Filipino mass were
significantly strengthened. "Filipino peasants differed in their devotion or sincere attachment to the
Catholic faith, although they had only a superficial
attachment to the existence of Christian dogma; Filipinos accepted the main image in the outward,

159

ceremonial side of Catholicism. Peasants preserved
remnants of old, tribal truths," which carried with
it a group of rites and ceremonies. Generally, as
Levtonova notes, "along with the perceptions and
adaptations from Catholicism went the rites and
principles of dogma, which to a great degree accompanied local traditions, mirroring the Filipino psychology" (51, pp. 14-15).

In the situation in the Philippines, "the aristocrats of the Catholic church acquired all-embracing power. The country became the arena for management by a monastic order of 'corporations,' and the
life of the local population fell under the full
control of parochial vicars." This situation also
promoted the stability of religious ideology (50,
pp. 23-24, 256-266).

However, the relations between church and peasant became hostile very quickly. The Catholic
church soon became the largest landowner and the
main expropriator of peasant land. In the eighteenth to the first half of the nineteenth century
the Catholic church was the biggest landowner. Other landlords had only begun to acquire holdings.
Nevertheless, a basic portion of the peasants in
this period were still hereditary owners of small
plots. The right of individual landownership was
strongly developed in the village. The "society"
itself was not the village; the basic peasant population lived in small administrative centers, or
pueblos. The stability of peasant landownership was
promoted by "the right of the first user, who played
an important role in a situation where a large
amount of free land is available" (50, pp. 28-32;
58, pp. 95-99).

The evolution of peasant social conceptions in
the colonial era was to a great degree related to
changes in the structure of the ruling classes. A
new, privileged segment of local society, so-called
principals or caciques, appeared during the colonial
period.

The principals were exempt from taxation and
labor obligations to the government. As the kabesery or headmen of the barangay, they were the lowest

link of the colonial administration (51, pp. 10-11).
Opposition and antagonism between peasant and prin-
cipal was evident right up to the middle of the
nineteenth century. "Relations of peasant and kabesa were based on tradition, and it spread among all
the large peoples of the Philippines through a system of mutual moral obligations (in Tagalog, utang
na loob, which literally means internal duty) between persons in any one social unit (family, barangay). According to this system, it was as if the
members of the barangay, fulfilling the 'inner
duty,' would devote themselves to the protection and
defense of the peasants in their barangay. Peasants, accordingly, had to respond to them with devotion, respect and full obedience" (51, p. 13).

If we disregard the Christian trait of nepo-
tism, the choice of godfather and godmother promoted
a strengthening of similar blood relations. "The
majority of peasants chose the kabesa of the barangay or estate as godfather" (51, p. 13).

In the first half of the nineteenth century in
the Philippines, and above all in central Luzon, es-
tate-type private landownership had appeared. By
the second half of the nineteenth century up to half
of the cultivated land had crossed over into the
hands of the monastic order and landlords. The
peasants became tenants on land which earlier had
been theirs by inheritance (50, p. 126, pp. 130-
131).

It was at this time that the Spanish clergy,
especially the Catholic order, became the object of
hatred for the peasantry, who now dealt with new
kinds of large landowners from the local elite who
had formed comparatively "peaceful" relations with
peasant tenants. It is true, however, that some had
often been forced into long servitude to landlords
(50, p. 182). However, this dependence was closely
tied up with relations of another kind.

Generally, in a number of agricultural regions
of central Luzon, and especially in territories
nearest to Manila, stable systems of primarily paternalistic relations had formed.

Among the factors in the social order having
great importance for the evolution of peasant consciousness we must note the following. A new elite,
the principals, had gradually moved away from the
peasantry in its cultural orientations. The principals were exposed to strong Spanish influence in
language, education and culture. The bond to the
Spaniards and Spanish culture led in the second half
of the nineteenth century to the emergence of an
educated leadership in Philippine society, the illustrados.

This intelligentsia, by its very conception,
had developed under the influence of Western bour-
geois ideology and "subsequently turned out to be
more receptive and psychologically prepared for
learning the spiritual and cultural values of the
West" (49, pp. 37-39; 51, pp. 27-28). In this way
newly educated groups were different because of the
absence of any ideological or cultural tie with traditional society. A definitive cultural severance
between elite and peasant had taken place (20, pp.
18-19; 58, pp. 101-102; 130, pp. 37-39). The peasants were left without their old leaders but were
oriented ideologically to the past. Simultaneously
under the influence of the European systems of social ideas, at the center of which stood an independent, liberated individual, in whom class prejudices
had already died, the newly educated layer of society invariably had to resort to a search for support,
and had turned at the end of the nineteenth century
to the people, the peasant masses, for this support.

The peasants of the different islands and territories were found at different levels of socio-
economic evolution. They had entered the process of
losing their land and into commercial-monetary relations to different degrees. The largest socio-economic shifts were characteristic of the farming regions of Luzon contiguous to Manila, the economic
and political center of the colonies (20, p. 18).
The socio-economic movements in the rural localities
of different regions, above all in Luzon (on the
loss of peasant economic stability, in relation to
the spread of an export culture, the emergence of
large private landownership, of landless peasantry
and spread of tenant relations, see 20, pp. 41-55),

and the above noted cultural and political changes
(introduction of Spanish centralized organs of government, civil jurisprudence and taxation instead of
common law and traditional public mechanisms, i.e.,
"Spaniardization" of the apex of society) made a
strong impression on the peasantry. The intrusion
of a new order and new value system had been per-
ceived by a sizeable mass of peasants as the destruction of the ordered ideological order.

Forms of protest by the working rural mass never really ceased during the entire colonial period.
Flight into the mountains, formation of groups and
insurrectionist camps, attacks on small towns and
estates--such were the more common forms of protest
of the rural mass on the many islands of the Philippine archipelago. Protest was directed mainly
against monks promoted to civil service in violation
of accepted custom (50, pp. 50-61, 171-194). Here
we should note the following circumstance. Although
sometimes a member of the principals was placed at
the head of the revolt, peasants themselves were
nonetheless often at the head of the group. The absence in society of deep-rooted class conceptions
promoted the formation of leadership from peasant
ranks. Moreover, the religious aspect had an exclusive role in these movements. The monastic order
was seen by peasants as "leaders who had profaned
the Christian truth." They proclaimed that the goal
of the movements was the establishment of the "true
Catholic religion" (50, p. 59). The religious moti-
vation behind the movements was strengthened by the
appearance in the country of a new clergy, drawn
from the people. The movements began to take on a
religio-syntactic character.

It is important to stress that in several peasant movements everything had become more clearly directed against the principals and the colonial administration, at least since the beginning of the
nineteenth century. The peasants advanced demands
for equalization of rights with the principals, liberation from obligations and changes in the poll tax
(50, pp. 176-177).

Nevertheless, right up to the end of the nineteenth century, the dominant form of peasant struggle was religious sectarianism. The peasant

movement of the 1840's in the Tagalog region of Luzon, led by Apolinario de la Crus, serves as one of the more clear examples of this (50, pp. 186-192).

The bond of the Filipino intelligentsia with European culture had great importance for the peasants of Luzon. Even at the end of the nineteenth century, significant variations among different religious movements of Filipino peasants in terms of the evolution of their social consciousness were already present. The peasantry of central Luzon was the most developed. Here the rift between intelligentsia and peasant mass was rather quickly cut short. The educational reforms of 1863, which had laid the beginning for the formation of a new, "co-opted" intelligentsia, including members from peasant and urban petite bourgeoisie strata, had promoted this (51, p. 32). This facilitated a union which took shape in Manila of a revolutionary democratic liberation movement with peasants living near the regional capital. The experience of <u>Katipunan</u> is evidence of this. Katipunan was a secret revolutionary society which had led preparations for an anti-Spanish revolutionary uprising in 1896. It has been shown that the head of Katipunan, Andres Bonifacio, had come from the poor of Manila, and another leader and ideologue of leftist persuasion, Apolinario Mabini (who had become in 1899 the prime minister of the Philippine Republic), was a peasant son (51, p. 158, pp. 170-171).

During the liberation struggle against the Spanish government in 1896-1898, led by principals, illustrados and urban groups, peasants everywhere joined the movement. The forms, character, goals and leadership in this struggle showed the primarily traditional orientations of the peasant, as it combined forms of religious hysteria with outbursts of class hatred and hostility. The movements' groups were basically sects and robbing gangs. Religious movements and uprisings, the foundation of theocratical monarchic mini-governments, the weakening of large estates, or <u>hasend</u>, attacks on towns and in many cases robbery which finally evolved into terrorism, were the forms of this struggle (130, pp. 67-72, 83-131).

Between the 1890's and the 1920-1930's, differences appeared in the struggle between various groups of peasants. As the movements of the peasantry of mountainous regions such as Bohol, Cebu, Leyte, Samar and Negros gravitated toward more indigenous actions and often degenerated into robbery, several movements differed rather strongly in their socio-economic direction (49, pp. 71-72; 130, pp. 121-131). The peasant struggle developed along several lines in this period (130):

1) traditional mystic-religious tendencies;

2) movements of a transitional type--here the peasant participated in secret societies led by rural groups and in reform-religious modes of a modern kind; and

3) movements approximating a class type.

Movements of the first two types were undoubtedly the most important. Powerful movements of the transitional type dated from the 1920's to the 1930's, when traditionally violent actions were combined with participation in elections, as in <u>Tanggulan</u> and <u>Sakdal</u>. Nevertheless, traditional ideas about the goals and methods of the struggle were still maintained, being inclined toward "heroic" actions (the words of Pedro Abad Santos, the founder of the Socialist party in the Philippines), and the death of the leader meant the death of the entire movement (97, p. 13).

The movement founded by Aglipay was an example of a movement of the religio-reform type. Aglipay founded the Philippine Independent Church. A Protestant church, it canonized as sacred heroes the leaders involved in the national liberation struggle of 1896-1901, and acted with open avidity toward the Catholic hierarchy. In the 1920's, half a million peasants and small urban bourgeoisie supported the basic line of the petite bourgeoisie Republican party (49, p. 65). Objectively, the anti-Catholic struggle of Aglipay stimulated many radical demands of the peasantry. So, if the peasant movements of the 1930's in general did not raise a question about redistribution of land, it was because of the rela-

tion of land to the Catholic corporations, since the
latter treated the demand for the redistribution of
land between tenants as if it were a transferral of
government land.

Finally, a portion of peasantry in regions bor-
dering Manila felt the strong influence of urban
groups and progressive intelligentsia. The specifics of historical development alone (absence of developed government, traditional elite-bureaucratism
and ethical-theocratic ideology) facilitated the influence of different intelligentsia, at first Spanish, and later and more widely, European culture
with its important achievements. In the final analysis, this conditioned the relatively quick formation of a modern intelligentsia "who had been receiving education on the level of European culture
for that time and had had it influence the liberation ideas of bourgeoisie nationalism," and later
socialism (49, p. 49). An intelligentsia of the
modern kind, familiar with socialist ideas, was then
in only infant form. However, it was in direct contact with people, and began to receive greater acceptance in the Philippines from the date of its
very first action (49, pp. 73-77).

Without pausing for an entire decade, the
"agrarian disorder" was still unable to attract the
attention of progressive intellectual teachers, advocates and other members of the intelligentsia to
give attention to the peasantry's problems. In
1917-1919, spontaneously formed peasant groups and
organizations of different rural regions of Luzon,
who had advanced agrarian-type demands, "found"
their first leaders who could stand for peasant
class interests (49, pp. 86-87).

However, right up to the 1920's and 1930's the
two aspects of the protest--the spontaneous struggle
of the peasantry, agonizing anxiously over its path
of reform in society, and the struggle of the progressive urban groups, the intelligentsia--still had
not come together even on Luzon. This merging was
possible only with the socio-economic shift of the
1920's. A more important element in these shifts
was the destruction of paternalistic relations between landlord and tenant.

At the end of the nineteenth century and first decade of the twentieth century, a more typical form of personal relation in the economies of the farming regions of Luzon where tenancy was dominant, particularly Nueva-Ecija, Bulacan, Pangasinan and Pampanga, was a paternalistic relation based on a long, handed down bond between the landlord and the tenant, the _kasama_. The only exception to this, as already noted, were the groups of small, economically independent peasants. However, in the nineteenth and twentieth centuries, both of the following factors, so important to the peasantry, had begun to run aground: the possibility of finding a plot of land and the guarantees the paternalistic system gave. Above all, the stock of uncultivated government land in the very populated provinces of Luzon had already disappeared.[78] The spread of absenteeism on Luzon had even greater social consequences. Since the end of the nineteenth century a significant number of large landowners, _hasenderos_, had lived in the cities or the capital, and the running of the farms passed into the hands of their intermediaries. Absenteeism and the transfer of management functions to intermediaries from outside brought about a deterioration of traditional relations between tenant and landowner.

The system of tenant relations in rice-producing regions, still present even at the beginning of the twentieth century, included the following features: expenses in tilling, harrowing and reaping were borne by the tenant; for seed and transport, by the landowner. Expenditure on threshing and the maintenance of irrigation canals was divided half and half; the product after all deductions were made was also divided halfway (97, p. 4). The landlord-hasendero usually lived in a rural community. He conveyed his patronage by giving the tenant no-interest loans of rice for food (the practice of _rasyon_), helped in times of illness, and provided material support upon the birth of a baby, weddings or

---

[78] The policy of "homesteads"--the colonization of isolated land--conducted by the American government since the beginning of the twentieth century was a failure in general (see 130, pp. 51-56).

funerals in the tenant's family. He did not object
to the traditional practice of "polo"--the free collection by the peasant of the harvest remains from
the reaped fields. The tenant knew that even in a
bad harvest he would have enough food. The landlord
provided instruction for the tenant's children. In
return, the tenant did much work in the way of "personal service" that was done without pay (prepara-
tion of fuel, work in the home, etc.).

Thanks to his participation in the funerals and
weddings of the peasant, the landlord "often stood
with a peasant family like an outside relative or
favorite (compadrazgo), due to his participation in
the baptism of the child and several other actions."
The peasants often had a personal interest in how
they stood with the landlord by making sure they
fulfilled the relations of "utang na loob," the inner duty, the mutual moral obligation (49, p. 67).
As Kerkvliet notes, the landlord had in these conditions material "interests, social prestige and political advantages" (97, p. 5).

The system began to "crumble to pieces" at the
end of the nineteenth century. The children of the
landlords, having been educated in Europe and returned home, went to work in the cities and deserted
their duties as farmers (100, p. 59). Even though
military service in the time of the liberation
struggle in many situations promoted closer, personalistic ties between the landowner and his tenants,
these relations were nevertheless nearing their end.

In the 1920's the economic integration of the
Philippines with the United States (U.S.), which
promoted the strengthening of money relations and a
bourgeoisie system of values, "corroded" even more
the paternalistic practice in rural areas. The new
generation of hasenderos would not have anything to
do with their land. The appearance in the village
of the overseers, katiwales, had a number of disas-
trous consequences for the peasants: a sharp de-
crease in the participation of the estate in the extraordinary needs of the peasant, the practice of
"rasyon" was discontinued, traditional "polo" was
supplied by outside organizations, written contracts
took the place of "good understandings" (97, pp.

6-7). In those cases where the landowners remained
in the community their relations with the peasants
also became rigid and assumed the character of economic and political pressure, of sheer strength.

This process was especially characteristic of
Pampanga. The political elite of Pampanga, repre-
senting the large landowners and always notably conservative, continued their rigid, arbitrary pressure
tactics on the peasantry. Here relations between
landowners and tenants assumed the character of open
or latent confrontation (100, p. 46, 53, pp. 60-61).

The deterioration of paternalistic relations in
various rural regions of Luzon, which marked the
demise of the old system of relations for a large
mass of landless peasantry, incited mass protest
movements that had a class character. Although Filipinos, and particularly Luzonites, were traditional
peasants, the active struggle was quite strong.
However, as already noticed, from time to time in
this struggle traditional orientations would domi-
nate. In the 1920's and 1930's conditions were ripe
for a massive unification of progressive strength
between the cities and the spontaneous class movements of the peasantry of Luzon. This unification
went through several stages, the most important being the creation of the National Conference of Peasants (NCP) in 1922-1924, which then joined with the
Union of Proletariats, Santos' founding in 1933 of
the Socialist party in Pampanga, the most visible
spokesman of peasant interests, and analogous organizations in other provinces (49, p. 105, pp. 146-
149; 97, pp. 23-27).

The struggle of the Luzon peasantry in the
1930's, and especially in the second half of that
decade, was clearly centered around socio-economic
class demands; it was as if it combined the previous
experience of hostile action with the new experience
in legalistic forms of struggle and mass campaigns.
Kerkvliet enumerated the following aspects of the
struggle in this period: attacks on shops, demonstrations in barrios (administrative centers), at
army outposts, in the capital, petitioning of the
ruling organs, burning the fields, strikes, ultima-
tums to the Labor Department and so forth (97, p.

14). Violent action as a rule followed quickly
after legal means, such as petitions, had been
used.[79] Local peasant class-type organizations, having gradually absorbed greater numbers of peasants,
began to form a solidarity evident in their coordi-
nated action and material support during strikes.
Toward 1938 there were nearly forty peasant and farm
labor organizations. In that year two of the largest ones, having sprung up from various small groups
of peasant organizations--the 70,000 member AMT organization of Pampanga and the 60,000 member National Conference of Peasants from Nueva-Ecija, Pampanga
and Bulacan--closed ranks (49, p. 244; 97, p. 23,
41).

The demands which the peasants in local actions
and in strikes had advanced had basically centered
on improvement of economic conditions: the demand
for loans in rice or money from the landowner, lowering of the interest on grain loans, an increase in
the tenant's share of the harvest (in Pampanga, for
example, from 30% to 50%), decreasing the peasant's
share in the cost of irrigation and others. Sometimes the demand that the right of peasants to participate in organizations actually be recognized was
put forth (97, p. 18, 19; 132, pp. 38-39). At the
end of the 1930's the Luzon peasantry was using such
forms of struggle, without preliminary clearance
from the authorities, as the strike and implementation of new legislation on tenancy and others. By
1938 the central Luzon peasants had become active
participants on a national front led by communists.
Peasant organizations rose up (49, p. 241). During
this time the unequal development of peasant action
was evident even on Luzon. Peasant action was concentrated on primarily three provinces of central
Luzon: Bulacan, Pampanga and Nueva-Ecija (97, p.
16). Here development of peasant class consciousness was accelerated, and according to the scale of
the increase of peasants in class conflicts, the
last remainder of paternalistic practices and traditional "understandings" would be eliminated (49, p.

---

[79] See a detailed survey taken in the 1930's in Nueva-Ecija, Pampanga and Bulacan (97, pp. 21-40;
also 132, pp. 38-39).

261).

In this way, at the end of the 1930's on central Luzon the process of a merger between the active spontaneous peasant struggles, which contained utopian ancient millennial hopes and racial socio-economic demands, traditionally gravitating toward short-lived armed standoffs, on the one hand, with advanced modern thought on the other, the bearers of which were the progressive intelligentsia of the cities, confining themselves basically to Marxist ideology, had definitely begun. This unification, being stimulated by the class aspects of the peasant struggle and the peasantry's class self-consciousness, left its mark on the subsequent path of peasant movements.

A significant number of peasants bordered on a nationalistic pro-Japanese ideological attitude in the 1930's. As research has noted, in the 1930's ideas and slogans of racial brotherhood and spiritual and cultural proximity between Japanese and Filipinos, which were initiated into Japanese-Philippine relations on the eve of the Second World War, were rather popular in the Philippines. The objective precondition of this phenomenon was the inclination of the Filipino intelligentsia toward a realization of national originality in the face of conditions of close dependence on the U.S. and other kinds of foreign interference in national life (90, pp. 62-63). There were many pro-Japanese groups in the intelligentsia. One of these, the party "Sakdal," thanks to the outstanding quality of the leadership of Benigno Ramos, played an important part in the preorientation of a number of Luzon peasants toward primarily nationalistic and pan-Asiatic goals. Nevertheless, for the peasant mass sakdalism was above all the means of struggle for "freedom from tenant-landlords, caciques, moneylenders and police" (90, p. 162).

The Japanese occupation of the country dealt a shattering blow to the pro-Japanese and pan-Asiatic illusion of the peasantry, stimulated several chauvinistic groups, and simultaneously strengthened class tendencies in the peasant struggle. In May 1942, on the border of the provinces of Pampanga, Tarlac and Nueva-Ecija, a national army, mostly

peasant in composition, was created, the Hukbalahap
(<u>Hukhbong</u> <u>Bayan</u> <u>Laban</u> <u>sa</u> <u>Haron</u>, the People's Army
against the Japanese), or Huks, who were putting up
a stiff resistance to the occupiers. In the anti-
Japanese struggle the communists played a large
role.[80] Although at first the struggle was against
the invaders, on Luzon the class attitude of the
peasantry and the hostility to landlords came
through rather clearly; the landlords were forced to
live in the cities. "Many peasants were influenced
by the call of the communists, which was not to consider any union with those landlords who might be
ready to participate in the general anti-Japanese
struggle." There were occasions of spontaneous violence with the landlords and of anxious solidarity
within Huk ranks. On the most active regions of
central and southern Luzon the Huks created peasant
organs of self-government and selected village committees on defense, religion and especially ways of
rent payment (49, p. 283; 129, pp. 16-17; 132, pp.
117-127, 139).

At this time the armed struggle itself and the
destruction it engendered had to some degree stimulated the revival of several historical features of
the peasant struggle: gravitation toward extremism
and anarchy, which relatively quickly upon the weakening of political leadership degenerated into ban-
ditry, the survival of the "charismatic" leader and
the domination of personal devotion to the leader
over faithfulness to the ideas of the movement (49,
pp. 279-281). Radicalism and extremism still retained a definite influence on the peasant masses.
This was evident within a group of the leading party
cadres even in the postwar years.

After the end of the Japanese occupation in
1945-1946 the Huks acted not as an army but as a
mass political organization operating a national
peasant union, which often wielded substantial power
in certain places. In the rural towns of central

---

[80] On the resistance movement in the Philippines,
the formation of the Huks and the role of the
communists in the anti-Japanese struggle see 49,
pp. 264-321, 333; 32, pp. 65-211.

Luzon an indigenous type of "dual government" took
shape. Having reorganized the veterans in Liga, the
Huks concluded a union among the democratic peasant
powers, brought about talks with the elites, secured
a number of concessions on agrarian problems, actively participated in political controversies and
created a wide front of democratic strength--the
Democratic Alliance.

1945-1946 was a period of greater maturity
within the peasant movement. At this time the peasants of central Luzon, who not long ago had participated in the armed struggle, now actively participated in the political struggle, in democratic
movements and elections. In the 1946 elections candidates of the left-wing party took impressive vic-
tories in a number of Luzon provinces thanks to support from the peasants. The Huk Luis Taruc was
victorious in the election in the second Pampanga
district for leader of the civil council, the candidate from the Democratic Alliance receiving 39,000
votes against his opponent's 10,000, the candidate
for the Liberal party (133, p. 25). The governor of
Pampanga in 1945 was also one of the popular Huk
leaders (115, p. 58).

However, the period of active political struggle for the central Luzon peasantry, even though it
was beneficial for the experience in new kinds of
struggle and the maturation of social ideas, was to
continue for only a short while. Soon after the
elections in 1946, which had shown the real political power of the peasantry, the elite, army and
landlords began an offensive for "democratic power"
against the peasantry, especially on Luzon. Many
peasant leaders were thrown into prison. The landlords armed bandits for struggle against the peasants. In Tarlac, Pampanga and Laguna they carried
out a number of destructive raids on the peasantry.
The police began a policy of terrorism in rural areas (132, pp. 241-246; 133, pp. 33-38).

For a great number of Luzon's peasants, not
very long ago having defeated the Japanese army, the
very natural and only possible way out was an exit
to the mountains for an armed struggle. First they
numbered hundreds and then thousands. A spontaneous
revival of Huk groups began.

From 1946 to 1948, the Huks confined themselves
basically to armed self-defense, and did not probe
for the start of talks with the rulers or for participation in political debate and elections. The
local population widely supported the Huks, their
land and their friends, by lending them food and the
necessary information on the formations of the government troops. Contact with the rural peoples was
very close. Basically the Huk groups played the
role of armed guards for the peasants, and in this
way were forced into encounters with the landlords.
Simultaneously, the Huks carried out a wide propaganda campaign among the peasants (133, pp. 42-43).
In this period the class consciousness of the peasants of central Luzon's provinces, where dozens of
Huks were especially active, invariably grew.

Generally, the protracted experience of armed
struggle and the relatively short period of legalistic political activity was unable to change all
aspects of the peasant's world view. The basic mass
of peasantry remained religious. The preservation
by the Huks of the baptism ceremony testified to
this. It is important to note that the christening
of the Huks' children was done by a member of the
ruling elites. Some of them would christen the baby
"in the name of the liberation struggle"; others,
such as Luis Taruc, in the name of god, and the
overwhelming majority of young parents did just that
(133, p. 35).

A strong attachment to the land or local senti-
mentality was not dominant in a number of Huks (115,
pp. 100-101). Comparatively slight experience in
political debate carried through into naive revolutionary ideology and voluntaristic organizational
principles.[81]

---

[81] We refer to the following words of a direct par-
ticipant in the struggle: "A small handful of
people were in a position to change their entire
world, if those who were inspired by the idea
kept to it. One novel of Rizal could have
overthrown the entire system of Spanish government" (115, p. 52).

Nevertheless, the struggle of the peasantry under the government and its direct contact with the communists further promoted the formation of ideas on the character and fate of society. The following words of one peasant from the mountain camps of the Huks are instructive:

> Today the landlords are in power. . . . At any moment the landlords might call the police in to defend their physical being and property. . . . The peasants are fated to be the slaves of the landlords.
>
> With a change in government all this would change. Work would be given to the people, to the basic and devoted use of simple people. All would be led by committee, and the people would choose these committees, not subjecting themselves to division of any kind. . . .
>
> Between all of us, good, comradely relations were formed, and as in our camp, no one would offend or cheat the other or act against him. We all had equal rights and would help each other. . . . I managed to get into the ruling cabinet of my country, and they regarded me as a comrade (115, p. 70).

In 1949, the peasant struggle began an important turn "to the left" in form and direction. The Communist Party of the Philippines (PKP), at the head of the movement by this time, assessed the situation then taking shape as revolutionary, which was immediately preceding a full-scale societal explosion. This was to no small degree related to the success of the Chinese revolution, and faith in the quick reduplication of the "Chinese experience" in the Philippines, the strengthening of a number of groups of intelligentsia and peasantry, as well as a number of extremist communist parties. The PKP broke off from the Democratic Alliance and set a course of armed conflict as the only means for seizing power and rebuilding society (115, p. 58). The main instrument of this struggle had to be the so-called Army of National Liberation, which had formed in the bases of the mountain retreats at this time. "Many Huk commanders were sure that all the problems before the Filipino people could be resolved only by way of a societal armed uprising" (49, p. 373).

Experience showed the error of these
suppositions. After 1950 the situation began to
change. These changes were mostly attributable to
the appearance of Ramon Magsaysay, at first Defense
Minister, and then President of the Philippines.
Meaningful communication with the peasants began simultaneously with an intensification of military action against Huk strongholds. The Huks were offered
amnesty. There was a proclamation on peaceful measures to resolve land problems on Luzon.

The psychological effects of these changes were
enormous. Magsaysay, who had at first talked of the
necessities that should be coming to the common
"Tao" or ordinary Filipino, was trying to establish
his popularity. Many peasants, tired from the long
struggle, began to come down from the mountains and
return to peaceful work. Massive support of the
Huks, which at first had fed the movement, quickly
began to weaken.

However, Huk leaders did not appreciate the
meaning of these changes. Armed groups continued to
remain in the mountains, and became more estranged
from their peasant bases in the valley and from
peasant support. The departure of the peasants in
the valley from their previous selflessness and
willingness to take risks to support the Huks produced contempt for the "unprincipled" peasantry.[82]

Armed struggle in these conditions was doomed.
The destruction of the party secretariat in Manila,
of the party faithful and center of armed struggle,
the destruction of the only just mended network of
ties with the local population--such were the land-
marks of the defeat of the peasant movement (115).
Remaining hotbeds of activity had been suppressed by
1953.

---

[82] "Someone from the Huks," writes a direct partici-
pant in the movement, Pomeroy, speaking about the
situation in 1950, "became bitter against the
people. The people, he said, were unprincipled"
(115, p. 166).

The suppression of the radical center of the peasant movement had a number of heavy consequences for the fate of the entire movement. The peasants of central Luzon suffered repression and were demoralized, and the more active of its elements, the local leaders, were killed. The remaining Huks turned to their only mass stronghold, the Luzon peasantry. The PKP was declared illegal and a great portion of its very best, most experienced workers were killed. The publication and tendentious interpretation of the party's seized documents marked the start of a wide anti-communist campaign, which long delayed the diffusion of communist ideas into the masses.

The consequence of this was the spread of reformism among the peasants. Its clearest manifestation was the establishment in 1953 of the Federation of Free Farmers (FFF).[83] The mass radical peasant movement, centered on central Luzon, went into a period of long abatement, to climb again only in the 1960's, in new conditions closely related to changes in all of Philippine society.

---

[83] The FFF, arising from the "remnants" of the revolutionary peasant movement, represented a turn in the thinking of reform and of the Catholic elite toward the necessities of the poorer peasantry; the new, more pliable course of the Philippines on questions of agrarian reform served as fertile ground for the promulgation of a range of basic options. The basic goal put forward by the organization was the improvement of the economic position (through union, cooperative and technical progress) and "spiritual well-being" (through the stimulation of religious aspirations) of the Filipino peasantry within the limits of "democratic revolution." Its basic principles were legality, solidarity with the ruling organs and nonparticipation in the political struggle. The FFF collaborated with the ruling organs under Magsaysay, participating in peasant cooperatives, in "development projects," and in the construction of wells, roads, schools, and irrigation works. They tried to act as intermediaries be-

The Peasantry of Central Luzon in the 1960's:
Social Relations, Political Consciousness, Social
Behavior

As noted above, even in the 1930's the policy
that was dominating the peasant movement, having
taken a more clear class character, was related to a
large group of peasant tenants in central Luzon who
had lost the vertical, paternalistic ties with their
landlords. Therefore, an analysis of the social relations in the 1960's in the rural regions where absenteeism was widespread is advisable. We will use
the materials of the field research of 1963-1964 in
the barrio of Kabukiram[84] as a premier example
(131).

Bulacan was an absentee region. Not only the
landlord, but also those managing the farms, the katiwales, did not live in the village. The basic
mass of the village population consisted of tenants
and agricultural laborers. There were no important
differences in the position and status between one
or the other group; the status of tenants was very
stable, and the transfer from one group to the other
and back again took place often. Consequently, hierarchical coordination between them was not important. Tenant-kasamas remained landless at least
into the fourth generation (131, p. 107, 108).

The conditions of tenancy were basically those
of the 1920's. However, the active struggle of the
Huks in the 1940's and 1950's had made a definite
impression on them. So, if expenses were divided
half and half between tenant and landlord, then the
rent of the landlord took up half or less than half
of the harvest (131, p. 26, 126). However, chronic
indebtedness did not engender any efforts by the
tenants for some sort of minimal guarantee. After
the debt was paid (credit most often was forwarded

tween landlords and metayers in order to get more
advantageous terms for tenant contracts and so
forth (78, p. VII, 2, 11).

[84] The name of the barrio Takahashi gave was fictitious.

by the landlord himself or his intermediary, and the
interest was often higher than 100% annually) many
peasants utterly refused to part with the rice. By
1963-1964 there was a tendency toward a fixed rent
in money or natural goods, in which the tenant had a
better material benefit (131, p. 126).

Historically, in the nineteenth and twentieth
centuries, three types of property had formed:
church, landlord and middle class--businessmen, government servants and so forth, who owned land before
and after the war. In Kabukiram the latter of these
constituted the majority; the majority of these were
managed without middlemen (131, p. 135).

Strong economic dependence of the tenant on the
landlord, as the researcher notes, did not constitute the durability of a vertical relation. The relations between them remained plainly economic.
Property owners, with rare exceptions, never entered
into national political life or the everyday life of
its citizens. Some relics of paternalistic practices still remained (tenants sometimes gave small
gifts to the property owner during his visits; many
owners were inclined to look upon the loan of rice
to the tenant as an act of philanthropy, although
not without a high interest rate). However, this
did not play an important role in the relations of
either side. The tenant often did not know the name
of the property owner, especially when work was organized through middlemen. Even when the property
owner lived in the municipality, many tenants did
not know his business, genealogy or family (131, p.
117).

In this way, vertical socio-economic relations
and relations of personal dependence were absent.
It was not surprising that arguments and conflicts
between tenant and property owner were frequent.
Although in the majority of cases the tenants lost,
in general the tension in land relations promoted
some lessening of land rents (131, p. 126).

A system of horizontal relations among peasants
existed at this time in the village. Much of it had
a traditional and almost obligatory character to it.
As is known, the attraction of supplementary work in
the off-season is a fact of life in rice farming.

The cooperation of labor, the traditional exchange
of labor and service, so characteristic in the description of the traditional Javanese village in
Chapter One, were widespread in the Luzon village.
However, in the researched regions these forms were
already outdated.

In Kabukiram, among the three forms of organized agricultural labor--family labor, traditional
mutual help and hired paid labor, the third form was
predominant. Family labor was used for tillage,
harrowing and other jobs. The traditional exchange
of labor services--the palusong--played an auxiliary
role and usually was for tillage and harrowing; the
low quality of work which palusong produced and the
expense of feeding the workers helped incline the
farmer to transfer these jobs to hired labor. It
was not only the absence of means that induced them
to have recourse to this method. Such traditional
forms of mutual work in nonrural regions as batalis
and bayanihan still had great importance at this
time. The composition of groups engaged in palusong
and batalis was not constant (131, p. 61, 120).

The basic rural work of the church was dependent on hired labor. The overwhelming majority of
village families participated in hired labor. When
both a tenant and his family were hired as laborers
the wages quickly added up for him and the others.
The accounting system of the landlord made the personal labor of the tenant subject to registration
and payment (131, p. 61). The highest single payment was earned by migrant workers. The migrant laborers were seasonal work groups. Usually a group
of twenty to thirty workers, sometimes over one hundred, led by a kabesa, concluded an agreement with
the farm for a definite kind and volume of work
(131, pp. 63-64).

At this time several traditional forms of social collectivism continued to preserve their
strength and exerted influence on the forms of organization of agricultural production, often to the
detriment of the landlords' interests. Accordingly,
the peasants continued to exercise their right to
graze cattle on small rice fields without the per-
mission of the property owner or the tenant. The

peasants would also cut down the grass on the edge
of rice fields for cattle. The farmer did not have
exclusive rights to the use of the grass and leaves
on his own fields. Peasants who did not plant because of the difficulty of getting water to their
crop simply used the open land of other peasants
that had water, and property owners did not inter-
fere in these matters (131, p. 119). Much of village tradition "divided up" the farm in definite
ways for the tenant so as to manage the land's distribution and use. Consequently, the tenant did not
have the right to participate in harvesting, he
could only use hired help. Furthermore, unemployed
village inhabitants received indirect shares of the
harvest, in the form of the collection of the remainder of leftover, unharvested rice (the practice
of polo) or the remainder after threshing. Neither
the tenant nor the property owner had the right to
participate in its collection. According to another
custom, "_pumpong_," the reaper took home a little
more harvested rice besides the paid portion. As a
result, if the tenant received about ten _cavans_ of
rice for one _ha_, then the losses from traditional
custom made up a fairly good share--two to three ca-
vans. At this time any metayer could exercise the
right of "collector." Both tenant and landowner became reconciled to this custom, which lessened the
risk of a bad harvest on any single plot (131, pp.
121-123).

Generally, we can say that in the researched
Philippine villages horizontal relations, both traditional and modern, predominated over all economic
vertical relations. Horizontal relations left an
imprint of class solidarity on the poor in conditions of extreme poverty and sharp hunger. Property
owners were forced to accept several customs as an
inevitable evil, against which they were powerless
in regions with established traditions of peasant
protest. On the other hand, a significant portion
of landowners in these regions of central Luzon, occupied in business in some way, were rather indifferent to the profitability of their farms.

In this way, important preconditions for the
development of an active class struggle existed in
the rural areas of central Luzon. Changes in Phil-

ippine society were reflected greatly in the administrative-political structure. The highest posts in the municipalities were occupied by industrialists, landowners and businessmen. To some degree a tendency toward a democratization of the administrative-political system appeared through the election of the leading organs of the barrio, the barrio council. So the position of <u>kapitan</u>, head of the council, was filled in 1964 by a small landowner, having only 1.5 ha himself, and often looking for work as an agricultural laborer (131, pp. 114-116). A questionnaire of the members of the councils of eight barrios in the municipality of San-Leonardo (Nueva-Ecija), conducted in 1964 in Valsan's research, made this tendency manifest: three members were landless, among those having land 40% had one ha or less, while 60% had more than one ha (with a maximum of three ha) (134, p. 325). Nevertheless, the tendency toward democratization could still not effect significant changes of political life in the rural localities. The conclusion that Valsan drew concerning the administrative-political structure of Nueva-Ecija was that on the municipal level "administrative personnel were usually found under the influence of large landowners and were interested primarily in supporting order and lessening taxes" (134, p. 10). The research of Takahashi in Bulacan found municipalities under the influence of conservatives in the Congress of the Nationalist party. Here on the level of the municipal organs the interests of the tenants "were not represented," and for that reason the tenants appeared fully indifferent to municipal politics (131, p. 115).

In spite of isolated cases of class differences the peasantry basically remained apathetic. This protracted apathy was to no small degree related to the lack of change within traditional forms of peasant consciousness because of the relatively short duration of the peasant struggle (end of the 1930's to the end of the 1940's). Several regions of Luzon had still not shaken off the more archaic features in the peasant consciousness.[85] But what is

---

[85] We should note, for example, that much farming work was accompanied by ritual (58, p. 125).

especially important for our analysis is the form of
peasant protest and the peasant's value system,
since many ethical norms inherited from archaic societies continued to live.

A wide range of material introduced by Podberezskii, touching upon moral norms in the Philippines, allows us to make some assumptions about how
they could influence the peasant's social behavior.
Cooperative service among peasants, undertaken often
as a moral obligation, could objectively serve as a
consolidating factor even though based on archaic
principles. At this time "cooperative" service between "small" and "big" persons had grown into a
particularistic-personalistic relation (58, p. 52,
53, 60). The ethical norm of "utang na loob" was
more important from the viewpoint of influencing
peasant social behavior (58, pp. 52-53).

The establishment of the Philippine peasantry's
class self-consciousness, presupposing an independent orientation of a person's socio-political life,
and the possibility of an individually conscious
choice of a class line of social behavior, had still
to overcome large moral norms and taboos characteristic for traditional societies. This norm--the
feeling of a bond with other people's attitudes of
an inner duty ("The individual was inseparable,"
wrote Podberezskii, "from the group as a person, and
related to them through the relations of 'utang na
loob'") (58, p. 64)--had many manifestations: the
creation of the moral principle of <u>hiya</u> (shame), of
aspirations "not to lead, but to know one's place,"
the avoidance of criticism and positions of being
critical, a sufficiently deep fatalism, and in general adherence to traditional norms and ideas (58,
pp. 62-65). With total justification Podberezskii
notes that hiya, presupposing "the approval of the
action of an individual from within, from the influential person," condemned any break of traditional norms of behavior as if it were the same as a
class-antagonistic attitude (58, p. 62).

Traditional ethical norms in concrete applica-
tion led to the spread of ethics of personal selfless service to the leader of the government, whether the leader was a political personality or group.
Santos noted that "the inclination toward heroic

actions" was also found inseparably linked with
these norms and the culture of the leader himself.
The experience of armed struggle in the 1940's could
not stimulate such ideas and the period of legal
struggle, as noted above, was relatively short.

The long period of apathy and even fear of active struggle characteristic of a great portion of
the Luzon peasants, having been deprived of their
leaders, indicated an incompleteness to the process
of formation of self-consciousness. However, this
period itself turned out to be a learning experience
for a large number of peasants in overcoming traditional "anarchism and heroism" and inclinations
toward hasty acts and in making more experienced
choices of more mature ideas about society and its
formation.

When the Catholic FFF began its campaign for
support on the ruins of the armed peasant movements,
it began its effort with fear of the peasants acting
in an organized fashion, even in central Luzon. Actually, local political figures and administrators,
related to the landowners, hindered the actions of
the peasants in new organizations through various
prohibitions, threats and dispersal of meetings.
The landlords themselves acted either through persuasion and bribery, or through threats of arson.
Eventually these reformed organizations underwent
great effort in order to overcome peasant indiffer-
ence and apathy (78, p. 4, pp. 49-53). Gradually,
however, its leaders succeeded in convincing a large
mass of peasantry in the necessities of union for
the peaceful struggle of its own interests.

The work of the FFF, and afterward a number of
other local organizations, promoted the use of ad-
mistrative-political structures among the peasantry.
The peasant began to turn to the FFF central leadership, for example, for help on questions on fertili-
zation, technical steps and so forth, for answers
that in normal channels would never have gotten out
of Manila (78, p. 45). Although such steps often
ended up in nothing (on account of the extreme bureaucratization of the FFF), the peasants nevertheless gradually turned to inherently unsuccessful activity within the legal structure.

184

It is important to note that the actions of
peasants in these organizations from which rural exploiters such as tenants and farm laborers were excluded (78, p. 21) effectively destroyed paternalistic practices in rural localities. But, as
Podberezskii stresses, paternalistic practices and
relations to landlords as father or benefactor were
still held by some of the peasantry (58, p. 27).

In the middle of the 1960's a revival of peasant movements took place in various regions of Luzon. This revival was closely related to important
changes in the general political situation and in
agrarian politics in the ruling groups. Although
the legislative measures of the 1950's touched upon
improvements in tenant relations, they were not realized in practice, and in 1963 a law on tenant organization was passed (20, pp. 198-203). Even the
peasants of Luzon had not actively participated in
the campaign for new legislation. However, they
gradually began to turn to this process. In the
middle of the 1960's local political leaders often
formed unions in the villages which were pushing for
speeding up the implementation of agrarian reforms.[86] Upon the initiative and leadership of the
PKP, now in underground activity, the legal Free
Farmers' Union, the MACAKA, was created in central
Luzon in 1963. Its goal was the mobilization of the
peasantry for control over the implementation of
agrarian reforms and the promotion of cooperatives
among the peasantry.[87] The work of a number of urban

---

[86] The widening struggle of urban and rural groups
for agrarian reforms in the 1960's and beginning
of the 1970's, and armed conflict in the rural
localities in this period, made use of the unpublished materials of Bai and other organizations,
and engendered schisms.

[87] Its field of activity was restricted basically to
the province of Tarlac in central Luzon. The
growth of influence and unity of this organization was greatly hindered by the fact that the
communist movement of the Philippines engendered
and propagated dissidence (in 1967 the PKP paid
workers, peasants and other people associated

185

democratic organizations was instrumental in setting
up sides to the struggle for the implementation of
agrarian laws. In 1959 the Philippine Agrarian Reform Movement acted basically through organizations
that used publications, conferences, radio and tele-
vision, mostly following the line of the progressive
intelligentsia. The creation of the Philippine
League of Rural Cooperatives in 1969 was an example
of this, and was at least one advocate of peasant
interests in the governmental apparatus. It also
was active in the organization of mass demonstrations.

At this stage the peasantry again assumed a
significant political strength, although fragmented
and not as independent as it was at the end of the
1930's and 1940's. But after a long period of peasant apathy, a unification of organizations representative of very diverse social groups acted
against the landlords' oligarchy. The acceleration
of agrarian reforms via legislative reform was one
of their means.

Simultaneously during the 1950's and 1960's a
group of peasants continued to carry out armed conflict with the government army. A tendency toward
armed forms of struggle was always characteristic of
a substantial part of the Philippine peasantry. In
the new historical conditions of the 1960's, related
to the spread of Maoist ideas in the Philippines,
this historical feature received a new impulse.
Even in the 1950's a "showdown" took place between
various movements. A definite rift had developed
between the basic peasant mass and the "new generation of Huks"--the radical direction of a number of
peasants as well as intelligentsia, or lumpenprole-
tariat, who were more and more popular with a number
of Huks. This group, already far estranged from the
peasantry and its age-old ideology, was fertile soil
for the diffusion of Maoist ideas, especially the
theory of the "encirclement of the city by the country." These extremists, basically Maoists who had
left the PKP in 1967, successfully attracted a large
number of "new Huks" to create in Tarlac province

---

with it to spread protest and dissidence).

the so-called New People's Army in 1969.

Nevertheless, in several Luzon provinces in the 1960's armed groups still continued to play a social role of their own as a "guaranteer" of peasant interests. This was true in Pampanga. The Philippine journalist Lachica, having devoted a special work to the Huk struggle in the 1960's, noted that an overwhelming portion of peasants in such provinces as Pampanga, Tarlac, Nueva-Ecija and Bulacan supported the Huks. Moreover, 75% of the supporters were in Pampanga, where the landlord oligarchy was notably the most conservative and reactionary (100, p. 28, 46, 53). The observations of the author about the durability of clan relations among the Pampanga peasantry, as well as his critique of the peasant idea of communism, which amounted to the redistribution of land, are interesting (100, pp. 25-26, 32).

The exceptional fragmentation and dissidence of insurrectionist strength was the characteristic feature of armed anti-government struggle right up to the 1960's (100, p. 12). At the beginning of the 1970's the armed stuggle became more and more transformed into an isolated movement, not so much among the peasantry as among unclassified elements, moving away from the main path of socio-political reform.

Finally, a substantial mass of peasants even on Luzon still remained on the plane of mystical-religious orientations in its social behavior. The defeat of the radical peasant movements at the beginning of the 1950's managed to turn the peasant masses of less developed regions of Luzon toward mysticism in the 1960's. The regions with mature class relations were not the centers of such mystical movements. One of the larger movements, <u>Lapiang Malaya</u>, formed in 1967 in southern Luzon. The head of the movement presented himself as a medium tied to the spirits of dead heroes of the national liberation struggle. Generally the leader advocated a call for social justice united with messianic hopes, the truth in a second coming, spiritual practices incorporating incantations, the use of icons, amulets and so forth (130, pp. 257-258).

In the 1960's and 1970's a whole range of similar messianic-type movements were present among the
peasant mass of Luzon, the Visayan islands and the
Christian population of Mindanao. Despite the simi-
larity in forms of organizational struggle and leadership (i.e., a religious type: its rituals, icons
and faith in the supernatural quality of the leader)
and despite the adequate mass character of the movements, enveloping nearly 280,000 people, here there
was no tendency toward union. Every one of these
centered around one charismatic figure, and between
them, to the contrary, there was rivalry and antipa-
thy (130, p. 262).

In this way, the rift between the leading class
group and remaining groups of Filipino peasantry was
not overcome even on Luzon, the most developed region of the country.

To show the strong and weak sides of the Filipino peasant movements in the 1940-1960's we should
consider the fate of one of the more famous of its
leaders--Louis Taruc, who was called the "con-
science" of the Philippines (133, p. viii). Taruc
grew up in a peasant family in Pampanga, and later
in Bulacan. The religious conditions of village
life had affected him greatly since his very child-
hood. In the 1940's in Manila he was witness to
demonstrations by the workers, with whom he sympa-
thized. But his main feeling remained, according to
his words, of sympathy for the needy peasants. "For
centuries," he wrote in his autobiography, "land to
the landless was the peasant cry." By his thinking,
the history of the last four hundred years "was a
history of constant uprisings, and their fundamental
reason was the land hunger of the peasant" (133, pp.
12-13).

In the middle of the 1930's he became the deputy of Santos, who was then forming the Socialist
Party of Pampanga.

Taruc had a calling for peasant leadership, and
this was apparent in the years of armed struggle
against the Japanese, as he was at the forefront of
the military leadership of the Huks.

At the time when the terror began against the
peasants and the peasant leadership was persecuted
in 1965, like hundreds of peasants Taruc fled to the
mountains, and again became one of the military
leaders of the struggle.

During this time Taruc was always a religious
person as were the overwhelming majority of peasants
he led. A person of exceptionally high moral qualities and a favorite of the peasants, he remained
comparatively not very theoretically inclined. In
his own writings, nationalism, industrialization and
socialism were related to the concept of democracy
and were the more important concepts. Communism was
a "vague theoretical idea" for him (133, p. 27).

The close bond of Taruc and his class appeared
at the time when the Huk movement had become isolated from the basic peasant masses, who had been
reoriented to the liberal politics of Magsaysay. At
that time Taruc decided to come down from the mountain and yield power.

His fate, as it turned out, was prison. Here
the ideas of socio-religious "salvation" in the
Christian-democratic interpretation, characteristic
for a few of the Filipino and foreign Christian figures, gained influence, but not without the exceptionally strong influence of the Catholic missionary
Douglas (133, pp. viii-xviii).

Taruc left prison a Christian proponent of social reform: "I believe that several forms of
Christian democratic socialism are best for our system of government and that these can solve the socio-economic problems of my country and my people"
(133, p. 6). In the concrete conditions of the
Philippines, especially Luzon, with its estabished
tradition of an active class peasant struggle, such
a position could not let him realize his goal as one
of the central figures of the peasant movement.

So, in the 1960's the objective situation in
the rural localities "fed" three directions of peasant protest: the legal struggle for reform by the
peasants of the more economically developed provinces, armed struggle in regions where a conserva-

tive landlord oligarchy dominated and the mystical
direction among the peripheral rural and urban mass

The position of Luzon had changed significantly
from the beginning of the 1960's. Radical measures,
undertaken by the Marcos government in 1972 after
his introduction of an extraordinary plan (the establishment of a ceiling on landed property, a program for the liquidation of metayage and the transfer of land to tenants) helped transform one
thousand tenants to landholders (117, p. 21). Having begun the realization of radical agrarian legislation objectively cleared the path for the formation of capitalist relations in rural communities
and for socio-economic differentiation among the
peasants, the existing tenants. The political situation in the village began to change greatly.

The PKP had already raised the question of the
meaningfulness of including the poor in cooperatives, which for quite a while were primarily a
means for unifying wealthy peasants.[88]

In such a way, the revolutionary action of the
more mature, in terms of class relations, groups of
landless peasants on the Philippines had fulfilled
their mission in stubborn struggle. Thanks to many
beneficial objective conditions it could significantly change the fate of the landless peasant.

The tenant peasants of the researched region
present a relatively "clean" type of class-active
peasantry. The characteristic features of the peasant attitude were: the disappearance of personal
relations; the attachment toward defending his property; armed confrontation against the landlords as a
class; solidarity with their brothers in class relations; tenants and agricultural workers not free of
several traditional vestiges; an ability to personally realize action on the socio-political arena;
and gaining of experience in a peaceful but forced

---

[88] A resolution was concluded between the PKP and
Marcos in October 1974: the communists were forbidden to work in governmental organs, even with
any established public organs (117).

struggle. During the 1950's and 1960's the peasants' preservation of ethical norms and traditional
ideas, as well as particularistic and personalistic
feelings for the struggle became the characteristic
attitude. Invariably they gravitated toward a more
secret, hostile method of struggle, despite its lack
of accord with the objective conditions.

CONCLUSION

The study of the historical conditions of the
formation in the 1950's and 1960's of social consciousness and stereotypes of social behavior among
segments of the rural labor masses in Asia, as well
as the various forms of their contemporary appearance, lets us make a definite statement. As already
noted, among the important moments in the formation
of the class features of the social attitude of the
peasant in Asia we must take note of the following
two. First would be the liberation of the peasant
from the archaic (in origin), traditional rela-
tions--lineal, tribal, clan and so forth, which we
have labeled horizontal, inasmuch as communal unity
assumed the conditional equality of all of its members. Second would be the liberation of the peasant
from hierarchical relations, still arising in archaic communities and having been incorporated into
traditional government formations, where the exploiter opposing the direct producer was the government
official, and the hierarchy itself was administra-
tively sanctioned and ideologically based--these relations we have labeled vertical. The peculiarity
of these relations was their non-particular "social"
nature, that is, they were sanctioned by the character of both society and government.

The traditional peasantry we examined have a
rather conservative social attitude. Here, in communities contiguous to one another, the archaic horizontal relations of the lineal or clan type were
fundamentally overcome. At this time vertical traditional types of relations maintained an important
strength. Right into the middle of the twentieth
century the community leadership acted as the authoritative bearers of administrative, economic and
ritual functions. The more archaic functions of societal mechanics showed stability, having been in-
scribed in the governmental structure. Paternalistic relations, having developed with the sanction of
the governmental hierarchy, had a special stability.

Ancient religious beliefs within the limits of such
a structure fed both horizontal and vertical relations and remained in the peasant consciousness in
inviolable ideas of a peaceful, harmonic paternalistic family, which was seen by the peasant to include
both society and government. From here the inevitable conformism of the peasant in relations with the
organs of power, both local and central, came naturally. The enlistment of such peasantry into a
struggle with such overall national importance could
be realized, as a rule, only through the traditional
mechanics of village power.

The social attitude of the caste peasantry was
notable for a certain contradiction. Caste relations are archaic in origin and in contemporary
times act primarily as a horizontal relation. Existing caste groups use traditional organs of government and are oriented toward age-old traditions
and groups; they have solidified membership by birth
into a "unity" and have joined this cultural unity
to the socio-caste system of assigning positions to
all its members. In this way, caste relations act
as an effective brake on individualism and variations from traditional relations and forms of consciousness. As regards the vertical relations of
the landless rural population, these have a dual
character. On the one hand, these are often in accord with a single hierarchical caste division within society. On the other hand, these relations do
not have an administrative base but do have a purely
private nature. Sometimes arising in vertical relations, paternalism can have a private, personal
character, which makes it unstable depending on the
idiosyncrasies of the situation.

Although "ideally" the ideological suppositions
of caste society had been drawn "to cement" this society, in reality, in conditions of the actual evolution of India, the caste division there had over-
grown into isolationism, opposition and rivalry
among the various caste groups. In the absence of
rigid governmental centralization and legislative
incorporation of the caste hierarchy the appearance
of localized variants was inevitable. Ideas about
inequality, about rivalry and about the possibility
of changes in one's existing position became only

recently important features of the consciousness of
a significant mass of rural Indian laborers. From
this came social activity among various groups of
rural agricultural laborers, although at first this
had appeared, it is true, among caste group activ-
ists. However, in contemporary India they objectively could grow and grow into class-type activity.

Both these segments--communal peasantry and
caste peasantry not having crossed into a class po-
sition--could retreat to the primarily traditional
position; the members of the first differed in their
conformism to social behavior, the second were active, although the activity was basically not of a
class type.[89] A comparison of these two groups shows
that administrative positioning and "state-fostered"
vertical relations were more important and, in essence, the insurmountable barrier on the path to
formation of the peasant as an independently active
and class-oriented individual.

The peasants of regions where landlords were in
the last stages of landownership, and were nearing
private ownership, seemed to us more prepared to assume a class form of consciousness. The absolute
personal power of the landlord (inasmuch as he acted
as a private individual) was not socially justified
and ideologically valid. Simultaneously they often
acted to demolish the peasant's image of traditional
horizontal relations. Paternalistic relations,
which could also develop on the basis of private
landlord ownership, had simultaneously an accidental
and private character in historical perspective, and
were relatively quickly destroyed.

---

[89] "Solidarity within the limits of any kind of
group," writes Baljit Singh, researching a village in Uttar-Pradesh, "were based on envy, hostility and evil dispositions in relations with
other groups; the organization of the spheres of
social relations were also conditioned not by
personal choice or friendship but by traditional
rivalry or familial-kin strife" (67, p. 37).

Generally, the private character of exploitation let the peasantry more quickly realize its hostility to the landowner. Nevertheless, a comparison of two of the examined groups of peasants in Iran and the Philippines shows that great obstacles stood on the path to such realization. The oppressive and unlimited power of the landlords did not allow the peasantry to break the bonds of dependence. The governing religion (particularly Islam) had in conditions of extreme dependence and poverty increased peasant fatalism. Paternalistic relations between landowner and peasant also could act as a brake. Of these, however, paternalistic relations of a private character were, in historical perspective, the stage immediately preceding the realization by the peasant of his opposition to landed property. Actually, on the territories of landlordism the destruction of paternalistic relations (at least the diffusion of absentee landlordism) directly and invariably led to the peasant's realization of his fundamental class interests. In this way, the tenant peasants of Luzon, who worked relatively independently, outside immediate personal contact with landowners, in the absence of any relations due to their mere physical presence or of paternalism, constituted more fertile ground for the formation of a class attitude.

At the present time, the analysis of social consciousness and social struggle of even the relatively developed peasants, in terms of class attitude, exposes the many weaknesses of this group. It exposes as well the significant detachment of the peasant's advance-guard from the general mass of rural workers that conditioned the inevitability of back-stepping in the development of peasant movements.

In conclusion, we must add that the preceding analysis presents only distinct and small localized variations in the social attitudes of Asian peasants. Such variations are indeed almost infinite, and research into such variations continues to be important.

GLOSSARY

abangan	Syncretic element which includes Buddhist, animist, Muslim and Hindu beliefs and practices
adat	Unwritten code of local customs and traditional practices
adhivasi	Settlers, transient groups who roamed in search of work
Adiyan	Farming tribe of Kurichi
advaito vedanto	Most influential of the schools of vedanto, an orthodox Indian philosophy
agrahar	Gifts of land by the Brahmans
Ahirs	Cattle-breeding and herding Indian caste
Akali	Sikh separatist party
alipins	Group of tenant farmers in the barangay
AMT	Aguman ding Malding Talapogolra, or General Workers' Union
anubhavis	Peasants openly supportive of the CPI
arbabi	Belonging to a large landlord
Bagdi	Caste of field laborers of West Bengal
barangay	Unit of administration consisting of fifty to one hundred families under a headman

bargadars	Tenants
barijibi	Betel raisers
barrios	Village or rural community, an administrative unit
bast	Taking sanctuary in an inviolable place, holy to Islam
batalis	Mutual aid for non-farming purposes
Bauri	Scheduled caste of West Bengal
bayanihan	Mutual aid for non-farming purposes
bhadroloks	Respected people, intellectuals
Brahma	Central god of the Hindu triad, the creator
caciques	Powerful Philippine landowners
caliph	Successor to Mohammed as the temporal and spiritual head of the community and religious faith of Islam
cavan	Measure of grain equal to seventy-five liters
cheris	Pulaya settlements
Cherumas	Untouchable caste of Kurichi
Chetti	Farming tribe of Kurichi
chotolok	Socially humble people, regarded as second class
compadrazgo	Social relationship arising between the godparent and the godchild and its parents
Daccata	Derived from dacoity and refers to the cult of Kali

dalang	Puppeteer of the Javanese puppet theater
dang	One-sixth of the land of a village
danyang	Javanese guardian spirit
dashtban	Village official who protects villagers' fields from damage and theft
datu	Barangay chief
deko	Bailiff or messenger
dervish	Muslim mendicants noted for their forms of devotional exercises usually leading to a trance or ecstatic dancing
desa	Javanese village
deshmaji	Headman of the Jati Sabha
desiatina	Old Russian unit of land measurement, amounting to just over one hectare
devaswan	Autonomous system of education
dhar	Internal village political organ
Dharam Devata	Bauri diety who rules the moral activities of man
dharma	Body of principles by which all things exist; conduct that establishes a morally sound life
Dharma Sastra	A Brahmanical collection of rules for life
dihgan	Village head who acted as a government tax collector

Dom	Low Bauri caste, considered untouchables
dukun	Magician, sorcerer
Duryodhana	Eldest son of the Kurus' King, who began war with the Pandavas to secure the throne
fakirs	Hindu ascetics
genten	Exchange of labor help on basis of strict reciprocity
Goala	Higher Bauri caste
gotong royong	Mutual cooperation, mutual assistance
gotra	Exogamous lineage grouping
grama	Group of families
grumbul	Hamlets; Javanese administrative unit
Gujars	Cattle-herding caste of northwestern India
gunina	Bauri shaman
ha	Abbreviation for hectare
hajj	Holy pilgrimage to Mecca
haqqi-jivar	Right of peasant to ownership deed of any dead land he reclaims
Harijans	Untouchables
hasend	Large estates
hasenderos	Large landowners
hiya	Shame
Hugli Zilli	Association organized to up-

Bauri Unayan Samity	lift status of Bauri in Hindu community
Hukhbong Bayan Laban sa Haron	The Hukbalahap or Huks, the People's Army against the Japanese
Ilavan	Another name for Izhavas
illustrados	Philippine educational or intellectual leaders
Imam	Caliph who is the spiritual and secular head of Islam
imamat	The "office" of the Imams
iqta	Government land assignments
Irava	Another name for Izhavas
Izhavas	Socially humble caste of Kerala
Izhuvan	Another name for Izhavas
jajman system	A reciprocal socio-economic arrangement between families of different castes, one performing services for the other
jajnma ownership	Absolute landownership in Malabar, free of any government supervision
jajnmi	Landowners under jajnma terms
Jan Sangh	Prominent right-wing political party
Jati Sabha	Caste council made up of the headmen of different villages
Jats	Peasant tribe or caste of northern India and Pakistan
Javatan Pendidikan Majarakat	Dept. of Community Education

Jayabaya   Prophecies that describe how
                        messianic kings will come to
                        rule in the future

jihad   Holy war

joft   Parcel of ploughed land

kabesa   Headman of the barangay

kabesery   Headmen of the barangay

kadkhuda   Village elders; village head-
                        man

Kali   Malevolent Bauri diety

kanam   Tenure system that resembles a
                        mortgage in which the kanamdar
                        pays a traditionally fixed sum
                        to the jajnmi and then pays a
                        fixed rent every year, either
                        cultivating or subleasing the
                        land

kanamdar   Holder of kanam tenure

kapitan   Head of the barrio council

karma   The sum total of a person's
                        good or bad actions that are
                        held to determine his specific
                        destiny in his next existence

Karshaka Sangam   Labor union that supported the
                        communists

kasama   Tenant or landlord in share ten-
                        ancy

Kashyap   Name of a Bauri gotra

Katipunan   Philippine nationalist organ-
                        ization founded in 1892

katiwales   Overseers

kavu   The temple where Pulayas wor-

	shipped the demons
kawulagusti	"Servant to sir"
Kayasthas	High Hindu caste of Bengal and Uttar-Pradesh
kelompok	Groups
kelurahan	Javanese administrative unit comprising five to eight desas
kentol	Descendants of an original village upper class
Khalsa	Dominant order of Sikhism, founded in 1699
khutor	Separated farm
Kisan Sabha	Leftist Indian political organization dedicated to helping the peasantry
Koli	Higher Bauri caste
kordah malaki	Peasant landowners
kromo	Javanese "high" language
Kurukshetra	Land of the Kurus
Kurumabas	Farming tribe of Kurichi
kuttam	Overall Nayar caste assembly
Lapiang Malaya	Religious movement that became a militant political sect in the 1960's
Lembago Sosial Desa	Village Social Institute
lurah	Head of the kelurahan or kampong; elder
MACAKA	Free Farmers' Union

maharlikas	Prominent independent warriors of the barangay
Mahishyas	Third highest caste of Bauri
majlis	Village council
Malacca	Malay kingdom founded in 1400 that extended its power over the Malay peninsula
Manasa	Highly respected Bauri diety
Mataram	Islamic kingdom that arose late in the sixteenth century
Mehesvar	Pulaya diety
Meno Bauri	A Bauri subcaste having the highest status
menumpangs	"Boarders"
mertelon	Arrangement where sharecropper takes on more work and receives a third of the harvest
metayage	Arrangement where one cultivates land for a share (usually one-half) of its yield, receiving tools, stock and feed from the landlord
metayer	One who works under the metayage system
Moplahs	Muslim caste group of Kerala
moral	Leader of the Bauri panchayat
morol	Village headman
mubashir	Bailiff; collector of landlord's share of the harvest
Muchi	Low Bauri caste, regarded as untouchables

mufakat	Unanimous agreement arising from deliberation
mujtahids	Religious class of high status
mullahs	Learned teacher of Islam
Mulo Bauri	Bauri subcaste having the lowest status
muqta	Government land assignees
murabs	Water overseers
musjawarah	Meeting, discussion, deliberation
nagas	Contract laborers
namamahays	Tenants who owned their homes and had some rights
namaz	Islamic worship
Nambudiri	Higher Kerala caste
Nasakom	Cooperation of nationalists, communists and religious people
Nayadi	One of the lowest untouchable castes of Kerala
Nayars	Higher Malabar caste
ngedok	Arrangement where sharecropper is responsible only for care of the crops and receives only a fifth to a tenth of the harvest
ngoko	Javanese "low" language
Oraon	Formerly noncaste group of West Bengal
pakars	"Leg men" who did odd jobs for the headman
palagoro	Variety of traditional duties

	and services village officials receive from villagers in lieu of a salary
palusong	Cooperative work based on exchange of labor between farming households
panchayat	Village council
Pandavas	The five sons of the legendary dynastic hero, Pandav, victorious in an epic war with the Kauravas
panembhana	Sacred personage
Parayi	Kerala slave caste
patti	Internal village exogamous groupings that can serve as administrative units
pehlevism	Nationalistic ideology centered around the Shah and Islam
Pembanguman Masjarakat Desa	Village Community Development
Pen mas	Dept. of Community Education
pishnamaz	Prayer leader
poligars	Subordinate feudal chiefs
polo	Gleaming of cut palay left on ground from reaping
prijaji	An official; the Javanese upper class
principal	A leading man or one of the leading citizens
pueblos	Philippine rural community
puja	Hindu act of worship

Pulaya	Large Kerala slave caste
Pulaya Maha Sabha	Pulaya organization that tried to uplift Pulaya status
pulung	Special political spirit
pumpong	Custom of reapers' bringing home a sheaf of palay from among that cut
punden	Burial ground of a legendary ancestor of a Javanese village; any holy place
puranas	Tales of legendary India
Qajar	An Iranian dynasty that unified Iran following the downfall of the Zand dynasty from 1779-1925
raja	Sovereign or king
raja brana	A princely value
rajakaya	Princely wealth
rajapundut	The prince's property
rajasyapen	Princely wealth
Rajput	Generic name for a diverse people who claim descent from Kshatriyas of ancient India
Rama	Widely worshiped Hindu diety, embodying chivalry and virtue
rasyon	Practice of patron providing no-interest loans of rice
ratu	Sovereign or king
resih desa	Village cleansing ritual
rewang	Form of reciprocal labor extended freely with no precise accounting made

rih se	Hereditary ownership rights of the peasantry
rukun	Feeling of mutual support and harmony
rukun kampong	Village administrative unit encompassing four to five rukun tettanga
rukun tettanga	Lowest village administrative unit, encompassing ten to twenty-five main families
ryotwar	Arrangement where the peasant paid revenue directly to the state and had full ownership rights
Sadgopes	Higher Bauri caste
Safavid	Persian dynasty founded in 1502 by Shah Ismail
sagigilids	Socially degraded workers
sahra	Land parcels
Sakdal	Movement founded by Benigno Ramos which went into revolt on May 2, 1935 and was crushed
salar	Peasant cultivator attached to a sahra
sanketan	Temple rights
sanskritism	Assimilation of Brahman culture
Santal	Lower Bauri caste
sar-dang	Largest landowner of a dang, head of one-sixth of the village
sar-salar	Head of a group of salars

Sarekat Islam   "Islamic Association," Indone-
                         sia's first mass-based party

Sarv-Khap   "All-Khap," a Jat political
                         institution

sava   Assembly of the traditional
                         village council

saya   Form of labor help used for
                         large-scale work parties

Sayyids   Descendants of Mohammed

selamatans   Ritualistic communal feasts

Seljuq Turks   Any of several Turkish dynasties
                         that ruled much of western Asia
                         in the eleventh to thirteenth
                         centuries

Setengah gogols   People holding residential land
                         only

shaman   Magician or sorcerer

Shariah   Sacred law of Islam

Shasthi   Bagdi diety worshipped as pro-
                         tector of children

Shiva   One of the central triad of Hin-
                         du gods, the destroyer

Sitala   A chief Bauri diety

Sri Narayana   A famous caste association based
   Guru   on "one god, one caste, one re-
                         ligion"

surasa   Sense or inner meaning

Tanggulan   Sectarian movement led by
                         Patricio Dionisio in the 1930's

Tao   Man, peasant

tara   Arrangement of two to four ad-

	jacent small Nayar villages
taravad	Nayar matrilineal household
Tiija	Another name for Izhavas
timags	Free, fairly prestigious group in the barangay
tjakal bakal	Common ancestors of a Javanese village
tuyul	Land assignment in the Ilkan and Qajar periods
Umayyad	Dynasty which ruled the Muslim empire from 661-750
utang na loob	Inner duty, internal obligation
valluvan	Headman
verympattamdar	Holder of verympattam tenure, in which land can be held for one year or for several years with a gift paid at the end of the period, the verympattamdar either working the land or leasing it to another verympattamdar on similar terms
Vettovan	Slave caste of Kerala
Vijayanagar	A great empire of southern India from 1336 to 1614
Vishnu	One of the central triad of Hindu gods, the restorer
waqf	Islamic grant of land to be held in trust and used for charitable or religious purposes
Ya	Hail!
yogakshema	1908 movement to obtain certain social reforms and study of the English language in schools

zamindars   Revenue collectors who under
                   British rule had rights to large
                   amounts of land by paying the
                   British a large fee taken from
                   the farmers

Zoroastrians   Followers of the religion of the
                   prophet Zoroaster

1. Marx, Karl. The German Ideology. Vol.
    III.[91]

2. Marx, Karl. Kapital. Vol. II, part 25.

3. Marx, Karl. The Theory of Surplus Value.
    Vol. III, part 26.

4. Marx, Karl. An Introduction to the Economic
    Thought of 1857-1859. Vol. I, part 46.

5. Marx, Karl. An Abstract of Louis Morgan's
    Book "Medieval Society." Vol. I, part 46.

6. Engels, Frederick. Anti-During. Vol. XX.

---

[90] The original bibliography was incomplete by Western academic standards, and I have attempted to
supply the missing information. The original
bibliography did not include the publisher for
any of the entries, nor page numbers or editor
names for journal entries. For the most part, I
have found these items, interpolated them, and
produced standard entries. Sometimes the edition
cited in the original did not match with the version found in the Library of Congress (LC). In
these cases, I have provided the information from
the original bibliography (year and place of
publication) first, followed by (LC) and the new
publication data I found. The few entries I
could not find I have indicated in notes. Additionally, sources 1-73 are Russian language
sources whose titles I have translated. Sometimes the different LC version I found was an
English language version, and I have indicated
this. I have also provided a transliterated
title for the Russian language journals. I used

7. Engels, Frederick. The Origin of the Family, Private Property and Goverment. Vol. XXI.

8. Lenin, Vladimir Ilich. The Oppressor of Land and Liberalism. Vol. V.

9. Lenin, Vladimir Ilich. What Is To Be Done? Vol. VI.

10. Lenin, Vladimir Ilich. The Agrarian Program of Social Democracy During the Russian Revolution of 1905-1907. Vol. XVI.

11. Lenin, Vladimir Ilich. "Peasant Reforms" and the Proletariat-Peasant Revolution. Vol. XX.

12. Abaya, Hernando J. The Untold Philippine Story. Moscow, 1970. (LC) Quezon City: Malaya Books, 1969 (in English).

13. Alaev, Leonid Borisovich. Southern India. Moscow: Nauka, Institute of Asian Peoples, 1964.

14. Alaev, Leonid Borisovich. The Social Structure of the Indian Village. (Uttar-Pradesh, Nineteenth Century). Moscow: Nauka, 1976.

15. Alaev, Leonid Borisovich. "The Origin of the Jat Khap." Asia and Africa Today. [Aziia i Afrika Sevodnia] No. 2 (1976), pp. 47-49.

16. Antonoba, Koka Aleksandrovna. The English Conquest of India in the Eighteenth Century. Moscow, 1958. (LC) Moscow: State Publishing House for Eastern Literature, 1968.

---

the LC transliteration system (trans).

[91] The works of Marx and Engels are taken from the second edition of Collected Works. Moscow: State Publishing House for Political Literature, 1956. The works of Lenin are taken from the Complete Collected Works. Moscow: State Publishing House for Political Literature, 1965.

17. Aleksandrov, Iurii Georgievich. "On the
     Social Structure of the Javanese Village."
     In Agrarian Relations in Southeast Asia. Ed.
     G.G. Kotovskii. Moscow: Nauka, Dept. of
     Eastern Literature, 1968, pp. 182-208.

18. Badi, Sharmsadin Mamedovich. Agrarian Rela-
     tions in Iran. Moscow: State Publishing
     House for Eastern Literature, 1959.

19. Balagtas, Francisko. "Tendencies Toward
     Change in the Philippines." Problems of
     Peace and Socialism. [Problemy Mira i Sot-
     sializma] No. 7 (1975), pp. 84-87.

20. Baryshnikov, Olga Gavrilovna. The Rural
     Economy of the Philippines (the Genesis and
     Development of Capitalism). Moscow: Nauka,
     1972.

21. Belenkii, Aleksandr Borisovich. The Nation-
     alistic Awakening of Indonesia. Moscow:
     Nauka, Central Dept. of Eastern Literature,
     1965.

22. Bongard-Levin, Grigorii Maksimovich.
     Medieval India (Historical Essays). Moscow:
     Nauka, 1969.

23. Bongard-Levin, Grigorii Maksimovich. India
     at the Time of the Maurs. Moscow: Nauka,
     1973.

24. Bodzinskaia, V.V. "Understanding Goals,
     Attitudes and Value Orientations in Sociolog-
     ical Research." Philosophical Science.
     [Filosofskie Nauki] No. 2, 1968.[92]

25. Gavrilenko, I.G. "The Dialectical Interac-
     tion of Natural and Social Factors in Socio-
     Historical Processes." A paper given at the
     First All-Union Academic Conference on

---

[92] The LC did not carry a few issues of this journal
early in 1968, including No. 2, so page numbers
cannot be provided (trans.).

<u>Problems</u> <u>of</u> <u>the</u> <u>Interaction</u> <u>of</u> <u>Society</u> <u>and</u>
<u>Nature</u>. Moscow. 23-25 Jan., 1978.[93]

26. Gopalan, A.K. <u>Kerala</u>, <u>Past</u> <u>and</u> <u>Present</u>.
     Moscow, 1961. (LC) London: Laurence & Wis-
     hart, 1959 (in English).

27. Danilov, V.P., L.V. Danilova, V.G. Rastianni-
     kov. "Basic Stages of Development in the
     Peasant Economy in the Agrarian Structures of
     Eastern Countries." <u>Agrarian</u> <u>Structures</u> <u>of</u>
     <u>Eastern</u> <u>Countries</u>: <u>Genesis</u>, <u>Evolution</u> <u>and</u>
     <u>Social</u> <u>Transformation</u>. Ed. V.G. Rastianni-
     kov. Moscow: Nauka, 1977, pp. 6-48.

28. Deopik, D.V. "A Hypothesis on the Origin of
     the Indonesian People." A paper given at the
     Malay-Indonesian Symposium at the the Insti-
     tute of Eastern Languages at Moscow State
     University, Moscow. Nov., 1974.

     a) Deopik, D.V. "The Relationship of the
     Central and Southern Parts of Eastern Asia
     2000 Years B.C." In <u>An</u> <u>Early</u> <u>Ethnic</u> <u>History</u>
     <u>of</u> <u>the</u> <u>People</u> <u>of</u> <u>Eastern</u> <u>Asia</u>. Ed. N.N. Che-
     boksarov. Moscow: Nauka, 1977, pp. 265-277.

29. Demin, Aleksandr Ivanovich. <u>The</u> <u>Rural</u> <u>Econ-</u>
     <u>omy</u> <u>of</u> <u>Modern</u> <u>Iran</u>. Moscow: Nauka, Dept. of
     Eastern Literature, 1967.

30. Demin, Aleksandr Ivanovich. <u>Modern</u> <u>Iranian</u>
     <u>Villages</u>: <u>Basic</u> <u>Problems</u> <u>of</u> <u>Socio-Economic</u>
     <u>Development</u>. Moscow: Nauka, 1977.

31. Doroshenko, Elena Alekseevna. <u>The</u> <u>Shiite</u>
     <u>Priesthood</u> <u>in</u> <u>Modern</u> <u>Iran</u>. Moscow, 1959.
     (LC) Moscow: Nauka, 1975.

---

[93] Neither this paper nor Deopik's paper (source 28)
   were found in the LC. It evidently is not unusual for papers presented at Russian academic
   conferences to take up to ten years to join the
   LC collection (trans.).

32. Drugov, Aleksei Iurevich and A.B. Reznikov.
    Indonesia During Guided Democracy. Moscow:
    Nauka, 1969.

33. Ivanov, M.S. "The Iranian Village of Oura-
    zan." Soviet Ethnography. [Sovetskaia Etno-
    grafiia] No. 2 (1959), pp. 107-112.

34. Ivanov, Mikhail Sergeevich. Current Iranian
    History. Moscow, 1969. (LC) Moscow: Mysl,
    1965.

35. Ivanova, Maria Nikolaevna. The National-Lib-
    eration Movement in Iran in 1918-1922. Mos-
    cow: Dept. of Eastern Literature, 1961.

36. Ivanova, A.I. "On the Evolution of 'Nation-
    alism' in Indonesia during the 1960's and
    1970's." Peoples of Asia and Africa.
    [Narody Azii i Afriki] No. 2 (1974), pp.
    28-37.

37. Irandust. "Notes on the Change of Regime in
    Persia." New East. [Novy Vostok] No. 15
    (1926), pp. 35-63.

38. Irandust. "The Path and Stages of the Peas-
    ant Movement in Persia." On Party. [Za Par-
    tiiu] No. 1 (1927), pp. 48-56.

39. The History of India in the Middle Ages. Ed.
    L.B. Alaev. Moscow: Nauka, 1968.

40. The History of the Middle Ages (XV-XVII Cen-
    turies). A Reader. Part II, Moscow, 1974.[94]

41. Caste in India. Ed. G.G. Kotovskii. Moscow:
    Nauka, Dept. of Eastern Literature, 1965.

---

[94] Part II could not be located in the LC. However,
Part I was published in Moscow by Prosveshchenie
in 1969, and sometimes the same publisher will
continue throughout a series (trans.).

42. Kotovskii, G.G., A.M. Melnikov and N.I.
    Semenova. <u>The Class Struggle in the Modern
    Indian Village</u> (<u>1947-1965</u>). Moscow: Nauka,
    1969.

43. Kozlova, M.G., L.A. Sedov, V.A. Tiurin.
    "Types of Early Class Governments in South-
    east Asia." In <u>Historical Problems of Pre-
    Capitalistic Society</u>. Part I. Moscow:
    Nauka, 1968, pp. 516-545.

44. Kolontaev, A.P. <u>The Decay of Rural Trades
    and Formation of New Branches of Small Indus-
    try in the Indian Economy</u>. Moscow: Nauka,
    1965.

45. Kotovskii, G.G. "The Agrarian Question in
    Southern India (Tamilnad and Kerala) During
    the Overall Crisis of Capitalism." Diss.
    Moscow, 1952.[95]

46. Kudriavtsev, Mikhail Konstantinovich.
    <u>Society and Caste in Hindustan</u>. Moscow:
    Nauka, 1971.

47. Kutsenkov, A.A. "The Evolution of the Indian
    Castes (in the Period of Capitalistic Devel-
    opment)." Ms. Moscow, 1974.[96]

48. Lalaiants, E.A. "The Decay of Javanese Rural
    Society (From the End of the Nineteenth Cen-
    tury to the First Half of the Twentieth Cen-
    tury)." In <u>Countries and Peoples of the
    East</u>. [Strany i Harody Vostoka] Vol. IV
    (1965), pp. 57-94.

---

[95] Neither this dissertation nor Parnikel's (source
55) have been published. The reader can most
likely find these dissertations at the Lenin
Library in Moscow (trans.).

[96] This unpublished manuscript could not be attri-
buted to any sources other than the author
(trans).

49. Levinson, Georei Ilich. The Philippines on
     the Road to Independence (1901-1946). Mos-
     cow: Central Dept. Of Eastern Literature,
     1972.

50. Levtonova, Iulia Olegovna. Characteristics
     of Modern Philippine History: From the
     1760's to the 1860's. Nauka: Central Dept.
     of Eastern Literature, 1965.

51. Levtonova, Iulia Olegovna. History of Social
     Thought in the Philippines (Second Half of
     the Nineteenth Century). Moscow: Nauka,
     1973.

52. Melnikov, A.M. "Several Agrarian Reforms in
     the State of Kerala (1957-1970)." In Modern
     India: Economics, Politics and Culture in 25
     Years of Independence. Moscow: Nauka, 1972,
     pp. 85-129.

53. Olshanskii, B.V. "Personality and Social
     Values." Sociology in the USSR.
     [Sotsialogiia v SSSR] Part I. Ed. V.N.
     Fokin and M.A. Pizshova. Moscow: Mysl,
     1966, pp. 470-530.

54. Pankratova, V.A. "Indian Communists and the
     Problems of a Unified Front of Left-Wing and
     Democratic (Political) Power (Based on Kerala
     State)." Communist Parties of Developing
     Countries in the Struggle for a Unified
     Front. Ed. P.A. Ulianovskii. Moscow:
     Nauka, 1976, pp. 118-146.

55. Parnikel, B.B. "On the Question of the Roots
     of Malaccan Literature and Its Place in the
     Literature Circles of the Indonesian Archipe-
     lago." Diss. Moscow, 1971.

56. Petrushevskii, Ilia Pavlovich. Farming and
     Agrarian Relations in Iran: XII-XIV Centu-
     ries. Leningrad: Academy of Sciences, Len-
     ingrad Branch, 1960.

57. Petrushevskii, Ilia Pavlovich. Islam in
     Iran: VII-XV Centuries. A Lecture Course.
     Leningrad: Leningrad Univ., 1966.

58. Podberezskii, Igor Vitalevich. Sampagita,
     the Cross and the Dollar. Moscow: Nauka,
     1974.

59. Historical Problems of Pre-Capitalist
     Society. Ed. L.V. Danilova. Moscow: Nauka,
     1968.

60. Rastiannikov, Victor Georgievich. Agrarian
     Evolution in a Differentiated Society: the
     Experience of Independent India. Moscow:
     Nauka, 1963.

61. Rastiannikov, Victor Georgievich. "Introduc-
     tion to Contradictions Within the 'Green
     Revolution'." In Developing Countries and
     the "Green Revolution." Ed. V.G. Rastianni-
     kov. Moscow: Central Dept. of Eastern Lit-
     erature, 1974, pp. 3-16.

62. Rakhmatullin, M.A. "Problems of Peasant
     Social Consciousness in the Works of V.I.
     Lenin." Historiographical Problems of Rus-
     sian History in the Feudal Epoch. Ed. L.B.
     Cherepnun. Moscow: Nauka, 1970, pp.
     398-441.

63. Sakharov, I.V. West Bengal: Ethnographic
     and Ethnogeographic Features. Leningrad:
     Nauka, Leningrad Branch, 1977.

64. Seidov, R.A. The Agrarian Question and Peas-
     ant Development in Iran (1950-1953). Baku:
     Academy of Sciences, Azerbaiyan S.S.R., 1963.

65. Semenova, Nina Ivanova. Sikh Government:
     Characteristics of the Socio-Political His-
     tory of Punjab From the Mid-Nineteenth Cen-
     tury to the Mid-Twentieth Century. Moscow:
     Central Dept. of Eastern Literature, 1958.

66. Simoniia, N.A. The Bourgeoisie and the For-
     mation of Nation in Indonesia. Moscow:
     Nauka, 1964.

67. Singh, Baljit. The Developmental Path of the

Indian <u>Village</u>. Moscow, 1963.[97]

68. Smirenskaia, Zhanna Dmitrievna. "The Green
     Revolution and the Problem of the Decay of
     Traditional Relations (Based on Hindustan)."
     <u>Developing Countries and the</u> "<u>Green Revolu-
     tion.</u>" Ed. V.G. Rastiannikov. Moscow:
     Nauka, Dept. of Eastern Literature, 1974, pp.
     63-108.

69. <u>A Report on the Research of Proto-Indian
     Texts</u>. Ed. Ui.V. Knorozov. Moscow: Nauka,
     1975.

70. <u>Social Psychology: Short Essays</u>. Ed. G.P.
     Pregvechnovo and Ui.A. Sherkovina. Moscow:
     Politizdat, 1975.

71. Suprunovich, B.P. "The People of Kerala."
     In <u>Countries and Peoples of the East</u>. Vol.
     XX of <u>India</u>: <u>Country and People</u>. Book 4.
     Moscow: Nauka, 1977, pp. 86-95.

72. Uledov, Aleksandr Konstantinovich. <u>The
     Structure of Social Consciousness</u>. <u>Theocrat-
     ic-Sociological Research</u>. Moscow: Mysl,
     1968.

73. Frye, Richard Nelson. <u>The Heritage of Iran</u>.
     Moscow, 1972. (LC) Cleveland: World Pub-
     lishing Co., 1963 (in English).

74. Aiyar, Subbaima. <u>Economic Life in Malabar</u>.
     Bangalore: Bangalore City Printing and Pub-
     lishing Co., 1925.

75. Aiyappan, A. <u>Social Revolution in a Kerala
     Village</u>: <u>a Study in Culture Change</u>. Lenin-
     grad, 1965. (LC) London: Asia Publishing

---

[97] This is a Russian translation of a book which
originally was published in English or an Indian
language. The translated title was not available
in the LC, even though there were many titles
under this author's name. It could possibly be
located under a different English title (trans).

House, 1966.

76. Alexander, K.C. Social Mobility in Kerala.
    Poona: Deccan College Postgraduate and
    Research Institute, 1968.

77. Blanckenburg, Peter von. "Who Leads Agricul-
    tural Modernization: a Study of Some Pro-
    gressive Farmers in Mysore and Punjab." Eco-
    nomic and Political Weekly. VII, No. 40
    (1972), pp. a-94--a-112.

78. Cater, Sonya D. The Philippine Federation of
    Free Farmers: a Case Study in Mass Agrarian
    Organizations. Ithaca: Cornell Univ. Press,
    Southeast Asia Monograph Series, 1959.

79. Census of India 1961. Vol. VII, part 6-c.
    Village Survey Monograph of Kerala. Ernak-
    ulam and Kottayam Districts. Delhi: Office
    of the Registrar General, 1966.

80. Census of India 1961. Vol. VII, part 6.
    Village Survey Monograph of Punjab, No. 36.
    Kunran: a Village in Sangrur District. New
    Delhi: Office of the Registrar General,
    1962.

81. Census of India 1961. Vol. XVI, part 4.
    Village Survey Monograph of West Bengal.
    Raibakhini. Delhi: Office of the Registrar
    General, 1966.

82. Chattopadhyay, Gouranga. Ranjana: a Village
    in West Bengal. Calcutta: Booklands Private
    Ltd., 1964.

83. Critchfield, Richard. "'Green Revolution':
    Most Significant of This Decade." Science
    and Culture. 37, No. 10 (1971), pp. 459-463.

84. Darling, Malcolm Lyall. The Punjab Peasant
    in Prosperity and Debt. Bombay: Oxford
    Univ. Press, Indian Branch, 1947.

85. Datta, Ansu K. "Politics in Village India:
    an Enquiry into Jagannathbarh." Tropical

Man: _Yearbook 1970_. Leiden: E.J. Brill,
        1972, pp. 88-159.

86. Deb, P.C. and B.K. Agarwal. "The Green Revo-
        lution and Expenditure Patterns in Rural Pun-
        jab." _Society and Culture_. VII, No. 1
        (1972), pp. 1-8.

87. Frankel, Francine R. _India's Green Revolu-
        tion: Economic Gains and Political Costs_.
        Princeton: Princeton Univ. Press, 1971.

88. Geertz, Clifford. _The Religions of Java_.
        Glencoe: Free Press, 1960.

89. Geertz, Hildred. "Indonesian Cultures and
        Communities." In _Indonesia_. Ed. Ruth McVey.
        New Haven: HRAF Press, 1963, pp. 24-96.[98]

90. Goodman, Grant K. _Four Aspects of Philip-
        pine-Japanese Relations, 1930-1940_.[99]

91. Haar, Barend ter. _Adat Law in Indonesia_.
        New York: Institute of Pacific Relations,
        1948.

92. Gough, Kathleen. "Village Politics in Ker-
        ala." _Economic Weekly_. 17, No. 8 (1965),
        pp. 363-372.

93. Hadgrave, Robert L., Jr. "Caste in Kerala:
        a Preface to Elections." _Economic Weekly_.
        17, No. 4 (1964), pp. 1841-1848.

94. Jay, Robert R. _Javanese Villagers: Social
        Relations in Rural Modjocuto_. Cambridge:
        MIT Press, 1969.

---

[98] The second edition was printed in 1967, and there
    is some confusion as to which one the author
    cited. Nonetheless, the reader can find the
    Geertz article in both (trans.).

[99] Publication data on this source could not be
    located in the LC (trans.).

95. Kartodirdjo, Sartono. "Agrarian Radicalism
     in Java: Its Setting and Development." In
     Culture and Politics in Indonesia. Ed.
     Claire Holt. Ithaca: Cornell Univ. Press,
     1972, pp. 71-125.

96. Kartodirdjo, Sartono. Protest Movements in
     Rural Java. Oxford: Oxford Univ. Press,
     1973.

97. Kerkvliet, Ben J. "Peasant Society and
     Unrest Prior to the Huk Revolution in the
     Philippines." Ms. 1970.[100]

98. Koentjaraningrat, raden mas. "The Javanese
     of South Central Java." Social Structure of
     Southeast Asia. Ed. George Murdock. Chi-
     cago: Quadrangle Books, 1960, pp. 88-115.

99. Koentjaraningrat, raden mas. "Tjelapar: a
     Village in South Central Java." In Villages
     in Indonesia. Ed. r.m. Koentjaraningrat.
     Ithaca: Cornell Univ. Press, 1967, pp.
     244-280.

100. Lachica, Eduardo. Huk Philippine Agrarian
      Society in Revolt. Manila: Solidaridad
      Publishing House, 1971.

101. Ladejinsky, Wolf. "The Green Revolution in
      Punjab: a Field Trip." Economic and Polit-
      ical Weekly. 4, No. 39 (1969), pp.
      a-147--a-162.

102. Lambton, Ann K.S. Landlord and Peasant in
      Persia: a Study of Land Tenure and Land
      Revenue Administration. London: Oxford
      Univ. Press, 1969.

103. Lambton, Ann K.S. The Persian Land Reform:
      1962-1966. Oxford: Clarendon Press, 1969.

---

[100] This unpublished manuscript could not be attri-
buted to any sources other than the author
(trans).

104. <u>Link</u>. 14, No. 34 (1972).

105. Mayer, Adrian C. <u>Land and Society in Mala-
     bar</u>. New York: Oxford Univ. Press, Indian
     Branch, 1952.

106. Mencher, Joan P. "Kerala and Madras: a
     Comparative Study of Ecology and Social
     Structure." <u>Ethnology</u>. 5, No. 2 (1966),
     pp. 135-171.

107. Mencher, Joan P. "Nambudiri-Brahmin: an
     Analysis of a Traditional Elite in Kerala."
     <u>Journal of Asian and African Studies</u>. 1,
     No. 3 (1966), pp. 183-196.

108. Miller, Eric J. "Village Structure in North
     Kerala." In <u>India's Villages: a Collection
     of Articles Originally Published in the Eco-
     nomic Weekly of Bombay</u>. Ed. M.N. Srivinas.
     Calcutta, 1955. (LC) London: Asia Pub-
     lishing House, 1960, pp. 42-55.

109. Miller, William G. "Housseinabad: a Per-
     sian Village." <u>The Middle East Journal</u>.
     18, No. 4 (1964), pp. 483-498.

110. Mintz, Jeanne S. <u>Mohammed, Marx and Mar-
     haen: the Roots of Indonesian Socialism</u>.
     Leningrad, 1965. (LC) New York: Praeger,
     1965.

111. Moertono Soemasaid. <u>Statecraft in Old Java:
     Study of the Later Mataram Period: XVI to
     XIX Centuries</u>. Ithaca: Cornell Univ.
     Press, 1968.

112. Mukhopadhyay, Tarasish. "The Jajmany Rela-
     tionship in Rural West Bengal." <u>Bengal East
     and West</u>. East Lancing: MSU, Asian Studies
     Enterprise Paper No. 13, 1969, pp. 139-148.

113. Mulherin, Billie. "The 'Bekel' in Javanese
     History." <u>Review of Indonesian and Malayan
     Affairs</u>. Vol. 4-5, 1970-1971. Sydney:
     Univ. of Sydney, Dept. of Indonesian and
     Malayan Studies, pp. 1-28.

114. Oommen, T.K. "Agrarian Legislation and
      Movements as Sources of Change: the Case of
      Kerala." Economic and Political Weekly.
      10, No. 40 (1975), pp. 1574-1584.

115. Pomeroy, William J. The Forest: a Personal
      Record of the Huk Guerilla Struggle in the
      Philippines. New York: International Pub-
      lishers, 1963.

116. [The original text has no source 116.]

117. Pomeroy, William J. "Martial Law and the
      National Democratic Struggle in the Philip-
      pines." Political Affairs. LIV, No. 5
      (1975), pp. 12-19.

118. Raja, P.K.S. Medieval Kerala. Calicut,
      1966. (LC) Chidambaram: Crossword Press,
      1953.

119. Rao, M.S.A. Social Change in Malabar. Bom-
      bay: Popular Book Depot, 1957.

120. Rudra, Ashok, A. Majid and B.D. Talib.
      "Large Farmers of Punjab: Some Preliminary
      Findings in a Sample Survey." Economic and
      Political Weekly. 4, No. 39 (1969), pp.
      a-143--a-146.

121. Saradamoni, K. "Agrestic Slavery in Kerala
      in the Nineteenth Century." Indian Economic
      and Social History Review. 10, No. 4
      (1973), pp. 371-385.

122. Sarma, Jyotirmoyee. "A Village in West Ben-
      gal: a Socio-Economic Study." In India's
      Villages: a Collection of Articles Origi-
      nally Published in the Economic Weekly of
      Bombay. Ed. M.N. Srivinas. Calcutta, 1955.
      (LC) London: Asia Publishing House, 1960,
      pp. 180-201.

123. Selosoemardjan. Social Changes in Jogja-
      karta. Ithaca: Cornell Univ. Press, 1963.

124. Selosoemardjan. The Dynamics of Community
      Development in Rural Central and West Java.
      Ithaca: Cornell Univ. Press, 1963.

125. Shasmal, Kartick Chandra. The Bauri of West
      Bengal: a Socio-Economic Study. Report on
      the Life and Living of an Important Sched-
      uled Caste Community. Calcutta: Indian
      Publications, 1972.

126. Sinha Durga. Indian Villages in Transition
      (a Motivational Analysis). New Delhi:
      Associated Publishing House, 1969.

127. Singh, N.M. Village Leadership (a Case
      Study of Village Mohali in Punjab). Delhi:
      Sterling Publishers, 1968.

128. Smith, Marian W. "Social Structure in Pun-
      jab." In India's Villages: a Collection of
      Articles Originally Published in the Eco-
      nomic and Political Weekly of Bombay. Ed.
      M.N. Srivinas. Calcutta, 1955. (LC) Lon-
      don: Asia Publishing House, 1960, pp.
      144-160.

129. Starner, Frances L. Magsaysay and the Phil-
      ippine Peasantry: the Agricultural Impact
      on Philippine Politics: 1953-1956. Berke-
      ley: Univ. Of California Press, 1961.

130. Sturtevant, David R. Popular Uprisings in
      the Philippines: 1840-1940. Ithaca: Cor-
      nell Univ. Press, 1976.

131. Takahashi, Akira. Land and Peasant in Cen-
      tral Luzon: the Socio-Economic Structure of
      a Bulacan Village. Tokyo, 1969. (LC) Hono-
      lulu: East-West Center Press, 1970.

132. Taruc, Luis. Born of the People: an Auto-
      biography. New York, 1953. (LC) Westport:
      Greenwood Press, 1973.

133. Taruc, Luis. He Who Rides the Tiger: the
      Story of an Asian Guerilla Leader. New
      York: Praeger, 1967.

134. Valsan, E.H. *Community Development Programs and Rural Local Government: Comparative Case Studies of India and the Philippines*. New York: Praeger, 1970.

ISBN Prefix 0-89680-

Africa Series

16. Weisfelder, Richard F. THE BASOTHO MONARCHY: A Spent Force
    or Dynamic Political Factor? 1972. 106pp.
    049-0   (82-91676) $ 7.00*

19. Huntsberger, Paul E., compiler. HIGHLAND MOSAIC: A Critical
    Anthology of Ethiopian Literature in English. 1973. 122pp.
    052-0   (82-91700) $ 7.00*

21. Silberfein, Marilyn. CONSTRAINTS ON THE EXPANSION OF
    COMMERCIAL AGRICULTURE: Iringa District, Tanzania. 1974.
    51pp.
    054-7   (82-91726) $ 4.50*

22. Pieterse, Cosmo. ECHO AND CHORUSES: "Ballad of the Cells"
    and Selected Shorter Poems. 1974. 66pp.
    055-5   (82-91734) $ 5.00*

23. Thom, Derrick J. THE NIGER-NIGERIA BOUNDARY: A Study of
    Ethnic Frontiers and a Colonial Boundary. 1975. 50pp.
    056-3   (82-91742) $ 4.75*

24. Baum, Edward, compiler. A COMPREHENSIVE PERIODICAL
    BIBLIOGRAPHY OF NIGERIA, 1960-1970. 1975. 250pp.
    057-1   (82-91759) $13.00*

25. Kircherr, Eugene C. ABBYSSINIA TO ZIMBABWE: A Guide to the
    Political Units of Africa in the Period 1947-1978.
    1979. 3rd ed. 80pp.
    100-4   (82-91908) $ 8.00*

27. Fadiman, Jeffrey A. MOUNTAIN WARRIORS: The Pre-Colonial
    Meru of Mt. Kenya. 1976. 82pp.
    060-1   (82-91783) $ 4.75*

32. Wright, Donald R. THE EARLY HISTORY OF THE NIUMI:
    Settlement and Foundation of a Mandinka State on the
    Gambia River. 1977. 122pp.
    064-4   (82-91833) $ 8.00*

36. Fadiman, Jeffrey A. THE MOMENT OF CONQUEST: Meru, Kenya,
    1907. 1979. 70pp.
    081-4   (82-91874) $ 5.50*

37. Wright, Donald R. ORAL TRADITIONS FROM THE GAMBIA:
    Volume I, Mandinka Griots. 1979. 176pp.
    083-0   (82-91882) $12.00*

38.   Wright, Donald R.   ORAL TRADITIONS FROM THE GAMBIA:
      Volume II, Family Elders.   1980.   200pp.
      084-9   (82-91890) $15.00*

39.   Reining, Priscilla.   CHALLENGING DESERTIFICATION IN WEST
      AFRICA: Insights from Landsat into Carrying Capacity, Culti-
      vation and Settlement Site Identification in Upper Volta and
      Niger.   1979.   180pp., illus.
      102-0   (82-91916) $12.00*

41.   Lindfors, Bernth.   MAZUNGUMZO: Interviews with East African
      Writers, Publishers, Editors, and Scholars.   1981.   179pp.
      108-X   (82-91932) $13.00*

42.   Spear,   Thomas   J.   TRADITIONS   OF   ORIGIN   AND   THEIR
      INTERPRETATION: The Mijikenda of Kenya.   1982.   xii, 163pp.
      109-8   (82-91940) $13.50*

43.   Harik, Elsa M. and Donald G. Schilling.   THE POLITICS OF
      EDUCATION IN COLONIAL ALGERIA AND KENYA.   1984.   102pp.
      117-9   (82-91957) $11.50*

44.   Smith,   Daniel   R.   THE INFLUENCE OF THE   FABIAN   COLONIAL
      BUREAU   ON THE INDEPENDENCE MOVEMENT IN TANGANYIKA.
      1985.   x, 98pp.
      125-X   (82-91965) $ 9.00*

45.   Keto, C. Tsehloane.   AMERICAN-SOUTH AFRICAN RELATIONS 1784-
      1980: Review and Select Bibliography.   1985.   159pp.
      128-4   (82-91973) $11.00*

46.   Burness, Don, and Mary-Lou Burness, ed.   WANASEMA: Conver-
      sations with African Writers.   1985.   95pp.
      129-2   (82-91981)   A $ 9.00*

47.   Switzer, Les.   MEDIA AND DEPENDENCY IN SOUTH AFRICA: A Case
      Study of the Press and the Ciskei "Homeland".
      1985.   80pp.
      130-6   (82-91999) $ 9.00*

Latin America Series

1.   Frei,   Eduardo   M.   THE   MANDATE   OF   HISTORY   AND   CHILE'S
      FUTURE.   Tr. by Miguel d'Escoto.   Intro. by Thomas Walker.
      1977.   79pp.
      066-0   (82-92526) $ 8.00*

2.   Irish,   Donald P.,   ed.   MULTINATIONAL CORPORATIONS IN LATIN
      AMERICA: Private Rights--Public Responsibilities.
      1978.   135pp.
      067-9   (82-92534) $ 9.00*

4.   Martz, Mary Jeanne Reid. THE CENTRAL AMERICAN SOCCER WAR:
      Historical Patterns and Internal Dynamics of OAS Settlement
      Procedures. 1979. 118pp.
      077-6   (82-92559) $ 8.00*

5.   Wiarda, Howard J. CRITICAL ELECTIONS AND CRITICAL COUPS:
      State, Society, and the Military in the Processes of Latin
      American Development. 1979. 83pp.
      082-2   (82-92567) $ 7.00*

6.   Dietz, Henry A., and Richard Moore. POLITICAL PARTICIPATION
      IN A NON-ELECTORAL SETTING: The Urban Poor in Lima, Peru.
      1979. viii, 102pp.
      085-7   (82-92575) $ 9.00*

7.   Hopgood, James F. SETTLERS OF BAJAVISTA: Social and Econo-
      mic Adaptation in a Mexican Squatter Settlement.
      1979. xii, 145pp.
      101-2   (82-92583) $11.00*

8.   Clayton, Lawrence A. CAULKERS AND CARPENTERS IN A NEW
      WORLD: The Shipyards of Colonial Guayaquil.
      1980. 189pp., illus.
      103-9   (82-92591) $15.00*

9.   Tata, Robert J. STRUCTURAL CHANGES IN PUERTO RICO'S
      ECONOMY: 1947-1976. 1981. xiv, 104pp.
      107-1   (82-92609) $11.75*

10.   McCreery, David. DEVELOPMENT AND THE STATE IN REFORMA
      GUATEMALA, 1871-1885. 1983. viii, 120pp.
      113-6   (82-92617) $ 8.50*

11.   O'Shaughnessy, Laura N., and Louis H. Serra. CHURCH AND
      REVOLUTION IN NICARAGUA. 1986. 118pp.
      126-8   (82-92625) $11.00*

Southeast Asia Series

31.   Nash, Manning. PEASANT CITIZENS: Politics, Religion, and
      Modernization in Kelantan, Malaysia. 1974. 181pp.
      018-0   (82-90322) $12.00*

44.   Collier, William L., et al. INCOME, EMPLOYMENT AND FOOD
      SYSTEMS IN JAVANESE COASTAL VILLAGES. 1977. 160pp.
      031-8   (82-90454) $10.00*

47.   Wessing, Robert. COSMOLOGY AND SOCIAL BEHAVIOR IN A WEST
      JAVANESE SETTLEMENT. 1978. 200pp.
      072-5   (82-90488) $12.00*

48. Willer, Thomas F., ed. SOUTHEAST ASIAN REFERENCES IN THE
     BRITISH PARLIAMENTARY PAPERS, 1801 1770/73: An Index.
     1977. 110pp.
     033-4   (82-90496) $ 8.50*

50. Echauz, Robustiano. SKETCHES OF THE ISLAND OF NEGROS.
     1978. 174pp.
     070-9   (82-90512) $10.00*

51. Krannich, Ronald L. MAYORS AND MANAGERS IN THAILAND: The
     Struggle for Political Life in Administrative Settings.
     1978. 139pp.
     073-3   (82-90520) $ 9.00*

52. Davis, Glora, ed. WHAT IS MODERN INDONESIAN CULTURE?
     1978. 300pp.
     075-X   (82-90538) $18.00*

54. Ayal, Eliezar B., ed. THE STUDY OF THAILAND: Analyses of
     Knowledge, Approaches, and Prospects in Anthropology, Art
     History, Economics, History and Political Science.
     1979. 257pp.
     079-2   (82-90553) $13.50*

56. Duiker, William J. VIETNAM SINCE THE FALL OF SAIGON.
     Second edition, revised and enlarged. 1985. 281pp.
     133-0   (82-90744) $12.00*

57. Siregar, Susan Rodgers. ADAT, ISLAM, AND CHRISTIANITY IN A
     BATAK HOMELAND. 1981. 108pp.
     110-1   (82-90587) $10.00*

58. Van Esterik, Penny. COGNITION AND DESIGN PRODUCTION IN BAN
     CHIANG POTTERY. 1981. 90pp.
     078-4   (82-90595) $12.00*

59. Foster, Brian L. COMMERCE AND ETHNIC DIFFERENCES: The Case
     of the Mons in Thailand. 1982. x, 93pp.
     112-8   (82-90603) $10.00*

60. Frederick, William H., and John H. McGlynn. REFLECTIONS ON
     REBELLION: Stories from the Indonesian Upheavals of 1948
     and 1965. 1983. vi, 168pp.
     111-X   (82-90611) $ 9.00*

61. Cady, John F. CONTACTS WITH BURMA, 1935-1949: A Personal
     Account. 1983. x, 117pp.
     114-4   (82-90629) $ 9.00*

62. Kipp, Rita Smith, and Richard D. Kipp, eds. BEYOND SAMOSIR:
     Recent Studies of the Batak Peoples of Sumatra.
     1983. viii, 155pp.

          115-2   (82-90637) $ 9.00*

63.   Carstens, Sharon, ed. CULTURAL IDENTITY IN NORTHERN PEN-
      INSULAR MALAYSIA. 1985. 91pp.
      116-0   (82-90645) $ 9.00*

64.   Dardjowidjojo, Soenjono. VOCABULARY BUILDING IN INDONESIAN:
      An Advanced Reader. 1984. xviii, 256pp.
      118-7   (82-90652) $18.00*

65.   Errington, J. Joseph. LANGUAGE AND SOCIAL CHANGE IN JAVA:
      Linguistic Reflexes of Modernization in a Traditional Royal
      Polity. 1985. xiv, 198pp.
      120-9   (82-90660) $12.00*

66.   Binh, Tran Tu. THE RED EARTH: A Vietnamese Memoir of Life
      on a Colonial Rubber Plantation. Tr. by John Spragens.
      Ed. by David Marr. 1985. xii, 98pp.
      119-5   (82-90678) $ 9.00*

67.   Pane, Armijn. SHACKLES. Tr. by John McGlynn. Intro. by
      William H. Frederick. 1985. xvi, 108pp.
      122-5   (82-90686) $ 9.00*

68.   Syukri, Ibrahim. HISTORY OF THE MALAY KINGDOM OF PATANI.
      Tr. by Conner Bailey and John N. Miksic. 1985. xx, 98pp.
      123-3   (82-90694) $10.50*

69.   Keeler, Ward. JAVANESE: A Cultural Approach.
      1984. xxxvi, 523pp.
      121-7   (82-90702) $18.00*

70.   Wilson, Constance M., and Lucien M. Hanks. BURMA-THAILAND
      FRONTIER OVER SIXTEEN DECADES: Three Descriptive Documents.
      1985. x, 128pp.
      124-1   (82-90710) $10.50*

71.   Thomas, Lynn L., and Franz von Benda-Beckmann, eds. CHANGE
      AND CONTINUITY IN MINANGKABAU: Local, Regional, and
      Historical Perspectives on West Sumatra. 1985. 363pp.
      127-6   (82-90728) $14.00*

72.   Reid, Anthony, and Oki Akira, eds. THE JAPANESE EXPERIENCE
      IN INDONESIA: Selected Memoirs of 1942-1945.
      1985. 411pp., 20 illus.
      132-2   (82-90736) $18.00*